Loyalty
Demands
Dissent

Other Books written or edited by Sulak Sivaraksa

Seeds of Peace: A Buddhist Vision for Renewing Society

Siamese Resurgence: A Thai Voice on Asia in a World of Change

A Socially Engaged Buddhism: By a Controversial Siamese

Siam in Crisis

A Buddhist Vision for Renewing Society:
  Collected Articles by a Thai Intellectual

Religion and Development

Radical Conservatism: Buddhism in the Contemporary World

Search for Asian Cultural Integrity

Modern Thai Monarchy and Cultural Politics

Buddhist Perception for Desirable Societies in the Future

AUTOBIOGRAPHY
OF AN
ENGAGED
BUDDHIST

Loyalty Demands Dissent

SULAK SIVARAKSA

Foreword by
His Holiness the Dalai Lama

PARALLAX PRESS
BERKELEY, CALIFORNIA

Parallax Press
P.O. Box 7355
Berkeley, California 94707

Edited by Susan Offner, Laurie Senauke, and Alan Senauke.
Jacket and book design by Legacy Media, Inc.
Jacket photograph by Alan Senauke.
Photographs courtesy Sulak Sivaraksa.
Index by Michael Brackney, Brackney Indexing Services.

Library of Congress Cataloging-in-Publication Data

Sulak Sivaraksa.
    Loyalty demands dissent : autobiography of an engaged Buddhist /
by Sulak Sivaraksa.
        p. cm.
    Includes index.
    ISBN 1-888375-10-8 (hardcover)
        1. Sulak Sivaraksa. 2. Historians—Thailand—Biography
3. Buddhists—Thailand—Biography. 4. Political activists—Thailand—
Biography 5. Buddhism and social problems—Thailand. I. Title.
DS570.97.S85S35   1998
959.304'092—dc21
    [B]   98-9467
                                                                CIP

1 2 3 4 5 6 7 8 9 10 / 02 01 00 99 98

Contents

THE DALAI LAMA

FOREWORD

I first met Sulak Sivaraksa during my initial visit to his country about thirty years ago. Since then, our paths have crossed many times and I have much appreciation for his concern and sympathy for the plight of Tibet and the Tibetan people. We also share the aspiration to bring the Buddha's teachings of wisdom and compassion into society. To be compassionate, one needs to be engaged and involved.

Sulak has shown by example that we all have a responsibility towards our fellow human beings. We can truly bring compassion to bear and create peace within ourselves and in our communities. Truth is extremely important in human society. Earlier in this century truth seemed to have lost its value, sheer power seemed to command more respect. Nowadays, these ways of thinking have changed. Even the most powerful and prosperous nations are beginning to see that there is little to be gained from neglecting such basic human values as morality and compassion. Sulak has tried to proclaim this simple truth, even when it has placed him in danger.

He has also tried to draw attention to proper paths of social development that take account of the needs of people and the environment. Although material advances have contributed enormously to human welfare, they cannot create lasting happiness by themselves. I believe Sulak and I share a conviction that if we are to solve human problems, economic and technological development must be accompanied by an inner spiritual growth. And if we succeed in fulfilling both these two goals, we will surely create a happier and more peaceful world.

February 11, 1998

Editors' Introduction

Sulak and I embraced, bowed, and parted at the gate of the Berkeley Zen Center. It was February of 1992, and I was on my way from California to Thailand (or "Siam," as Sulak insists) to attend the fourth International Network of Engaged Buddhists (INEB) conference, a gathering inspired and initiated by Sulak. There had been a military coup in Siam exactly a year before—the seventeenth since 1932—and Sulak was once again in exile, indicted on charges of *lèse-majesté* for allegedly criticizing King Bhumiphol, and defaming the coup's leader, General Suchinda Kraprayoon. While I was free to travel to Bangkok and stay at his home, Sulak would remain at my house in Berkeley. The irony of this moment was not lost on either of us.

Ironies and contradictions mark Sulak Sivaraksa's life as social critic and philosopher, as writer and activist, as a bellwether of socially engaged Buddhism in Asia and the West. Truly, these complexities express his life. Sulak has always been at the crossroads: tradition and modernity, inside and outside, action and contemplation, orient and occident, loyalty and dissent. He is at once a royalist and a democrat. This has always been Sulak's way, "radical conservatism." It seems to have been written in his stars. But as you will read, his has been a long, difficult journey, intimately bound up with modern Siam's own tumultuous history.

Sulak was born in 1933, the son of an accountant for the British-American Tobacco Monopoly, just as Siam's absolute monarchy was yielding to an unsteady constitutional government, one to be shaken by frequent coups, dictatorships, and popular uprisings in the ensuing sixty years. During the Second World War, while Japanese troops used Thailand as a staging area, Sulak spent two years as a Buddhist monk, a kind of idyll and touchstone for the rest of his life. But at his father's request, he disrobed and finished his schooling at a French Catholic secondary school in Bangkok. He completed his university and law degrees in England and Wales, where he also worked as a writer and broadcaster for the BBC.

When Sulak returned to Thailand in 1961 at the age of 28, he was in a unique position to see the relative qualities of Asian and Western spiritual and intellectual traditions, as well as the vulnerability of his country and his people to the seemingly unstoppable force of Western development. He founded the *Social Science Review*, which became the intellectual voice of the generation, opened an international bookstore, and was off and running as an activist, lecturer, publisher, and "professional gadfly."

Now, thirty-seven years later, he has not slowed down a bit. Just this week I received e-mail bulletins from his Kalayanamitra Council, which is organizing against a Western-funded gas pipeline across Burma and Thailand that will "pipe" millions of dollars into the pockets of generals and corporations at the expense of local people and the environment. With his fierce individualism and Buddhist ethic, Sulak is still taking on those of his contemporaries who turned towards privilege and position while he went a different way. There may be insights and events that elude the pages of his memoir, yet the impact of Sulak's activism speaks for itself.

In Siam, Sulak is a controversial figure. People's movements, concerned students, and the press turn to him daily for perspective. Ministers, parliamentarians, and generals, many of whom grew up under Sulak's tutelage, often confide in him privately while attacking him publicly. The wider world has recognized Sulak's willingness to speak the truth as he sees it by twice nominating him for the Nobel Peace Prize in the 1990s, and awarding him the prestigious Right Livelihood Award in 1995, on the heels of his remarkable legal victory against charges of lèse-majesté. In Europe and North America, Sulak is welcomed at universities, international convocations, and Buddhist centers, where his urgent articulation of interdependence, sustainable development, activism, and spiritual conservatism cuts through cant and passivity. (For an overview of Sulak's social thought, I encourage you to read his *Seeds of Peace: A Buddhist Vision for Renewing Society*.)

Sulak can be demanding and hardheaded. Everyone who knows him, whether they love or condemn him, recognizes this. How many of us have received midnight phone calls or faxes with a laundry list of tasks to be done by morning? But he is generous of spirit and surprisingly open to criticism. His loyalty far outweighs his demands. I have often seen Sulak arrive somewhere and page through his worn address book, calling old friends and meeting them for the pure sake of friendship. Again and again in this memoir he recalls friends of thirty, forty, fifty years with whom he stays in close touch. His house in Bangkok is a refuge for many of us from around the world and from Siam itself. Thanks to Sulak, his wife Nilchawee, and his family, everyone can feel at home there.

My own life and work as director of the Buddhist Peace Fellowship have been immeasurably broadened through my friendship with Sulak and involvement with INEB. I know many people around the world who feel the same. Building on Sulak's connections, the common work of socially engaged Buddhism and the wider field of "buddhism" with a small "b" bridges nations and continents, venturing into bold projects and partnerships that are grounded in grassroots empowerment and social transformation. Sulak is the consummate networker, manifesting what Thich Nhat Hanh calls "interbeing" on the social, political, and organizational level.

In recent months, Siam's economic boom and the reckless development of all Southeast Asia have fallen like a house of cards. Once again Sulak's vision has proven painfully prophetic, as it was in his exile from the brutal 1976–1978 Thai dictatorship or in his famous speech at Thammasat University in which he predicted the tragic and bloody events of the following May, 1992. Being outspoken has often put him at risk, but Sulak never hesitates "to speak truth to power." This habit of truth springs from some deep source of conviction within him. Perhaps it is within each of us as well. With his blunt words and forceful melding of political philosophy, modern economics, and Buddhist wisdom, Sulak Sivaraksa's is a voice we might all attend to in this interdependent world. Listening to him, we are moved to find our own courage, to do what is right, to work for the benefit of all beings. His heartfelt loyalty and his dogged dissent are exactly what we need.

Alan Senauke
Berkeley, California
February 1998

P utting this book together has been like running a marathon. It has been an extraordinary team effort, with batons passed from person to person along the way. The book is based on a series of nearly thirty tapes of Sulak Sivaraksa telling the story of his life. They were recorded primarily in Berkeley, California, during his second exile in 1991–1992. Laurie and Alan Senauke took charge of interviewing and taping, and organized much of the transcribing and editing. I joined the project after it had been underway for a few years. I was handed a large brown envelope containing all the pieces to date. It fairly shouted the months of work contained therein, and whispered the months of work that still remained. The pieces in the package lay at different stages of completion—smoothly edited book chapters, a half-edited transcript, partially transcribed tapes, and many tapes not yet heard.

A manuscript shapes itself into a book in an uncanny sort of way, sometimes seemingly on its own. I spent hours with the material, living with it, moving through it, and becoming familiar with its soul. Sulak had recorded most of the tapes roughly in chronological order, carefully organizing his life and thought and the interrelationships between them. A few tapes were thematic, tracing the overlapping development of relationships and events. At times, this posed a problem of coherence, as I tried to fit everything together. Fragments of text lay uncooperatively silent for weeks, refusing to fit anywhere, until finally they began to shift themselves around. With some persuasion, they ambled over to the proper paragraph of the proper chapter and settled down exactly where they belonged. I generally integrated pieces from the thematic sections into the chronological framework where they fit best. For a long time I had wondered if this particular puzzle had come with the wrong pieces, but in the end all of the pieces fit.

Sulak has a powerful gift of speech—indeed it is his speeches that have always moved people to act, either to reject the status quo as he constantly urges, or to reject him and his challenges, even to the point of accusing him of defamation. While these tapes can loosely be called "interviews," they are more truly "monologues." For most anyone else, talking about one's own life in such detail, for ninety minutes at a stretch, would be a chore, if not impossible. In the case of Sulak, our biggest difficulty was in deciding how many of the vividly painted details should be kept. While the raw transcriptions were edited to transform his spoken monologue into written form, we did not add our own summaries or conclusions. The book is Sulak's own narration—his words, his peculiar turns of phrase, his style and cadence. You can hear him speaking from the pages.

The project was fascinating, not only in terms of form, but in terms of content. I was intrigued to see how someone perceives his life, how he interprets his actions and explains his motives. Sulak exudes an energy that cannot be suppressed. He senses that to act is the only way to live—to move, to speak, to write; that the world is waiting, languishing, dying, for want of more people who will act, and so, at least, he will act. Sulak sees himself as a mover, and he dares others to react to him as he pushes ahead, challenging our society and its false values. He does not just let things happen, molding his life in response. Instead, he makes things happen. He decides what is needed and does it. Now. Nothing is halfway or halfhearted.

Seeing into the life of a person through his own eyes fills one with profoundest respect and sympathy, a deep-rooted sense of companionship in this shared journey of life. Yet it is quite beyond the limits of most of us to muster the vision and energy that Sulak has, to initiate so many different organizations working on so many issues. He has devoted himself to work for justice and social transformation. His outspoken criticism of the injustices of our time has brought new and deeper understanding to countless people, and with it, the courage to join him in the struggle. His unflagging effort to challenge a complacent world is inspiring. Here is his story.

Susan Offner
Chiang Mai
February 1998

Acknowledgments

In 1982, Larry Stifel was instrumental in helping me to receive an invitation from the Rockefeller Foundation to be a scholar-in-residence at Villa Serbelloni, Bellagio, on Lake Como, in Northern Italy, to write *Phrases of Life,* my autobiography in Thai. Quite a number of friends hoped to see the book translated into English, Japanese, and Chinese, but it has proved too big a volume to allow such a project. Ten years later, when I was in exile from Siam due to my public lecture in August 1991 attacking the military coup that had taken place six months earlier, Larry persuaded the Foundation to fund my *Later Phrases of Life.* Unfortunately, Larry passed away before I could acknowledge my gratitude to him in print.

While in exile in the United States, my friends at Parallax Press in Berkeley encouraged me, in dialogue with Laurie and Alan Senauke of the Buddhist Peace Fellowship (BPF), to produce several tape recordings as material for my autobiography in English. Laurie could not transcribe all of the many tapes, and many other friends in the BPF volunteered to help. The Senaukes edited many of these transcripts, but I eventually left the Bay Area and returned to Siam in 1993 to fight the case of lèse-majesté (defaming the king) then in the courts.

I was given a tape recorder on which to provide more information for the forthcoming book. After my acquittal in 1995, I asked Susan Offner to continue editing the manuscript in Siam. She worked in collaboration with the Senaukes and did the work splendidly. Dennis Crean and the editors at Parallax Press kindly saw to it that the manuscript became really worthwhile for the reader. My longtime friends David Chappell, Grant Olson, and Donald Swearer offered valuable comments, as did Tom Ginsburg. Anchalee Kurutach helped with translations. Indeed, so many hands have been involved in shaping the book from transcribers of the texts to providers of photographs. Many names have not been mentioned, yet I feel grateful to them all.

I am also grateful to the military, the police, and the public prosecutors who tried to put me in jail. To my skillful and patient lawyers who worked for many months to defend me and to my many well-wishers and supporters from around the world, I owe a debt of gratitude. The trials against me and a number of other unpleasant events in my life have helped me to practice my Buddhist mindfulness, to be aware, to overcome anger, to cultivate seeds of peace, and to forgive, as well as to be grateful.

I am especially grateful to my wife, my children, my relatives, and my friends and foes. Without them, my life would not be as it is.

Sulak Sivaraksa
Schumacher College
Totnes, England
January 1998

◆

"No man can draw his own profile correctly because, as Thoreau said: 'It is as hard to see oneself as to look backwards without turning round.' The truth is that our friends—and our enemies—always know us better than we know ourselves." —W. H. Auden, from the foreword to *Markings,* by Dag Hammerskjöld

Beginning Anew

With great respect, we turn towards
Shakyamuni Buddha, the Conqueror of afflictions.
We have lived in forgetfulness for a long time,
as we have not had the opportunity to encounter the Dharma.
We have brought about our own suffering.
We have been blinded by our wrong perceptions for a very long time.
Our heart's garden is sown with attachment, hatred, and pride.
In us are seeds of killing, stealing, sexual misconduct, and lies.
Our everyday deeds and words do damage.
All these wrong actions are obstacles to our peace and joy.
Let us begin anew.

We are thoughtless, straying from the path of mindfulness.
We are a storehouse of suffering, worries, and anxieties
due to wrong perceptions.
And we have become weary of life.
Because we do not understand others,
we maintain ill-will against them.
Even after our dispute with them has been resolved,
we continue to feel enmity,
making the rift greater.
There are days when we are unwilling to speak to each other,
unwilling to look each other in the face,
and we create internal formations.
Now we turn to the Three Jewels.
Sincerely recognizing our errors, we bow our heads.

We know so well that in our consciousness
are buried all the wholesome seeds—
seeds of love and understanding,
and seeds of peace and joy.
But if we do not know how to water them,
and we always allow sorrow to overwhelm them,
how can they spring up fresh and green?
When we chase after a distant happiness,
life becomes but a shadow of reality.
Our mind is always occupied by the past

or worrying about this and that in the future.
We cannot let go of our anger,
and we long for what we have to be permanent,
thereby trampling on real happiness.
As month follows month, we are sunk in sorrow.
So now we recognize our errors and begin anew,
fragrant as a breath of fresh air.

With all our heart we go for refuge,
turning to the Buddhas in the ten directions
and all the bodhisattvas, noble disciples, and self-achieved Buddhas.
Very sincerely we recognize our errors
and the mistakes of our wrong judgments.
Please bring the balm of clear water
to pour on the roots of our afflictions.
Please bring the raft of the true teachings
to carry us over the ocean of sorrows.
We vow to live an awakened life,
to learn the path of true happiness,
and to practice smiling and conscious breathing.
Diligently, we live in mindfulness.

We come back to live in the wonderful present,
to plant our heart's garden with good seeds,
and to make strong foundations of understanding and love.
We follow the way of mindfulness,
the practice of looking and understanding deeply
to be able to see the nature of all this,
and so to be free of the bonds of birth and death.
We learn to speak lovingly, to be affectionate,
to care for others whether it is early morn or late afternoon,
to bring the roots of joy to many places, helping people to abandon sorrow;
to respond with deep gratitude to the kindness of parents, teachers,
and friends.

We ask the Lord of Compassion to be our protector
on the wonderful path of practice.
We vow to practice all aspects of the path with energy
so that our practice may bear fruit.

From *Plum Village Chanting and Recitation Book*, Berkeley: Parallax Press, 1998.

Dedication

This book is respectfully dedicated to the memory of the late Siamese senior statesman Dr. Pridi Banomyong, whose centenary will be celebrated on May 11, 2000.

Mr. Pridi was an exemplar of a socially engaged Buddhist—in the fields of education, economics, and politics. Hopefully, his centenary celebration will serve to remind the Thai public of the dangers of consumerism and globalization and urge us to look to our Buddhist roots to seek economic and political self-reliance, as Mr. Pridi experimented with from 1932 to 1947. In this way, Siam can leave behind its blind acceptance of the Western development model, discarding the name Thailand and its false connotations of material progress. Together, we can build Dhammic societies as Mr. Pridi envisioned, serving as an example to our neighbors of an alternative to consumerism.

Loyalty
Demands
Dissent

CHAPTER 1 | *Early Years*

I was born March 27, 1933, nine months to the day after the ratification of the first provisional constitution. I jokingly say that I must have been conceived on this very important day of the Siamese revolution. My grandmother noticed that my right index finger was always pointing at someone, which she interpreted to mean that I was born to be a leader. She told my mother, "You must take care of this boy. He will be somebody."

My father's story

On both sides of my family, the men came from China and the women were Siamese, which was common among the merchant and upper classes. Generation after generation of Chinese men came to Siam, married Siamese girls, and became Thai.

My father's father

My paternal grandfather was a well-to-do farmer in the Canton region of China, with a Chinese wife and two daughters. He had a younger brother, a hot-tempered man who liked to gamble. This brother quarreled with a neighbor and shot him. The man died, and by the Ching Dynasty's law, my great uncle would have faced capital punishment. So he asked my grandfather to escape with him to Siam. He supposedly swam with a sword in his mouth, carrying on his back my grandfather, who could not swim. Then they walked into Suotow, the big city, and took a boat to Bangkok. This occurred around 1870.

My grandfather and his younger brother got jobs in a small fac-

My grandparents' house on the Chao Phya River

tory that produced lime for whitewash. Soon they started their own business and crossed over the Chao Phya River to settle. They had two factories, one for each brother, and did wonderfully well. They bought big houses and more land. My grandfather married a Siamese woman and had eleven children. Five daughters and three sons lived to be adults. My father was the youngest. My grandmother became pregnant once more but died in childbirth along with the baby, and my grandfather remained a widower.

It was customary for Chinese men who married Siamese girls to continue to send money back to their families in China. Their sons often returned to China to be educated and to marry Chinese women. But their Siamese wives wanted their sons first to be ordained as Buddhist monks for a brief time, so most families compromised. My eldest uncle was ordained a Buddhist monk for a short time before going to China with his father to marry a Chinese girl. My second uncle also went to China with his father but refused to marry a Chinese girl. And my father refused to go to China altogether. By his time, the younger generation felt they were Siamese and had no particular loyalty to China. In fact, my father could not even speak proper Chinese.

At that time, many elder Chinese returned to China to die. Even if they died in Siam, they wanted their bodies sent back to China to be buried. But my grandfather was different. When he returned to China to have his eldest son married, his Chinese wife said, "You are now old. You should not return to Siam. Your son is also my son. Both of you should settle down here in our country." The old man asked, "What about my other children over there?" and she answered, "Why worry about those half-barbarians?" My grandfather got very angry. "I've been working there and sending money back to you, yet you call my children half-barbarians. If that's how you feel, I will go back and stay with my family over there, and I will not even send my body here when I die." After his death he was cremated, which was unusual for the Chinese, and his ashes were interred in a stupa with the ashes of his Thai wife. This was the end of our family's connection to China.

My father's name was Nam Chua in Chinese, Chalerm in Thai. He was born on November 15, 1902. Since my grandmother died soon after my father was born, he was raised by his eldest sister, who was twenty years older. Her daughter Banjong was only two years younger than he. They were very close friends. They went to school together and were the two most educated in the family. Both attended Christian schools, and she became a Christian. At that time, to become Christian was considered to be more progressive, and Buddhism was viewed as decadent, old-fashioned, and superstitious. However, my father was never interested in becoming a Christian, and later on, Banjong learned that there was more to Buddhism, and she became Buddhist again.

My father's two brothers both went to the same American mis-

My father (front row, center) with his family

sionary school, Bangkok Christian College. But they left school early because, in those days, if you could write some English and Thai, you were very much in demand to join the new civil service or to work for the newly arrived European companies. My father insisted on completing his high school education. There was no higher education at that time. So, after graduating from primary school at the Bangkok Christian College, he went on to secondary school at the French Catholic Assumption College.

My father wished to be as educated as the Europeans. He wanted to learn their language and their way of thinking. He was very Westernized. He liked to speak English—even kept his diary in English—and he liked to dress in the Western style. He wore neckties, never removed his shoes in the house, and ate with a fork and spoon, whereas my mother and aunts ate with their fingers. My father began working at the age of twenty and soon joined the British-American Tobacco Company as a clerk, then as an accountant.

My mother's story

My mother's family was financially much better off than my father's, and they can trace their family lineage further back. My maternal great-great-grandmother Lady Lim was well-to-do, having married two Chinese merchants; the second after the first had died. Like other members of the nobility and upper classes, she sponsored the build-

Wat Salari, sponsored by my great-great-grandmother

ing of a temple, Wat Salari in the north of Bangkok. This was a customary way of propagating Buddhism and providing a spiritual, medical, educational, and cultural center for the community. The monks' lifestyle served as a model of harmonious living for the lay members of the temple.

My maternal great-grandfather had several wives in Siam and China and twenty-five children. He had three daughters, Ngern, Mee, and my grandmother Mae, who were born to the same mother and very close to one another. This was about a century and a half ago. My grandmother's cousins controlled the rice trade in Bangkok, with branches in Batavia, Singapore, Penang, Hong Kong, Canton, and Suotow. They were the first Chinese to buy steam rice mills from the Germans, and eventually the family owned

My great-aunt Lom Hemajayati

thirteen rice mills. They also had ocean liners, imported many items from China, and became quite rich.

My mother, Supan, was born on April 9, 1908. Like my father, she was the youngest. Her mother Mae had one more pregnancy and died in childbirth. She called her two aunts "mother," and was adopted as the daughter of her elder aunt Ngern. I have always thought of both my great-aunts as my grandmothers.

They all lived in her wealthy cousin's household—there were more than one hundred people living in the same compound, like a small town. This millionaire great-aunt of mine, Lom Hemajayati, knew all of the high society. King Chulalongkorn and the princes and princesses all knew her. Members of the royal family came to her seventieth birthday ceremony, and the whole of Bangkok attended her daughter's wedding. Our family legend has it that when my great-aunt met the king, she offered him just two oranges. The king said,

"This woman is very unpretentious," and he ate both oranges. Later, when he built his marble temple, my aunt ordered tile from China and offered it to the temple. The king said to her, "I will be the earth, and you are the sky." I don't know whether he really said this, but that's how it was passed on to me.

After my great-aunt Lom Hemajayati died, there were quarrels among the many children and adopted children. Unlike the British, who recognized only one wife and left all or most of their money to the eldest son, the Thai and Chinese recognized all wives and children, so wealth did not remain consolidated for long. Few of them knew how to earn money—only how to spend it—and eventually, their enterprises collapsed. This was just about the time I was born.

My parents

But my grandmother Ngern was as capable as any man and started an enterprise of her own—a dry dock where the big junks that carried rice and salt got hauled and scraped clean. Her dock was not very far upstream from my paternal grandfather's lime and whitewash factories, and that's how my mother and father met.

My mother went to secondary school, which was quite unusual for a girl in those days. When my parents met, they fell in love right away. This was a little unusual as well, since among the well-to-do, marriages were usually arranged. My parents arranged their own wedding, despite the fact that the astrologers said they were not well-suited for one another. My mother was very determined to marry my father. But the astrologers were right. Their marriage did not last long. I was their only surviving child. When I was five my mother left my father and remarried. Secretly my father had married my mother's half sister Prasop and set up another household before I was born. They had four children. The eldest son Tu was one year older than me.

My early years

I was born in a modern nursery run by an American nurse. In the old days, Thais were typically born at home with the help of a midwife, but my father was very Westernized and my mother claimed to be progressive. This nursery was something new so they agreed on it, but I was the last in the family to be born there. The Thais didn't like the way the Europeans were running the hospital. People said that in hospitals and nurseries they saw spirits and ghosts of those who had died. That was their belief. The Europeans also introduced new ideas. For instance, a baby was only allowed milk every four hours, even if it was hungry and crying. In earlier days there were wet nurses if mothers didn't have enough milk, but by the time I was born, children were drinking cow's milk and milk in tins imported from the West. Whenever I cried, my grandmother Mee would give me milk. She would say, "What does this foreign nurse know about babies? I have brought up so many children and grandchildren." She used to bathe me with hot water and massage my fingers so that I would be able to hold them properly when I danced.

At the time when I was born, we lived in the big family compound. Because of our polygamous society, we were all related in one way or another—half brothers, half sisters. Many other people came from China claiming to be relatives. Since we produced rice, everyone had free rice, and each household cooked its own food to go with the rice. Every morning we would offer food to more than one hundred monks who would come on foot and by boat. At lunchtime, we would take food to the abbot and other masters at the temple next door whom we supported. This practice is also traditional. During the Buddhist retreat season, we invited the monks to preach at our house every night. Our household, the temple, and the Buddhist ceremonies were interconnected. It was a wonderful atmosphere in which to grow up.

We lived on the Thonburi side of the river, and the year of the Siamese revolution was also the year of the 150th anniversary celebration of Bangkok and the royal house of Chakri. Thonburi (Dhana-pura) was the original capital of Siam, across the river from Bangkok. In 1782, General Chao Phya Chakri took the throne from King Taksin of Thonburi and moved the capital to Bangkok. It is said that King Taksin cursed the usurpers and predicted that if Bangkok and Thonburi were to become linked with a bridge, it would signal the end of the dynasty. To celebrate the 150th anniversary of the new capital in 1932, the Memorial Bridge was built in honor of the dynasty's founder, King Rama I. In an effort to avoid the curse, it was constructed as a drawbridge. In June, revolution came anyway, bringing an end to the absolute monarchy, and replacing it with a constitutional monarchy. (See Appendix II.)

My stepmother Prasop

By this time, my mother's family fortune was coming to an end. At first we didn't realize it, because we lived in a big house with beautiful gardens maintained by four gardeners from China. But we lost one rice mill after another, until all thirteen were gone. We mortgaged the house and could-n't meet the payments, but because great-aunt Lom Hemajayati was so generous and good, the British bankers allowed her to live there until the end of her life. I was five years old when she died, and then we all had to leave the house. Our family moved across the river to Bangkok, and my other aunts and uncles moved elsewhere.

After we moved, my father and mother began to quarrel, and she walked out on him. I stayed with my father, and my stepmother Prasop came to live with us. I must say, my stepmother was very kind to me. Every now and again, my mother would come to see us. My father always thought very highly of her. He felt that he was the one who had made the mistake, but my mother never forgave him for secret-ly setting up house with her half sister.

That's how I was brought up on the Bangkok side of the river, and

I've lived in that part of Bangkok for nearly sixty years now. In those days, the area was not yet developed—just orchards, canals, and a few houses. We had mangoes, coconuts, bananas, betel nuts, oranges, pomeloes, durians, custard apples, and many other kinds of fruit. It was wonderful! Each area had a temple at its center and was more or less autonomous.

Although our new house was much smaller, my father invited his sisters to live with us, so our household included my stepmother, two aunts, and two or three servants. Later on, my father's eldest brother came to live next door with some other relatives. Other families that lived nearby also became like relatives. Neighbors would call us brother or sister, and we called them parents, aunts, and uncles. It was like that until about thirty years ago, but this kind of community is mostly gone now.

When I was five or six years old, I began school, a few hours a day at a small school next door, and then a larger school nearby. But I didn't get on with the teachers and never liked to be told what to do. So my older cousin Banjong arranged for me to attend the best school, St. Mary's, where she herself taught. She was very close to the missionaries.

St. Mary's, an Anglican school, was much better organized than my earlier schools. The teachers were all women and very devoted, and I stayed there for almost four years. Even though it was run by Thai people, they followed the Anglican style. We went to chapel in the school and were taught Catechism every morning. On the whole, I quite enjoyed myself there. For the first time, I stayed long enough to make a number of good friends. My younger half brother Pravit was a student there, too. He was very smart, particularly in mathematics, and always did well. I didn't do as well, but Banjong had a soft spot for me nonetheless and felt that I could be a leader.

After my first year at St. Mary's, in 1939, the name of the country was changed from Siam to Thailand by Field Marshal Pibunsongkram. Because he admired Hitler's idea of a great Aryan race, he pushed the idea of the great Thai race. We were taught to hate the Chinese, except for our fathers and grandfathers. Pibun, called the "Great Thailander," decreed that our country must be entirely Buddhist. Muslims and Christians were barred from entering the civil service.

He wanted to fight the French, who were being defeated by the Germans, and take back the four provinces that had been lost to the French in 1893, during the time of King Chulalongkorn, Rama V. I was too young to participate, but my half brother, one year older, was more or less conscripted to join the demonstrations. He was forced to walk all day to hear the prime minister denounce the French. On the way back, he collapsed and never regained his health. He died at the age of thirteen. My father never forgave the prime minister for this.

During my second year at St. Mary's, we no longer had chapel. Field Marshal Pibun made sure that Christianity was not taught. The school changed its name to the Peoples' School, and we started praying in the Siamese Buddhist way. My cousin recommended that I be selected to lead the prayer. We praised the Buddha, the Dhamma, and the Sangha before each lesson.

At first, Siam was neutral in the Second World War. But Pibun was interested in the Japanese, Nazism, and fascism, and he thought the Germans would win. The Japanese pressured the French to return the four provinces, and, in 1941, the Japanese army arrived. In theory they did not "occupy" our country, but in fact, they did. They were allowed into Siam to send their troops to fight the British in Malaya and Burma and to engage the Dutch in Indonesia. In 1943, they took over our school building, and we had to leave. Because of the aerial bombing, the school had to relocate several times. The area was full of Japanese disguised as merchants and dentists, but when the war

Three brothers in our militia uniforms

came, they all put on their uniforms. Officially, we declared war against the British and Americans. Luckily, our minister in Washington, Seni Pramoj, refused to communicate the declaration of war to the Americans. Still, the Allies bombed Bangkok. Our house was in a Japanese area that was fire-bombed, and we had to evacuate.

In the middle of my fourth year of primary school, my father decided I should attend his old school, Assumption College, for my secondary education. The Catholic college maintained its religious regimen, insisting that we say our prayers in the Catholic way and cross ourselves. In each classroom hung a painting of Christ, with either Mary the Mother of God or the Sacred Heart. We all wore uniforms—blue shorts and a white shirt. But Pibun, the Great Thailander, made schoolchildren join the militia, so every week we had to dress up like small military men with green shorts and a soldier's cap. Previously, classes had been taught in French and English, but by that time they were taught only in Thai.

Unfortunately, or fortunately for me, only a fortnight after I entered secondary school, the school was heavily bombed along with the rest of Bangkok. The Ministry of Education closed all schools in the capital, and many were relocated to the countryside. My school moved to Sri Racha, near where my mother and stepfather lived. My father asked whether I would like to go there, and I said no. First of all, I didn't like school. Second, I didn't want to be apart from my father. But my father was very conscientious about schooling. Banjong had not yet settled into a new school, so he asked her to come every day to teach my brother, my cousins, and me. I didn't like it at all.

We moved back to the place where my father grew up—on the Thonburi side of the river where my grandfather used to have his lime and whitewash factories. My family still lives in that area—brothers, sisters, and lots of cousins. Then, because of the bombing in Bangkok, we moved even further out from the city—thirty or forty miles—to the next province. My father had to commute to work every day by train. I was very happy out in the countryside. My cousin came along to teach us.

Most days I went out to see the folk dramas. During vacation I even went to an opium den to visit an old servant of my father. He had been with my father when he was very young, because his family had sold seashells to my grandfather to make lime. We knew his whole family. He had become an opium addict, but he was fond of me and I was fond of him. During the war cigarettes were scarce, but my father worked in the Tobacco Monopoly and had extras. I used to pinch them from his box to give to this old servant so he could trade them for opium. He took me along to the opium dens, where children were not usually allowed. In fact, few Siamese went there. The dens were supposed to be for Chinese laborers, but nobody checked.

It was a new world for me—men lying half-naked on bamboo mattresses, glistening with perspiration. The furnishings were imported from China, and there were Chinese pillows made of wood or clay. The opium was melted on a lamp and put into a long bamboo pipe. The men smoked it and had beautiful dreams. I never tried opium, but the smoke had a wonderful smell. I liked the company, and I heard all kinds of things. The men there considered themselves wicked. One chap had only one leg and a crutch, and he would boast, "Last night when a big bomb exploded in Bangkok, I pointed my crutch at Bangkok and the fire went out. I can make magic." I believed him.

Oddly enough, I learned some of my first Buddhist prayers in the opium dens. I learned all these supposedly magic words. They talked about all kinds of superstitions—on such and such a day you must face in one direction; on another day you must face the other direction; sometimes you must take three steps before you go outside; when you leave home you must put water on your head. I was fascinated by their talk. Of course, my father never knew I was there. Our old servant Mr. Leang warned me that my father would be upset.

It was fashionable in that crowd to be tattooed. Tattoos were considered magical. If you had a tattoo on your knee, snakes would never bite you. If you had a tattoo on your chest, you became very manly and women would fall in love with you. I wasn't interested in girls at that time, but I believed all the superstitions and wanted to have my body tattooed. I told my father, "I want to have some tattoos," and he became furious. He was very good to me, but he drew the line. "This silly thing will remain with you all your life. If you regret it later, you won't be able to get rid of it. When you grow up, if you want to have a tattoo, go ahead. But while you are under my care, you cannot have a tattoo." I never got tattooed.

I had gone to a Protestant school and a Catholic school. With most of the schools closed down, my father decided that it was a good time for me to be ordained as a novice and to learn something about Buddhism. A learned monk from the temple next to our former home was a well-regarded astrologer. He said it was a good idea for my half brother and me to be ordained, which was customary for all young boys in Siam. He saw some dark periods at the end of my father's life and said that if his sons were ordained, it might help him. So my brother and I entered the monastery in 1945.

We were supposed to be ordained for at least ten weeks, but for a boy of twelve that was difficult. My brother didn't want to be ordained at all. My father said he would give each of us a bicycle—a big gift—if we stayed two and a half months. After the time was up, my brother went back to school, but I liked the monastery so much I stayed on for another year and a half.

CHAPTER 2 | *Life as a Novice Monk*

'd always found school oppressive. We were supposed to be on time
to line up and salute the flag. The teachers never smiled, and I nat-
urally wanted to outsmart them. If they asked me to write from A
to Z for homework, I just wrote "A to Z." At the Christian schools,
they taught that Christ was the Lamb of God, but I'd never seen a
lamb, and it didn't mean much to me. I didn't mind making friends,
but the kids my age liked going to the movies, reading comics, and
other things I didn't particularly care for. I felt different. I liked traditional music, dance, drama, and going to the temples to listen to
sermons. I liked being with older people; I could sit and listen to them
for hours.

Being in the monastery was the first time I really enjoyed life.
Once you were ordained as a novice, a *samanera*, you were treated as
an adult. In our culture, different pronouns are used when talking to
children. Kids are looked down upon. But when I was ordained, although I was only twelve years old, twenty-five and thirty-year-old
monks used adult pronouns when they spoke to me. My master, Phra
Bhadramuni, had a strong influence on me. He was a great astrologer,
and his life was kindness itself.
He was sometimes very stern
to the other students, but he
was always kind to me. When
I was a novice, I used to go
and massage him, and he
would teach me. He told me
that I must always do my best
and not settle for anything
mediocre. Instead of seeking
fame and riches, I should

My teacher Phra Bhadramuni

*As novice monks
(I'm in the center)*

strive for excellency. Other monks in the temple were also important influences on my life. I loved the whole monastic atmosphere.

The temple gave me liberty. I could study whatever I wanted, and I became addicted to reading. Before, because I had been forced to read, I never got into it. But at the temple I would pick out books, even large volumes, and read them from cover to cover. I read all kinds of books—religion, history, literature. I've loved books ever since. I also became interested in traditional medicine, fortune-telling, and arts and crafts, which at school we'd been told were old-fashioned. I learned to meditate from a lay teacher who was well known for his insight-meditation technique.

As a novice you have to be observant. I was very good in this way, and my teacher gave me the sort of acknowledgment I never got at school. At school, if you learn your lessons by rote, you are considered capable. But in the temple you have to observe ceremonies and other monks' behavior in order to learn. You must be attuned to your own culture. Most of my contemporaries stayed at the temple for only a few months. They found the life too antiquated, but I felt like a fish in water. I wanted to stay for good. In school I never got to the top of the class, but at the temple my teacher felt that I was smart. I was the only one who dared to ask the abbot questions. In our culture, children and even grown-ups are not encouraged to ask questions, especially of an abbot. The abbot looked very formal and severe, but I asked him all kinds of questions, and he liked that, too.

Although I was the youngest, the superior of my house felt that I was special, and of course I liked that. In our temple, Wat Thongnopphakhun, there were thirteen houses, each headed by a superior, with five or ten monks, as well as novices and lay attendants. Our superior, Phra Bhadramuni, later became the abbot. When he was ill and had to go to the hospital, he gave the house key to me. I was twelve years old and in charge. I got senior monks to help, and together we had the house properly cleaned and everything carefully arranged. When he returned from the hospital, my master was very pleased that I had done as he would have wished.

At home, my father had treated me specially, and I was spoiled. He always felt a little guilty, that I was like an orphan because my mother had walked out on him. We slept in the same bed, and he told me tales. I enjoyed his company, but I treated other people badly. I never made my bed. I demanded whatever sort of food I wanted. My father would consult with me and tell the cook what I wanted. If the rice was too hard, I would complain and not eat it. If it was too soft, I wouldn't eat it either. I was a terror. At the temple, there were no servants. I had to make my own bed, wash my own dishes and clothes, and go out to beg for alms every morning. The culture of the temple was wonderful, and we were very proud to follow the rules established by the Buddha. Everyone was equal. Even my master washed his own dishes.

I attuned myself to the temple's system, but I also rebelled. Every morning and evening we were supposed to go to the consecrated assembly hall for prayers and meditation. One morning when we went, the hall was locked. The monk who was secretary of the temple wasn't there to unlock it. Nobody complained openly, but they

Wat Thongnopphakhun school, built by and named after my great-aunt Lom Hemajayati

gossiped about him. So I complained openly. I even wrote notices and posted them on the temple—that this monk was no good, that he was corrupt. He was furious. I was a troublemaker.

This life was Buddhism with a capital "B." I began to understand the distinction between Buddhism for educated people and popular Buddhism. I learned that a spirit house, which is said to house the guardian spirit of every household, is not quite Buddhism. In the temple, we are supposed to preserve the pristine teachings of the Buddha. Of course, some monks also become astrologers and so on—not for pay, just to help people. Buddhism and culture are intertwined.

During the Second World War there was bombing all around the temple because of the Japanese factory next door. Fortunately, bombs never hit the temple, but it was dangerous. The abbot asked us, "Since there's bombing here, would you like to leave?" One monk said he wasn't sure. Another lay attendant said he might leave. The abbot asked me, and I said, "Wherever the master is, I'll go along with him." He was pleased with my answer, but still decided that I should evacuate first. He felt that the children should be safe, and he would follow later. We moved about eight miles from our temple. In those days we had to go by rowboat, and it seemed far away. Although this temple was just on the outskirts of Bangkok, it was quite rural. The people were very devout. When we went out for alms, they offered a lot of food. It was a different atmosphere. On the full moon, new moon, and half moon, we walked all the way back to our temple in the city to perform the ceremonies.

I came from an upper-middle-class family and had only known people from that class. At the temple I met people of all classes. Because Phra Bhadramuni was a well-known astrologer, all kinds of people came to see him: princes, nobles, merchants, rich, and poor. Although he treated them each according to their rank, he was very polite and kind to everyone. At the end of the war, King Ananda Mahidol returned from Switzerland, where he was educated. There were big ceremonies and great joy. My teacher was invited to arrange the flowers for the altar in front of one of the large Buddha images at Bangkok's Marble Temple, and he invited me to help him. The king walked by to pay his respects. Had I not been a monk, I would never have seen the king face to face like that. When you became a

monk, all social barriers were removed. I felt that I could go anywhere. I've felt very close to the monkhood ever since.

In the early morning, as soon as there was enough light to see the
lines on the palms of our hands, we went out to beg for almsfood,
sometimes walking together in a long line, sometimes walking alone
or with a senior monk. There were many people offering food then.
Traditionally, the monks would eat together first, the novices would
eat after, and the boys who looked after the temple would eat last.
We had prayers and chants to promote mindfulness about the simple acts of daily life. At mealtimes, we cultivated the awareness that
meals are only to prevent hunger from arising and to keep the body
strong. The monks recited this in Pali at every meal. Every time monks
put on their robes, they recited "These robes are not put on for beauty but to protect us from cold, heat, and insects. Do not be attached
to the robes." When going to sleep, the monks recited, "This is our
house. It is only temporary, just to protect us from cold, wind, and
rain. Do not be attached to its beauty." When taking medicine: "It is
only to keep us well so we may help others." Food, clothing, shelter,
and medicine—these are known as the four requisites.

When we finished our meal, we would express our gratitude to all
who offered food to help us survive. In turn, we would help them by
offering the teaching, the Dhamma. If we didn't offer the Dhamma
or if we misbehaved, we would be considered thieves, and our food
would burn like hot iron in our throats. But the merit of giving and
receiving was not just for ourselves. It was shared among all beings,
living and dead. Following the morning meal, we had prayers in Pali,
taking refuge in the Buddha, the Dhamma, and the Sangha. Then
we would recite other verses from the scriptures. Afterwards, we had
sitting meditation. The novices did cleaning work for a short time
before the day's last meal at eleven in the morning. Sometimes the
monks were invited out. Since my master was well-known, many people came to offer food at lunchtime. All of us at the temple benefited from this, so that despite the war, we were not starving. After
lunch, there was a little time to rest. Then we had formal teaching.
For several hours we studied the life of the Buddha, Buddhist history, the discipline *(vinaya)*, and the discourses *(suttas)*.

Pleasures of the Rains Retreat

For the three months of the rainy season, monks don't travel. This is called the Rains Retreat. Throughout most of the year monks are encouraged to travel freely and to propagate the teachings. Traditionally, monks walk everywhere, but in the rainy season they might step on and harm the sprouting plants, so from July through September we were not allowed to travel or to spend the night outside the temple without special dispensation. And so, during the rains, all the monks would assemble, and many laypeople would also come to the temple for the preaching and ceremonies each night. Young men were often ordained while the best teachers were in residence. The Rains Retreat is also called the Buddhist Lent, because some laypeople would give up smoking, drinking, rude speech, fishing, and so on for this time. Others would vow to do good things. It was a good opportunity to practice Buddhism, to be mindful.

During the Rains Retreat, we had a sermon every night. Usually we heard Jataka Tales of the Buddha's earlier lives. In Buddhism you are not required to believe in previous lives if you don't think it's helpful to you, but the stories are still wonderful. Our culture is an oral tradition, and many people came to listen—mostly older women and young people.

There was no television in those days, but we had this preaching. I went to listen to sermons every night in the *sala*, the preaching hall. This is how I came to know Buddhist culture at its best. There was a nun, about eighty years old, wearing white, who noticed me. She said, "It's wonderful how this twelve-year-old boy comes to listen every night. At the end of the Rains Retreat we must invite him to preach." She proposed it to all the ladies, and they accepted. The abbot said, "Okay, give it a try, but you have to learn to sing and chant." So they gave me a small part in the story of the Buddha's next-to-last life as Prince Vessantara, one suitable for a young novice. I had to recite the verses telling how beautiful the forest was, what kinds of animals and plants lived there. I learned all about ecology and even some tricks to train the voice, like swallowing a whole boiled egg.

That year I collected more money than any other preacher, not because of my ability—to be honest I chanted very badly—but because

I was so young. Most boys my age hardly read, much less preached to the public. They had to carry me up to the high pulpit. People offered all kinds of delicious fruit—bananas, pomeloes, oranges, coconuts.

The end of the Rains Retreat is followed by the Kathina ceremony. The village offers robes to the whole community of monks. They offer other things as well and make donations to repair monastery buildings. Often two villages would collaborate.

The monks go their own separate ways at the end of the Rains Retreat. Those still in the temple on the last day perform a ceremony known as Pavarana. Once a year, each monk must come forward in order of seniority—beginning with whoever was ordained first, not by age or rank—to request of the whole assembly: "Out of pity for me, out of your generosity and kindness, if you have heard, or seen, or suspected that I have done anything wrong, please speak so that I will have an opportunity to change and behave properly." This was a helpful ceremony for me. I have used it in some of our groups: "Please tell us what we have done wrong so we can change." In the temples today, this sincere request is often just a formality. The same with the Kathina. Now the abbot usually receives the robes instead of the monks who are most skillful or whose robes are in rags. The Pali Canon spells out the meaning of these ceremonies very clearly, and it is wonderful when we can create the essence from the form. Unfortunately, they are now often performed as empty rituals.

When schools reopened in 1945 after the war, my brother left the temple. I stayed for one more year even though my father wanted me to come home. I had needed his permission to be ordained and leave home, but once one joins the monkhood, nobody can ask you to leave unless you are expelled. I enjoyed life at the temple so much that I didn't want to leave. I hated the thought of going back to school, wearing shorts, and being treated like a child. My father said, "I have land for you; I will build you a house." He would invite me every evening to see the house being built. But I was not interested in houses. I was interested only in the monkhood.

British troops came to Bangkok after the Japanese. There were also lots of Indians and Pakistanis, British and Dutch. There were bars for the foreign troops, and outside the bars were noodle shops for the taxi drivers and chauffeurs who drove the officers. Each evening I had to walk back to my temple past these shops. I had never been especially interested in food before, but now it smelled so good. I began to think, "Perhaps going back to school and my family might not be too bad after all."

My father continued his pleas: "What happens if you want to leave the monkhood at the age of twenty or twenty-five? What will you do for a living? In this competitive world, you need to have some skills. By the time you are twenty, I may be gone. Who will support you? After your education, if you want to rejoin the monkhood, I won't object." Finally I agreed. I left the temple and returned home to be with my father in the house he had built for me.

Our house on the Bangrak Canal

fter leaving the monastery, I returned to Assumption College. When the war was over, the old Catholic brothers came back. Since the Great Thailander Pibun regarded French Catholics as spies, most of them had gone to India, and some joined the Free Thai Movement against the Japanese.

I had missed almost two years of school while living in the temple, and so I didn't do very well at first. I thought I was fairly smart, but at school I found I didn't know how to answer the questions. The teachers were mad at me all the time. They forced us to learn by rote and gave a lot of homework. They also used to beat us.

Assumption College in Bangkok

My younger brother had gone on ahead of me, and I felt ashamed. My father told Brother Hilaire, who was in charge of admissions, that I wouldn't go to school unless I was in the same class as my brother. The old man said, "He can go into the second year provided he takes French, not English." He was a Frenchman and wanted to promote his language. My father said, "To tell you the truth, Brother, French is not so useful in this country. We prefer English." The old man said he would test me in English to see if I placed in the second-year class. I didn't pass the test. I didn't even know how to conjugate the verb "to be." All my reading at the monastery had been in Thai. Fortunately, the man who tested me was a very kind old upper-class Thai Catholic. He said, "Of course, this is understandable. The boy has been away for so long; he was a bit nervous. Give him some extra lessons, and he will catch up. Then put him in the second year." That's how I got admitted to school.

After I'd been in school a month and a half, I failed the midterm examination. My father felt he had lost face. My brother took first place, but I couldn't even pass. In a few more months I was doing quite well, but I never caught up with my brother. Those who did well skipped straight to the fourth class, so he jumped ahead of me. I gave up competing with him.

The only thing I really enjoyed about school was making friends. I got to know people from different backgrounds. There were Hindus, Muslims, Confucians, and Sikhs. We learned to respect each other despite our different cultures and religions. I liked to learn about rituals, so I went to midnight Mass at the cathedral. The Mass was in Latin then, and I tried to get a translation so I could follow it. A former student, Phya Anuman Rajadhon (who later became famous), wrote a book called *Friends' Religions*, which explained various beliefs. I was always interested in books on comparative religion like his, that respected other religions and rites. I admired the Catholic brothers for their devotion to teaching, their honesty, and their chastity. But I felt their vow of obedience—not to question their superiors at all—was a bit too much.

Our Catholic school was known as the "farang" school because we went there to learn a foreign language. We often looked down on the Thai language or anything else related to our culture. At first I rebelled against the Thai teachers. In particular, we treated the teacher who taught Thai language quite badly. He was bald-headed, which in Thai culture suggests a hot temper, and he beat me. But I realized that he meant well, so I took care writing his next assignment, and we became very close. Later, he taught my son, and after his retirement at age seventy, I sponsored his ordination as a monk and supported him while he spent his last years in the order. The Thai teachers were often quite poor, and they sacrificed most of their time for the students' well-being. When I realized they meant well, I became devoted to them. A number of these teachers became lifelong friends.

Even after I left the temple, I still read many books on Buddhism. I read everything by Sujivo Bhikkhu, a famous monk who appealed to young people. I studied Buddhist prayers, learned the Thai translations, and was very proud to be a modern young Buddhist. The Venerable Phra Vimaladhamma (Choi Thanadatto) had a great influence on me. He was brilliant. I knew him when he was abbot of Wat Mahadhatu. He founded Mahachulalongkorn Buddhist University after the Second World War. He became very popular and did a lot of lecturing. I read all of his works. He said we should not be ashamed to pray loudly, so of course I then said my prayers very loudly. Unfortunately, he died young and was succeeded by the controversial monk, also known as Phra Vimaladhamma (Arj Asabho), who was demoted and put in jail by the dictator Sarit Thanarat in 1962.

My father's death

My father died in October of 1946, not even a year after I disrobed.

My father

When I left the temple he was still strong, but soon after he fell ill with cancer and suffered greatly. I was very close to him. He spoiled me in many ways, but he loved me, and I will always feel gratitude towards him. He was honest and hardworking and tried to build up the family. Of all his brothers and sisters, he was the most financially successful— he had a big income and a good position. He taught me that I should be independent; I should not yield to any authority or tradition if I didn't find it helpful. In the Thai custom, if someone gives you something, you bow respectfully with your palms together. But my father told me, "If you don't want to bow, don't do it. If they don't want to give you something unless you bow, they don't need to give it to you." In many ways, I would turn out to be very different from him. He was for industrialization and modernization and didn't have much time for our indigenous culture. We might have had clashes when I got older.

When he died, his body was kept at home for months. During the first week, there were ceremonies and chanting by monks every night. People came to pay tribute with flowers and reeds. Weekly, they returned for further rites. In the Mahayana and Vajrayana traditions, this chanting is supposed to help the deceased in their journey to the next world. In the Theravada tradition, monks are invited to meditate on the corpse to underscore the impermanence of life and the decaying nature of the body. Laypeople are also taught about impermanence and selflessness and urged not to lament the dead. Any merit that we acquire through these deeds is transferred to the deceased.

When my father died, the family fortune changed. He was not rich, but he had been well paid. He was always helpful to his family and supported his brother, his nephews, and his niece in her nursing studies. Because he had a fairly high position in the Tobacco Monopoly, he sometimes found jobs for relatives, although he was careful not to appear to have special privileges and wouldn't support anyone with the surname Sivaraksa. The politicians who controlled the Tobacco Monopoly took advantage of their positions, and there was corruption at all levels. But my father was against it. He was known to be honest. He felt it was an obstacle to share his name, because even if his relatives were good at their jobs, people would say they got their positions through favoritism. Two of my cousins actually changed their names.

(Ironically, some years later, my sister-in-law felt that my stepbrother couldn't move up in the hierarchy because we share the same name—I had become quite a controversial character by then. My stepbrother was proposed to be the navy's aide-de-camp to the dictator Thanom Kittikachorn, but when they saw his surname, they passed him over. His wife should be thankful to me, since Kittikachorn eventually had to flee the country!)

I didn't know we had no money, but by the time all the ceremonies were finished, we hardly had anything left and had to sell things just to get by. My stepmother had a nervous breakdown and went to a mental hospital. I was forced to become more mature. I was looked after by my aunt Lom, my father's elder sister, until my mother took me to live with her family.

Life with my mother

Living with my mother, I was exposed to Chinese culture for the first time: Chinese New Year, Chinese Half Year, and the Moon Festival. When the Chinese Communists took over mainland China, many people fled to Siam and elsewhere in Southeast Asia. The Chinese were good carpenters, laborers, and so on. We wanted to help them any way we could. I even wanted to learn Chinese, but I didn't get very far. At my grandmother's dry dock, there were Chinese workers, so I tried to practice speaking Chinese with them, but in a few months they all spoke Thai with me. They had to survive, so they learned Thai quickly. I felt ashamed that my Chinese was not all that good.

At this time, my mother was still living with my stepfather Thavorn Ratanachomsri in the countryside. Mr. Thavorn was a kind of country gentleman, living near Sri Racha in a small village called Bangphra, halfway from Bangkok to Pattaya. It used to take all day to go from Bangkok to Bangphra by road, but in those days we still went by boat through the Gulf of Siam.

Bangphra was divided into the old town by the sea and the new town by the road. It was a three-mile walk from the old to the new. My mother and stepfather lived in the old market by the sea. There was no electricity or running water. People collected water from a common well used by the whole village. I was a city boy. I'd never lived in the country before. It was a new kind of fun for me. I carried water and met people in the village. I learned folk dances and local ceremonies. We were only a hundred miles from Bangkok, but the culture had its own identity. People spoke with their own accent.

Nowadays, television has done away with regional speech, which is a great loss.

Today we have no legs for walking any more, but back then I walked through the orchards and deep shade. I learned how to enjoy nature. There were hot springs but no tourists or commercialism yet. It was untamed. When my mother walked to the hot springs before dawn, she carried a long knife in case she confronted wild animals. She might see tigers, bears, or elephants roaming free. But by the time I arrived, much of the countryside had been cleared for farms and roads, and few large animals survived.

My mother was very good at making friends and had a number of friends around the area. I became interested in these local people. One old lady gave my mother a piece of property that my half brother eventually inherited. Her name was Plaek, meaning "unusual." She kept her small piece of land very tidy, with all kinds of fruit trees, like bananas and jackfruit. She never had to buy anything. She would offer fruit to the temple first, then she would collect some for herself, and then she would give some to people she liked. The rest she used to barter with people for what she needed. People would trade her fish or shrimp. When neighbors had a Buddhist ceremony, she would bring offerings from her garden, and the neighbors cooked, sharing their cooked food with her. She hardly used money at all. She was a very strong lady with a very simple life. She died at the advanced age of eighty-five.

Miss Plaek spoke the old country language, which didn't distinguish between high or low, male or female. In the speech I was raised with, men would use one ending for a sentence, and women would use another. The middle and upper classes used different vocabulary. Addressing the king, I would speak to the dust under His Majesty's feet—that would be the appropriate kind of speech. But this old woman wouldn't make such distinctions. I later wrote an article about her that caused quite a stir.

Another lady I met became a nun in her later life. At one time she had been governess in a prince's household, and so despite her rural background, she knew about the upper classes and sophistication. She told me that later on she found all these class and royal distinctions to be unreal. That's how she became attracted to Buddhism. She wore white as a nun would, ate one meal a day, and studied with various meditation masters. She became very ill before her death, but she continued to be very mindful, suffering mindfully. These people in the countryside influenced me greatly. I learned that answers were found not only in books but from all kinds of people.

During this period, I stayed with various relatives, moving from one household to another among my mother's family. My mother and I were not very close, but she was an influence on me nonetheless. She and I have a lot in common. She had a strong character and strong will, so we clashed often. She was hardworking and artistic—a good cook and skilled at making beautiful arrangements with flowers and banana leaves. She was interested in a popular kind of Buddhism, including mysticism, charms, spirit possession, and fortune-telling. She would take me to different gurus who were possessed by the spirits of dead beings. In those days, I looked down upon this as a kind of "lowly" science. I was a bit too stubborn and puritanical and didn't like it. Perhaps I should have been more broad-minded. I would have learned a great deal. Looking back, my mother was very kind to me. I feel very sorry that I was harsh with her.

Back to Bangkok

I also visited my father's house every now and again. Because we were poor, my father's house had became a youth hostel. Country people who came to Bangkok to go to university would stay at our place, paying for food and lodging, and a little extra for laundry. Eventually, I returned there to complete my secondary schooling at Assumption College. I lived with my stepmother, who had just returned from the mental hospital, and my aunt. My stepmother was like a mother to me. She was very quiet and never hurt my feelings. She was very fond of her own son, but since I was one year his senior, she felt that any responsibility must come to me. She relied on me when my father died. I was thirteen or fourteen years old. I was very close to her.

When my aunt died, my stepmother was so upset that she had another nervous breakdown. So I ran the hostel myself, even though I was still in secondary school. The hostel was just like a boarding school. Most of the boarders were senior to me—students at the university or several classes ahead at school. Even so, many of them were my age, since I had spent time away at the temple. Some studied engineering, others chemistry, physics, or medicine. We all talked late into the evening. My background was Buddhism and Thai culture. But since many of them came from the countryside and greatly admired Bangkok, modern Western science was the answer for them, and Buddhist beliefs seemed old-fashioned. We had countless political arguments because in the late forties and early fifties there were so many coups—the army, the left wing, the right wing. We argued about the direction in which our country should be heading. It was a stimulating time, and some of these people have remained lifelong friends. Today, most are old and retired from government service. We still keep in contact.

Our house was next door to my uncle's home, so we had a large extended family. In the old tradition, my uncle had several wives and numerous children, some treated better, some worse. I was friendly with all my cousins, but I usually sided with the cousins who were disadvantaged.

Although I have a hot temper and was a spoiled child, I could be diplomatic, and my relatives tended to like me. My extended family had a good influence on me. But when the time came, I had my say. I called a spade a spade. People say I became a rebel because I was raised like an orphan. I don't believe this is true. I think I am a rebel partly because my father encouraged me to be a rebel and partly due to my past karma.

My first publishing efforts

When I was a boy of fifteen at secondary school, there was a small controversy. A minister of state wrote an article criticizing Prince Damrong as being old-fashioned. This minister had been educated in England. He was a mathematician, a minister of industry, and a great literary man. But Prince Damrong was one of my heroes. The first book I had ever read was his famous book on our war with the Burmese. Later, I read most of his other works. He wrote in order to preserve our culture and history, and he used to argue that the royal family was a great thing for our country—and it was. Prince Damrong had helped King Chulalongkorn develop our country, and he had started the National Library. He and his half brother Prince Naris were both great literary men. They were spokesmen for the absolute regime—for royalty—and I admired everything they said.

When the minister made this attack on Prince Damrong, nobody dared to respond. So I wrote an article in defense of the prince and sent it to a literary magazine. The magazine editor was so pleased to receive my article that he said, "We have been rescued by an unknown scholar." When he invited me to come to collect the royalties for my article, he was shocked to see how young I was.

At that time it was fashionable for teenagers to put together clandestine school magazines. They were mostly full of sex and dirty jokes. I thought to myself, "This is a good idea, but I want to be more constructive." I thought a clandestine magazine should encourage people to go to the National Library or museum, to visit Chinese or Thai temples. Since I had already been a monk, I was interested in books concerning religion. I followed the new magazines on Buddhism and was particularly interested in Buddhadasa Bhikkhu, who wrote about Buddhism in the modern context. On Sundays, I would visit the museum or National Library or see classical plays at the National Theater.

So a few of us started a magazine with these things in mind, but at the same time criticizing our class master. At first he was very pleased, but then he found out we were attacking him. Since the word "communist" was a bad word—supposedly antireligion and antination—he said I was a communist. He went to the old French brother in charge of the school to argue that I be expelled or else he would resign amidst a big scandal. The old man, Brother Hilaire, an old-fashioned disciplinarian, was furious. He said I was just like a train that never wanted to run on the rails. "Be careful. You are smart, but you are not mindful, and that will be your downfall." He used the Buddhist words *sati* meaning mindful and *pañña* meaning wise or clever. He said, "At your age, you'll never agree with me, but just remember—when you see something wrong, be silent. To say something untruthful is bad, and even to say something truthful, you must find the right occasion." At the same time, he was fond of me and felt our magazine was encouraging to others except for the subtle attack on our class master. He would not punish me, and he would not praise me. The upshot was that our class master did not resign, and I was not thrown out of school.

Because of this situation, I considered transferring to another school to prepare for university, but I felt that Brother Hilaire had forgiven me. The old man and I loved and respected each other, and I wanted to do something for him, so I decided to stay. I chose the art stream, not the science stream, which meant I had to start learn-ing French. My teacher was Brother Victorien. He was very severe, but we got on very well because he recognized my strengths

Working on my first publication

and weaknesses. I told him, "I don't like learning by rote, but if you tell me to read something, I can summarize it and explain it in my broken English." He agreed, and we became close friends. When I was arrested in 1984, my name became known in France because a French Catholic organization helped me, and we renewed our acquain-tance after all these years. He's now in his late seventies, and I see him quite often.

The next year, 1952, we felt we should have an annual school mag-azine like some other colleges did. By this time I had become respectable at Assumption, known by my published articles and poems. It was suggested that I be the editor of this new publication. I agreed, but insisted on forming an executive committee to share the work. The school used to have a magazine called *Echo de l'Assumption,* so we called our magazine *Echo,* or *Echo under the Locust Tree,* because of the beautiful locust tree in the schoolyard. Brother Urbain, the principal, said, "I'll give you full support—I'll write letters to the old boys seeking advertisements and articles; I'll give you a pass to get out of school—but the school is too poor to offer any money." My friends asked me, "How can we do it without money?" I said, "Simple. Our school is very prestigious. We have over two thousand boys in

the school, all sons of rich merchants and senior government officials. Ask these boys to get advertisements from their parents for five
or six dollars for a full page. Give them a ten percent commission and
see what happens." He asked, "What about selling the books?" I
responded, "Easy. We ask every class to take a group photograph.
They'll all want to have a book to see their own photographs."

With that in mind, I said to our committee, "I'll take responsibility for the overall publication. You are in charge of getting the
money for printing." The committee got busy, and we raised much
more money than we had expected. The chairman became especially interested because he made a lot of money on commissions.

I edited the magazine to represent the whole school. I asked the
teachers at all levels to encourage the boys to submit their work—
poetry, stories, news, anything. Second, I wrote to all the graduates
now at university and urged them to send articles and photographs
to tell us of their activities. There was a very good response. Third, I
looked for names of former students in old magazines from before
the war. Some of them had become very prominent. I went to see
them in person to ask for articles and help. And, I wrote poetry in

Brother Victorien and our class at Assumption

praise of the king. In our tradition, we praise the Buddha, but since we couldn't do that at a Catholic school, we praised the king and the queen according to Siamese tradition.

When the magazine came out, it was more like a book, and no one had ever seen anything like it. The year before was the fiftieth anniversary of the French brothers—the Order of St. Gabriel—teaching in Siam, so there were many activities, and many alumni came. As a result of editing this magazine, I became well-known at an early age to my schoolmates and the alumni network.

On to the university

I graduated from Assumption College in 1952. I was nineteen years old. I prepared to go to Chulalongkorn University. My first choice was to study Siamese language and literature. My second choice was political science. At that time you could also study at Thammasat University without taking entrance examinations because it was an open university. At Thammasat, you didn't have to attend classes. You could prepare on your own and take examinations for a degree. So I thought I would take two degrees.

I wanted to be independent of my mother, who still supported me a little, so I went back to my old school and said, "Now that I'm at the university, I have plenty of time. I'd like to teach part-time in the school. I could teach perhaps two or three hours a day." The principal was delighted. It was a great challenge. I would be teaching Thai to my contemporaries, only a year younger than me. But my mother got very upset. According to our Oriental culture, she felt she should support me even though she was a widow. When she told me she was unhappy, I bargained with her. I said, "If you want to support me, don't support my university education—that is almost free. If you want to support me, send me to England." My mother had inherited some property from my stepfather, who had passed away a few years earlier, so she agreed, thinking perhaps it was a good investment to send me to England for an education.

Since we had opened our country to the West, the elites were mostly educated in England. It was a very conservative, very royalist education. Those who overthrew the monarchy in 1932 had been mostly educated in France (although the French brothers at Assumption had been royalists). The temple where I had been ordained was a royal monastery. Thus, I tended to be conservative. I liked the princes and the monarchy. I had been more or less brainwashed by my education. From books, I felt I knew Piccadilly Circus, Charing Cross, Buckingham Palace, and Pall Mall. American education didn't even enter my mind. If you wanted to be somebody, you had to be educated in England. I also felt that my destiny was to preserve and propagate Siamese culture. It would be difficult to reach my own people without an English education because they wouldn't listen to you otherwise. I thought, too, that with an English education I would be in a very good position to make my culture known to the West, and that I might understand Western culture beyond what I had received secondhand from missionary teachers.

Moreover, earlier in the year, a very dear friend went to England to study. My friend wrote to me, and I was very much encouraged. If he could cope with the English language, I could also manage. I also found out that it wasn't very expensive. It cost about fifty pounds a month, which I thought my mother could afford. If she didn't agree,

My sendoff to England

it would be difficult, although there were a few scholarships available.

Some people said I should not go; others said yes. The decisive word came from my teacher at the temple, Phra Bhadramuni. In our family, when we had to make an important decision, we went to him. Although my mother and I often disagreed, we both respected this abbot. He used his astrological knowledge as well as Buddhism to help us decide. He looked at my horoscope and told my mother, "This boy, with proper encouragement, proper education, will go very far—his destination is no less than a minister of state." Of course, my mother was very pleased about that! We agreed that I would go.

The amulet I've worn since 1953

Phra Bhadramuni urged me to travel at an auspicious time, saying, "You must leave the house on a certain day; you must face the proper direction." I answered, "Yes, Your Reverence, but the plane leaves on another day." He said, "Never mind. Leave the house on the day I tell you. You can go stay with your mother while you wait, but you must leave your house on that day." I did what I was told. He came to see me off at the airport, and gave me a Buddha image made 150 years earlier by the monk Somdet Toe, a famous meditation master. It was supposed to bring good luck and everything wonderful. I felt very touched. I still wear this amulet on a chain around my neck. It reminds me of the Buddha, of Somdet Toe, of my teacher, and of my mother, who gave me the chain. I wear it in their memory. Without them, I would not have had a chance to have the education I did.

A big crowd from school came to see me off. They gave me a wonderful party. That was in June 1953, the month of the coronation of Queen Elizabeth II. I traveled a fortnight after the coronation because it would have been too crowded in London any earlier. It was my first time on a plane, the first time leaving my country. I was all by myself.

It took me three days to get to England by plane. We left Bangkok at dawn. The first stop was in Calcutta for lunch, then we took off again and spent the night in Karachi, Pakistan. I saw camels walking in the streets side by side with motorcars—a great excitement. That night we visited a Siamese lady. She was married to a Dutch man, the local manager of KLM airlines, but previously she had been married to Kukrit Pramoj, who became prime minister and a principal adversary of mine in later years. She gave us Chinese food, much better than the meal offered by the airline.

Very early in the morning, we took off again. Our lunch stop was somewhere in the Arabian desert. It was very hot and dry. I'd never seen anything like it. We spent the second night in Athens, Greece. We went to the Acropolis, the heart of Western civilization. I felt very much at home. The next day we flew to Rome for lunch, then on to Geneva to change planes. We finally arrived in London after three days of traveling.

My friend Maitri Tantemsapya came to the airport to greet me and took me to a hotel in South Kensington. He lived in Bournemouth, about one hundred miles from London. We had to report to the Royal Siamese Embassy. Our families sent money in Thai currency to the Civil Service Commission in

In London with my friend Maitri

Bangkok. That money was transferred to London and converted into sterling. The Commission was very careful and very thorough. The Thai government had been sending students abroad since the reign of King Chulalongkorn. They gave us a monthly allocation—about thirteen pounds a month—and paid for our food, lodgings, books, and miscellaneous expenses. (By the time I was a senior, I received a small stipend and paid for all but tuition by myself.)

We had planned to stay in London for one week. It was the coronation year, a good time to see Westminster Abbey, Buckingham Palace, and other sights. Although the coronation was over, it was a great occasion for me. London was still beautifully decorated. June is also the warmest time of year, although coming from Bangkok it seemed very cold.

We called on a senior Thai statesman, Mr. Direk Jayanama, who had been a friend of my father. He was a former ambassador to the Court of St. James's and had been foreign minister many times. In fact, he had been the first Thai ambassador to England. At the time, though, he was more or less in exile because of political turmoil. He had supported Mr. Pridi Banomyong, who brought democracy to Siam in 1932 and was later kicked out in the coup of 1947. He had been very kind to me as a young boy and as a novice in the monastery. We enjoyed a good visit with him and his wife.

Bournemouth

After this visit, we decided to go to Bournemouth. It was expensive in London, and there seemed to be no point in staying. It was a sudden decision. We checked out in the evening and took the night train. We got to Bournemouth at two o'clock in the morning. My landlady, Mrs. Woodhall, was very surprised to hear our knock on the door, but she was very kind. Bournemouth is a seaside resort in the south of England. The Thai Embassy liked to send their students to the south; it's warmer, and the southern accent was supposed to be better than the northern accent. At that time there was a big influx of Thai students coming to England, about eight hundred in all.

That summer we went to the annual meeting of the Thai Students' Association. This was a tradition started when Crown Prince Vajiravudh was studying in England during the reign of Queen Victoria.

He liked to form clubs in the English manner. He also liked drama, translating Shakespeare, and writing plays. He encouraged the Thai students to form a club, called *Samaggi Samagom,* meaning "united society." We usually met once a year in the summer. The idea was to meet in order not to forget our Siameseness. It was also a way to get to know each other so that when we returned home we could help each other in developing our country through the various trades, professions, or branches of the government.

This year's meeting of the Samaggi Samagom was in Scotland. My friend and I had to go back to London and catch a train to Edinburgh. The platform was crowded with Thai students going to our summer camp. It was great fun to meet these Siamese students, some of whom became prime ministers and chief justices and quite a few of whom became lifelong friends. It was also exciting to see the Scottish kilt and bagpipes, but it was a dreadful, rainy summer. They still had food rationing, so the food was awful—oatmeal and rice pudding. We nearly had a rebellion. It was very difficult to find or make Thai food. There was no coconut milk, no curry. The only place to find chilies was in the shop that sold birdseed. There was no duck nor duck eggs. Duck was thought to be unclean.

School still hadn't started, so returning to Bournemouth was more play than anything else. My friend Maitri came from a very well-to-do family, and he had the latest model motorcycle. In those days, a motorcycle was the thing. A car was a bit beyond most of us, although a couple of Thai students had one. I had only a bicycle, so Maitri showed me around the area—Bournemouth, Southampton, Christchurch, the towns around Dorset and Hampshire. Getting to know the English countryside was wonderful.

The girls liked to ride on the back of a motorcycle. It was something very new after the war. We didn't have anything of that sort at home. Although I didn't have a motorcycle, one or two girls were interested in me. I was shocked. In our country we didn't even touch each other's hands. Although I was nineteen, I had never dated a girl before in my life. I had been rather in love with my cousin in Siam, but I never expressed it. She knew I liked her, and I knew she liked me. On her graduation, she asked me to escort her home, but I didn't even hold her hand. One time in Bournemouth, a pretty English girl came into the classroom during lunchtime and kissed me. I nearly collapsed.

School started in September. I had to take an entrance examination. The English did not recognize our Thai education, so we had to start from scratch. I attended Bournemouth Municipal College. I had to prepare myself for the General Certificate of Education (GCE). If you wanted to go to a British university, you had to pass the GCE in at least five or six subjects at ordinary level, ideally one or two at advanced level. Since I didn't do very well on the entrance examination, I was put in a lower grade. I didn't like it. It was just like being at home—a foreign teacher and many Thai students. However, within a few weeks I proved that I was quite capable. Most of my classmates came from very well-to-do families, and they didn't take their studies seriously. They liked to take their girlfriends out late at night on their motorcycles. They didn't do their homework, and they didn't get very far. After a few weeks, I was promoted to the more advanced class and was separated from most of my classmates. That helped me.

At the beginning, I took six classes—English, Latin, French, mathematics, history, and British constitutional law. I thought I could take the examination in the Thai language so that I wouldn't have to study much. Since I enjoyed literature so much, I volunteered to take English literature as extra. This helped me a great deal. At first they didn't think my English was good enough. When I took the entrance examination, I wasn't used to English pronunciation, so I didn't do very well. But when they saw that I studied at night and progressed quickly, they allowed me to take English literature. For the most part, it was just getting used to English ideas and English accents.

My first friend at the Municipal College was a chap named Graham Ferguson. Before I went to England, I was told that the English are very reserved and don't make friends easily. Once they invite you to their home, it means the ice is broken, so I was very flattered when Graham Ferguson invited me to his home. His father was a fishmonger. Every night after six o'clock (when the long distance telephone was cheaper), Mr. Ferguson would call a seafood wholesaler in Grimsby in northern England, and they would chat: "What sort of fish have you? I need such and such." The fish would come by the night train and arrive at Bournemouth at five or six o'clock in the

*With my friend
Graham Ferguson*

morning. He would go to the train station to collect the fish and open his shop at seven o'clock in the morning. He would sell most of it, and give away the leftovers—some for folks to eat, some for cats. He enjoyed his work very much. They weren't rich people, but Mr. Ferguson earned enough to send his three children to be educated. Later on, when the big supermarket chains came, mostly from America, they could sell to their customers cheaper than Mr. Ferguson could, so the old man went bankrupt. He had a breakdown and died in a mental hospital. I felt very bad about it and have avoided supermarkets ever since.

The Fergusons had a small shop and lived upstairs in a nice English home. Behind the fish shop was their sitting room. Graham's mother and grandmother would sit by the fire. I went to soccer games with Graham and his father. I became very friendly with the whole family. When I failed the French examination, Graham's uncle recommended that his colleague Robert Barrett help me brush up on my French. His wife Edith wanted to learn Siamese, which was very unusual, so she taught me piano and I taught her Siamese. The three of us became close enough for them to ask me to call them by their Christian names, which was also unusual for these times in England. I took the Barretts to all the Thai student meetings, and they enjoyed being with the Siamese. All through these years we've kept contact. Edith visited me in Bangkok years later after Robert passed away. She died in 1997 at the age of eighty-three. I often went to see the

Fergusons and the Barretts on school breaks. Graham and I have known each other for over forty years now.

At the end of the year I took the examination. I passed five subjects—all except French. Most Thai students took at least two years to pass English, although the other subjects were easy for them. My success was partly due to hard work, partly due to good luck. I consulted with my tutor, Ernest Jones, after I passed. I told him, "I don't want to stay in England long. I just want to get my degree and go home. I don't care which university." My friend Maitri, along with many other Thai students, wanted to go only to Oxford. He was very snobbish. He dressed like an English gentleman with an umbrella and a pipe. Mr. Jones suggested, "If you're not choosy, why don't you write to them all?" So I filled out applications to them all, in long hand.

I got two or three good replies. The most encouraging response came from St. David's College at Lampeter in Wales. It said, "For us, six subjects is fine. We would love to have you." I wrote back, "Only five subjects. Any chance?" They wrote a very nice letter. The principal even asked me to telephone him—in those days long-distance calls were not common. I used all my pennies to make the call. He said, "Why don't you come and see whether you like the place. If you like it and you pass French, we will admit you. If you don't like the place, you need not stay." Mr. Jones, who happened to be Welsh, said, "Go. Lampeter is a very nice place."

So I went to visit Lampeter. From Bournemouth I went to London. I took the underground from Waterloo to Paddington station, then the train all the way past Cardiff, the capital of Wales, to Camarthen. We had to change trains again for Lampeter. We left at seven o'clock in the morning and arrived at five o'clock in the evening. It was a very long train journey, but it was interesting. When you got on at Paddington, you could see the contrast straight away. In Bournemouth or London, the English never spoke to you. They would sit in one compartment, very fierce, serious, looking away with their newspaper in front of them. But on the train to Wales, they started talking: "Where are you going? Yes dear, yes love," and so on. I liked the Welsh. They are very kind and unpretentious.

We got to Lampeter in the evening, and I looked around for the bus to go to the college. They all laughed, "There's no bus here! You just walk." It was a real country town. The college, which is very beautiful and old, is the first college founded in England and Wales after Oxford and Cambridge. At the college there was a letter waiting for me saying, "We have booked a hotel for you in town. Tomorrow you can take the French examination." It was very cold in the hotel. In those days there was no central heating. There was a big clock chiming every hour from the town hall opposite my hotel. I was so excited I couldn't sleep very well. The next day I took the French examination and passed. I was qualified to begin college in October. I was very pleased. No Thai student had ever gotten into a university with only one year's preparation.

That summer, before going to Lampeter, three of us—Maitri, myself, and Graham Ferguson—cycled through the south of England from Bournemouth to Land's End in Cornwall, and stayed at youth hostels. But the weather was very bad that summer. It rained almost every day. We got so wet, and Maitri wasn't very helpful. He was a bit of a dandy. I had to do all the cooking, washing, and cleaning up. I washed his socks and dried them, but I didn't do it very well. When it rained, soap came out!

The college at Lampeter

Life at Lampeter

Not only was I the first Thai student at Lampeter, I was also the first pagan. When I went there, it was fairly old-fashioned—all boys, no girls. Chapel was compulsory three mornings a week, three evenings a week, and at least once on Sunday. On Sunday we had to wear white surplices; on weekdays we had to wear black gowns to lectures, to chapel, when we met our professors, and when we left the college at night. Being a Buddhist, I didn't have to go to chapel—that would be against religious freedom. But I volunteered to go; it was good discipline for me, and it helped me to learn English. I enjoyed all the hymns and psalms and so on. The principal said to the other students, "Even the Buddhist comes all the time. Why don't you people turn up at chapel?" I was interested in all the rituals and ceremonies, and I got to know the Anglicans quite well. Many of them tried to make me into a Christian. They said, "Sulak, you're a nice chap, but what will God make of you? You haven't converted. You won't go to heaven." I said, "You people have been very kind to me. Your God must be even kinder. He won't throw me out."

Nobody could own a motorcar. Bicycles were the usual transportation for most of the students. We could not entertain girls in our own room unless there was a chaperon, and then only until dusk. By eight o'clock we had to be back in the college or in "digs," the lodgings approved by the college. We had a room each. There was a sink and a commode underneath your bed. The bathroom was very far away, and the whole college used the same one. We all ate together. It was very English—wearing gowns to dinner and eating properly. Grace was offered in Latin. They even had "high table," where professors and lecturers literally sat at high tables.

At Lampeter and other English colleges, studying was very light. If you were clever, you didn't go to lectures but worked on your own. At most, lectures were only in the morning. At ten o'clock everybody went to town for coffee, which in England meant tea, of course. The English took sports much more seriously than classes. If you're not a sportsman, you're not a gentleman. They laughed when I went to join them. I couldn't even hit a cricket ball. But I enjoyed walking, and it was beautiful countryside. You could walk for miles in exquisite surroundings with brilliant lakes and Welsh sheep all around. My friends

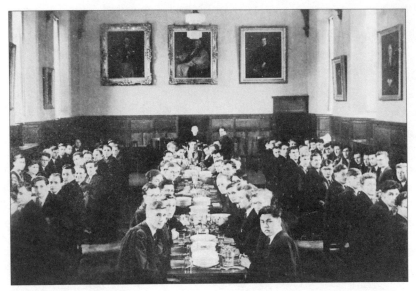

Dining in the English style

said, "Sulak, if you want to know English culture, you must go to the pub." At first I found beer very bitter, but finally I learned to like it and enjoyed going. I also found mutton awful but got used to it. At college I had no choice. We were required to eat three meals a day at the dining hall. The only meal that you could make for yourself was at tea time. I cooked rice and curry in my room and invited the other students to join me. It was great fun, and I became quite popular.

There were two cinemas a week—Saturday matinee and Tuesday evening. The students would date the local girls. To get back in after the eight o'clock curfew, they would come knocking on my window at one or two o'clock in the morning. I lived on the ground floor, so I would have to open the window for them to climb up. They made good use of me!

During the first term they held the freshman concert. They said to me, "You are Oriental. Why don't you do some Siamese dancing?" I said, "No, I didn't come here to be Siamese. I want to be like everybody else." So I joined them doing the French cancan. We wore black stockings and shorts and used our black gowns as skirts. We borrowed the girls' bras and had our scarves made into bosoms. It was great fun.

Each student had a "moral tutor." He was just like your father. Throughout your college years you could go to him with your financial problems, heartaches, and headaches. In Latin it was called "in loco parentis." My moral tutor, Frank Richard Newte, was a great Greek and Latin scholar. He was very good to me, but very shy—a typical Englishman and a confirmed bachelor. We played chess together, and he invited me to tea and for walks. Because it was a small college, each staff member at Lampeter had to take an extra job. Mr. Newte was the librarian and appointed me as his assistant. He said that since I was popular, I would be able to go to anybody's room to get books back. I was full of ideas. I thought I should keep statistics—how many books were out, how many were in. Mr. Newte, quite English, said, "What do you want statistics for? Statistics are only for the Americans. I am interested in whether they read it and whether they got the sense of it!"

I greatly enjoyed these Lampeter days. Lampeter was a very small college—only 130 students and sixteen professors and lecturers. Everyone knew everybody else. We could visit our tutor anytime, and the principal, Rev. J. R. Lloyd-Thomas, invited us for tea. His wife, Betty, kept in touch with me until she died in 1996. I made lasting friendships at Lampeter. Even now, when I go to England, I visit my friends.

I studied Greek (to the English, you are not educated unless you know Greek), English literature, ancient history, British and European history, general philosophy, and psychology—a general B.A. degree. There was no homework, but once a week we had to write an essay. At the beginning and end of each term was an examination, with a long vacation between terms. Each summer I was able to go abroad for vacation. The first time I went to Geneva, I stayed for three weeks. I thought I would learn French there, but I partied and didn't learn very much. The next year I went to France and stayed in a small château that had become a farm. The food was so good. In England, you ate to live, but in France, you lived to eat. I had my own bedroom. The first morning there was a knock at the door. A beautiful maidservant brought a *petit déjeuner* into my room: coffee, French bread, jam, cheese. Every morning I waited for the knock, but after that it was always an old woman. I was so disappointed.

They also let rooms to some old pensioners. I became friendly with one old lady. It bothered her a great deal that I wasn't a Christian. She said she would pray for me, since without a Christian baptism I would end up in hell. She said, "By the grace of God, you must become Christian." I answered, "With the grace of God, I don't have to become Christian."

Even so, I liked the lifestyle of a vicar in England. He could help people in need and conduct services one day a week and also have a wife and children. In a Buddhist monastery you can't do that. But Christianity as a religious philosophy never appealed to me. I felt it was limited to only one history. It could be true for that people, but I couldn't accept its claim to be true for all people. Why should the Jews alone be chosen, and why should the one Christ be born in that particular place? If Christ had been born as Jesus in one time and place and as the Buddha in another, I would have found it much more to my taste. God would be more encompassing. But I never argued when others tried to convert me to Christianity. And I never talked to them about Buddhism. They never asked.

I made many friends in the Church of England. Some of them now have high positions—Vicar of Hampton, Prebendary of St. Paul's, Dean of Rochester, Archbishop of Wales, and so on. Recently, a few have become interested in Buddhism. They say, "Sulak, you must have something good in your religion. When we tried to convert you, you were never attracted, yet you never opposed us. You were quiet and smiling, and you never once told us anything about Buddhism." I said, "I did not tell you because you did not ask. In Buddhism, we are told not to teach people unless they want to know. And even when they want to know, tell them just a little bit. If they want to know more, tell them a little bit more. Otherwise, it's just an advertisement, not the truth."

While at college, we didn't read much. They told us what to read during the vacation. When we came back for the new term, we had to take a test to see whether we had done the reading or not. All the English students pretended not to do any work. To appear to work was inappropriate for a gentleman. It meant you were a laborer. I didn't know they were just pretending, and as a result of not working myself, I failed my first examination in English literature. I wasn't too worried, since I could take the test again next term. It was only one subject. But I went abroad during the next vacation and took a job to earn extra money, so I failed the test again. I had been the first Thai to enter college after just one year, but now I had failed twice. Throughout my life I had never failed before. Even though it was just a minor examination, it hurt my ego tremendously.

I felt I might as well make the best out of my failure. I consulted with my moral tutor, suggesting, "What if I leave the college for a year and come back to take the examinations or just for the last term? I want to study law at one of the Inns of Court in London. I would like to become a barrister." I had been interested in studying law, hoping that I could become somebody important in Siam, perhaps prime minister or cabinet minister, and you had to know law to do this. He agreed, "I think you should apply." So I applied to one of the Inns of Court and was admitted.

Studying law in London

There are four Inns of Court: the Middle Temple, the Inner Temple, Gray's Inn, and Lincoln's Inn. They date back over one thousand years. I was admitted to the Middle Temple. In the Inns of Court, to become a barrister, you are required to "keep twelve terms," meaning that you have to dine in the hall three nights a term for four terms a year. When you become a lawyer, you're also supposed to become a gentleman. You must know how to dine, how to dress, how to speak, and so on. In England everything was so classy. Around the law court, they dressed in the old style: striped trousers, top hat, black jacket, and sometimes a morning coat with long tails. It was as if they had come out of a Charles Dickens novel.

When you were a barrister at law, you first became a lawyer of the outer bar, which meant you could argue the case far away from the judges. You were very junior and had to join a chamber. The head of the chamber was usually a QC or Queen's Counsel. He gave you a green bag for all your legal documents. You carried that to court with your gown and wig. When you became somebody more important, you got a red bag. Finally, you might become a QC, very limited in number and recommended by the Lord Chancellor. You then "take silk" and wear a silk gown instead of cotton. Your wig is now long, like a judge's wig. You no longer argue the case at the outer bar but at the inner bar next to the judge. You can even tap his throne. You can see these changes on the nameplates on the doors: "Mr. Norman"; later on "Mr. Norman, QC"; then "Sir Henry Norman, QC"; and finally "Lord Norman." All this custom and ceremony fascinated me.

During that term in London I also joined the Buddhist Society. They had one small room in those days at 16 Gordon Square, next to London University's School of Oriental and African Studies. Mr. Christmas Humphreys was the president. His book, *Buddhism*, had just become famous. I met a lot of Western Buddhists there. I became friendly with the president of the Pali Text Society, Ms. I. B. Horner. It had been founded by T. W. Rhys Davids in 1881 to publish Pali texts. It was good to get to know all these Westerners interested in my culture. At the same time, I was getting to know the leading English personalities from the law courts. From the legal profession they had risen to become prime minister and members of Parliament (MPs). I would go to the House of Commons and House of Lords to see how they worked. That was part of my education.

After two terms at the Inns of Court, I went back to Lampeter. I would travel to London each term to dine at the Middle Temple and maybe see a play. I stayed with my cousin, Sala Sivaraksa, who worked

A new "Bachelor"

at the Thai Embassy. I continued my law studies by correspondence course and took an examination every so often. Back at Lampeter, I passed my examination easily, and it was clear sailing from there on. The general degree course at Lampeter gave me a good background in European civilization and an understanding of the English and European mind. In philosophy, I began with the Greeks, then the Middle Ages, then Descartes, Spinoza, Locke, Hume, and Berkeley.

The idea was to stimulate us to think clearly and to argue properly. The same was true with history. The British system doesn't teach you everything, but it teaches you how to get to the truth, to examine the evidence. My last year I earned First Class Honors in philosophy. I had learned how to argue in the English way! When the time came, I received my degree. The superintendent of the Thai Students' Office in London was very pleased and came to my degree ceremony.

Thai Students' Association

Every year during the long vacation, I went to the Thai Students' Association reunion. After the first year in Scotland, it was held for two years at Brianston, a public school in Dorset, not far from Bournemouth. The second year I took part in a debate. I had never been a public speaker before, although I liked to attend debates in Bangkok and admired the eloquent speakers. When they asked for volunteers, I was shy. In our culture you never volunteer to do anything; people ask you. Maitri put my name forward, so I joined in. I prepared my talk, but I refused to use any notes. That year the superintendent of Thai students came to give a lecture before our debate. He was an old man and read from his notes. I thought, "Good lord, this excellent man is reading from notes, and I have no notes. In five minutes I have to go up there." But, I got up all my courage and spoke anyway. There was big applause, which, of course, I enjoyed. The next year I also took part in the debate dressed up in my national costume.

The association also published a magazine, called *Samaggi Sara*. The editor, Mr. Chaiwat, had come to England with Mr. Direk Jayanama. He eventually got a job with the BBC and became honorary editor of the magazine. He published a number of my articles, one of which, "Let's Speak Siamese," became well known in those circles.

My great weakness has always been that I want to reform things. I felt that the Thai Students' Association had much to offer beyond enjoyment. It should prepare and unite us to do something for our country and society. I proposed a reform of the association. They liked my speech, but when I suggested we do this or that, nobody wanted to work on it. My speech may have fallen on deaf ears, but the new editor of the magazine liked it. "What you said is true. Our magazine should have more meat. Why don't you join me on the editorial board?" (This editor was himself a rebel of sorts. Later he became a minister of state.) This was in 1957, the year 2,500 of the Buddhist era by Thai reckoning. They asked me to produce a commemorative magazine not simply for the association but for the whole Thai student community in Europe. There was no money to produce the magazine, but I accepted anyway.

I formed a committee and asked Thais from various European countries to be representatives, to send articles, and to find subscribers. I got some money from the ambassador. I wrote to all the European firms with offices in Siam and got enough advertisements to have the magazine produced. I collected articles and divided them into a European section and a Buddhist section. They were on themes such as the meaning of a European degree or marriage to an English or European woman. Ms. I. B. Horner wrote an article on the Pali Text Society. Edward Conze wrote a piece on the Western approach to Zen. I wrote something on the state of Buddhism in Europe at that time. I also quoted from various books concerning life abroad during the last hundred years. We included poetry and essays. It came out as a nice volume and was very well received by the Thai press. They said, "Usually students abroad write very poorly in Thai, mixed with foreign words. This is pure Thai, of high literary style."

We had a little money left from the magazine, so I proposed that any surplus go to the Fine Arts Department for conservation of mural paintings at various old Thai temples. The director general of the department said that if the students from abroad would take an interest in the preservation of Buddhist art, it would make a big difference. We started a very good cause, and a lot of people became interested in the preservation of Buddhist art.

Working for the BBC

Mr. Chaiwat suggested I submit my articles to the BBC, where he then worked. I sent an article concerning Siamese students abroad. Mr. A. C. Pointon, head of the Thai section, liked the article and wrote to me at Lampeter saying my article had been approved for broadcast. They would pay my train fare plus seven guineas. He also suggested I send more articles for his consideration. I enjoyed writing, and I didn't mind the money—seven guineas was quite a lot. I was in heaven. I had a big celebration and took my friends out for a good meal.

My first talk considered why the Siamese sent their students to Europe. This was in 1956, the one hundredth anniversary of the first Siamese Embassy to England. Mr. Pointon liked it so much that he sent my talk to the Thai ambassador and asked him to speak on the occasion of this anniversary. After my graduation, Mr. Pointon asked, "Would you like to become a part-time broadcaster here?" There were four Thais and one broadcast at about half past eight in our country. The pay was very good. I said, "Yes, why not?" and became what they called a "casual." They called when they needed me. We had to translate the news, and sometimes we were asked to write a feature article. They paid my way to visit various places, and I became interested in writing on different aspects of English culture. I wrote about a visit to Canterbury and about my old college. I learned a little about the operations at the BBC as well.

When I was about to return home, Mr. Pointon offered me a steady job. My broadcast was popular. At the same time, I was writing for the *Police Monthly*, and my broadcasts were occasionally published by the British Information Service, so I had a fairly wide audience. The contracts were usually three years. I had finished my education, and my original idea had been to get a degree and then go home. But I had started my legal education and felt it was a pity to leave it undone. Here was a way I could complete my law degree and earn a living without needing my mother to support me anymore. He said, "You don't have to decide right away, but leave your application here. You stand a very good chance since we know you." So I left the application and went home by boat to see my family.

Return to Bangkok

I had been away for five years, and Bangkok had changed tremendously. When I left in 1953, Bangkok was much the same as when I had been born in 1933. The area was full of rice fields and orchards. There were small signs of development, but there were still trees on both sides of the street and canals everywhere. Bangkok was on very flat land, and the canals provided our main transportation and livelihood. Thai people had always liked to live by the river. When we needed to expand the city, we just dug a canal. That's how Bangkok expanded.

Only small ships could come up the river because of the sandbar at its mouth. This prevented salt water from coming upriver, and we could grow all kinds of things: durian, mangosteen, oranges, mangoes, longan, lychee, all kinds of bananas, whatever you can think of. We had hardly any industry; it was all agricultural. Although the war had been over for several years, we were still very poor. Electricity was not working properly because the power plant had been bombed during the war. The water supply was also fairly poor because although Bangkok was expanding, the water system hadn't. This was the negative side of living in Bangkok, but there was plenty of space. Middle-class families had their own houses and yards. We built raised houses and dug a pond connected to the canals. We used the water for washing, laundry, and even fishing. We were self-sufficient.

The mayor and city council didn't do very much because we looked after ourselves. In fact, when I was a boy, Bangkok was just an amalgamation of villages. Each village was more or less autonomous. The *wat*, or temple, was the center of activities—educational, spiritual, cultural, even medical. If the wat was wealthy, there would be all kinds of artists around, so it became like a museum or art gallery. We had birthday parties and funerals there, and year-round we went to the wat for ceremonies and holidays. We used to live on floating houses around Bangkok, until the Great Thailander Pibun said, "This is not civilized." In fact, the Great Thailander wished to see an industrialized Bangkok full of chimneys and smoke instead of one full of spires, pagodas, and temples. He had come back to power in 1947 and opened the country to the Americans. We sent troops to the Korean War, and, for the first time, received American aid. The Americans started sending experts and officials to our country. When I left, I could see things were changing, but on the whole Bangkok was still intact.

When I came back, the first thing I noticed was that we docked at the new Bangkok harbor, about five miles downstream. They had dug the sandbar out to allow big ships to pass through. Bangkok wanted to be progressive, to develop, to compete with Singapore, which was still under British control. But with the new harbor, salt water came upriver and destroyed many of our orchards. Most of our temples near the river had murals and frescoes that were ruined by the salt. I couldn't see anything but roads coming from Bangkok harbor to my house. They had filled the canals and cut down all the trees. Dreadful!

In other respects, Bangkok was still beautiful. I had missed it. Outside Bangkok there were jungles and rice fields, entirely different from the English countryside. Just fifty kilometers from Bangkok was the biggest

Bangrak Canal completely filled in

pagoda, Phra Pathom, the place where Buddhism was supposed to have first come to our country. The area around the pagoda was full of palm trees. It made me feel very good to be back. My old friends at Assumption College made a big fuss. I was the first among us to return from England with a degree. They threw a party at a seaside resort.

All my relatives were very pleased. My mother wanted me to work. I was offered a job at the university and at the Ministry of Education. Mr. Direk Jayanama was by then head of a small company and dean of political science at Thammasat University. He offered to put me in touch with the chief of Shell Oil Company. If you worked for a foreign firm, you were much better paid and had a lot of privileges. But my heart was set on the BBC. My mother wasn't very happy about it, so we had to consult the abbot at the monastery. He said it would be good for me to return to England to acquire more degrees and more experience. It was good to have a foreign degree, but now quite a number of people had foreign degrees. My mother wouldn't have to pay, and I could even save a little bit of money to send to her. It was agreed that I should go back.

While home, I visited my cousin. Before I went to England, I had fallen in love with her but said nothing at the time. While in England for these five years, I had written to her, and she wrote back. Even so, in our culture things were very indirect. Everybody knew we were in love, but we never told each other. Before I returned to Bangkok, she had told me that a much older man was seriously interested in her. She was not in love with him but felt he might be the best man available for her at that time. A lot of people liked the idea of her getting married. I wrote back, "Go ahead," although I was not quite sure of my feelings. When I came home, I became very jealous. When I went to see her, we went out together for a meal. I was very angry. I didn't say I loved her but asked her, "Would you like to break your engagement and come with me? I'm going to England. The BBC will pay for our passage." She said no, it wasn't possible. She may have felt she would not be happy because I was so stubborn. Whenever we quarreled, she was always the one to ask for forgiveness. Perhaps she felt this older man offered more happiness in the long run. So that was that.

I spent the rest of my time in Bangkok publishing our magazine to commemorate the Buddhist year 2,500. I also learned how to type and how to drive.

Wearing the Thai costume, 1958

CHAPTER **5** | *Living in London*

Working at the BBC

I returned to England in January of 1959. London was cold and foggy, and nobody met me at the airport. I took a bus to the London terminal where the BBC sent the most junior man in the Thai section to meet me. This chap, Kriengsak Sirimongkol, happened to be a friend of mine. We had studied law together in London, and he had just joined the BBC with even less experience than I. We became very close. (Eventually, he became ambassador to Egypt, but he died very young.) Kriengsak took me to the BBC hostel, and I stayed there for a few weeks while I looked for housing. The next day I reported to the BBC and assumed my position.

There were four people working in the Thai section. The man I replaced was to become chief of the Thai section for the Australian Broadcasting Corporation. In London the chief had to be English, but in Australia the chief man could be a Thai. He offered me his flat to rent. It was very cheap but a long trip from work on the Underground and buses. I liked anything cheap, so I said okay. It was just one room with a stove. There was a telephone outside, and I shared the bathroom and toilet with

My BBC publicity photo

the landlady. Every time I used the telephone, I had to leave money or a note. To heat the water for a bath, I left money to pay for the gas. We were allowed only one bath a week. In Siam, we pour the water over ourselves. We had never heard of just lying in a big tub of water. I would fill the tub with fresh water three times to rinse off. The third tub of rinse water was very clean, but of course all the hot water was gone. My landlady complained bitterly. "Sulak, when we boil water for a bath, it's for the whole family." I responded, "By our custom we must have three rinses to make our bodies really clean." My landlady replied, "In this country you get into the bathtub, you wash with soap. That's it."

I had two jobs. One was to earn a living at the BBC and to send some money to my mother. The other was to pursue my legal education. Work at the BBC was fairly light since I was experienced, so I spent most of my time studying law. By that time I had passed Roman law and criminal law. Those were the easiest. The other three were much more difficult: contracts, torts, and real property. English land law is very complicated. I was also interested in studying Pali and spending more time on Buddhism. By that time there was a Buddhist *vihara* run by the Singhalese. I was very close to them. The monk in charge, Venerable Saddhatissa, wrote *Buddhist Ethics* and became well known later on. He asked me to lecture and help with ceremonies. I began to bring the Thai community to the vihara.

After being at the BBC for three months, we were sent to a formal training program lasting one month. They taught us how to use a microphone, timing, how to respect your interviewees, how to pro-

Broadcasting for the BBC

duce plays, and so on. One day, Mr. Pointon told me secretly, "Sulak, nobody in your country listens to the BBC Thai section. You know that, and I know that. So enjoy yourself. You are a creative artist, and I give you a free hand." We were all spoiled. The BBC sent me up and down the country to do reporting. I had my train fare paid, and I really enjoyed myself. I stayed with my old college friends—one in Guernsey, one in Jersey, one in Grimsby. Many of them were clergymen.

Mr. Pointon was very kind to us. He'd been in the Special Force 136, an intelligence agency involved with the Free Thai Movement during the Second World War, so he felt close to the Thai. Before that, he had been manager of the British Bombay Burma Company, so he spoke several Asian languages. He and his wife invited us to dine at their hotel. He brought us to his small, exclusive club where they served Oriental food. He also belonged to the East Indian Club, where they served good Indian curry.

The clubs were one of the great things about London. A foreigner usually could not participate in the clubs. Only those educated at Oxford or Cambridge could join the Oxford-Cambridge Club; the Tories could join the Tory clubs; liberals could join the Reform Club. Of course, the clubs were very chauvinistic. Men could go there to escape from their wives, but they always had to dress like gentlemen. I was interested in observing the different aspects of society, so I said I wanted to write about the clubs for the BBC. First, I went to the Royal Overseas League, a club open to all members of the British Commonwealth. Lord Louis Mountbatten, the earl of Burma, was the president of the club. He was a big man. When I went to the club, all the reporters were around him. Somebody told him I was from the BBC. He said, "Ah, you are Siamese, eh? Your king is coming to our country. I've known your king since he was a lad. We have the same tailor." I ended up doing a piece for the BBC on the tailor, Hawke and Curtis.

The director of the club saw me talking to Lord Mountbatten and asked if I would like to join the club. I said, "My country's not a member of the Commonwealth." He said, "Never mind, we'll make you an honorary member. You don't even have to pay." So I became an honorary member of the Royal Overseas League, which was very handy. I could entertain my friends and show off the elegant dining room. They served delicious roast duck. The club had various activities for the members. Because the Queen was patron of the club, ten to twenty members could go to the Queen's birthday party at Buckingham Palace. We also went to the Glyndebourne Festival, just outside London. They staged Italian opera with elaborate costumes and real jewelry, and they sang in the original Italian.

I also got a glimpse of upper-class English society through the Middle Temple of the Inns of Court. The Queen Mother was honorary treasurer, and she came once each year to dine at high table. She would drink wine from a silver chalice, then pass it to all the members of the high table, and finally to us all over the hall. We would stand up four at a time, drink, clean the top, pass it on, bow to her, and sit down. Sometimes, the Queen Mother would come to a tea party in our beautiful garden. She talked to me once when the Siamese king was planning a state visit, and she shook my hand. I loved shaking hands with royalty.

I continued to attend the annual meetings of the Thai Students' Association. Although I was no longer a student, they always asked me to speak. I encouraged them to include the monks at their meetings. At that time there were no Thai monks, but I thought they should get to know the Singhalese monks. They took my advice, and the monks would preach to them. I enjoyed working and studying in London. My plans were clear. When the examinations came, I would study hard and pass easily. In the summer I would tour Europe, and I would still have money to send home. It was a happy time.

But all good things must come to an end. Mr. Pointon retired, and the BBC brought in a new man, Mr. Kingsley. He was the opposite of Pointon—short, chubby, and bad tempered. He had run British broadcasting in Kenya when it was a colony, and he had a typical British colonial attitude. He used to bang on the table at staff meetings. On the one hand he appreciated me because I had ideas, but he didn't like me to correct him. One day, Kingsley made a rule that everybody had to come at nine o'clock in the morning and leave at five o'clock. I said, "No. We are creative writers. We do our half-hour broadcasting, that is our job." He became very angry and banged on the desk. I banged back and said, "You cannot treat the Thai in the colonial way. We were never colonized by the British." Then one day Kingsley called a meeting. "They want to make the Thai section redundant," he announced. As Pointon had said, nobody took the Thai section seriously. He said, "We'll close the section by the end of the month, give you six months' salary, and pay your airfare back home."

I had not finished my law exams. I had only completed the first part. I wanted to stay in London to finish the examination. It might take six months, or perhaps a little longer. Luckily, I had taken on another job at the BBC, teaching English by radio. They said they'd pay me for every recording as long as I continued and would hold my airfare for me. So I had money to survive for at least six months.

When I was back in Bangkok, a friend had told me about the Asia Foundation, something new from America. "They are interested in young scholars. In Southeast Asia they offer scholarships for people to study not only in America but in other parts of the world. If you need some money, you can apply." At the time I wasn't interested, but when my BBC job ended, I thought I might as well apply. The truth was that I needed a scholarship to finish my law exam.

I wrote to my friend Phya Anuman Rajadhon about the Asia Foundation. He was a man I had respected for a long time, an Assumption College alumnus. He was so diligent and extraordinary that he rose to the rank of deputy director general of the Customs Department. After the 1932 coup he was sacked, but because he was a great scholar, they asked him to join the Fine Arts Department, and he rose to become its director general. He was a fine scholar, but he kept a very low profile. I corresponded with him all through my years in England, and I regarded him as my guru. Our correspondence was later published in a book.

Phya Anuman himself went to the representative of the Asia Foundation, Mr. Harry Pierson. He wrote me a letter saying, "Never before has Phya Anuman himself come to my office. Please write your *curriculum vitae* and explain why you need the scholarship." He arranged for a woman to interview me. She was an American lady, very down-to-earth and outspoken, very tough. I told her, "I need only fifty pounds a month." I referred her to the Thai Embassy, the Office of the Superintendent of Thai Students, to my old college in Wales, to the Middle Temple, and to my former boss at the BBC. She checked all my references and made a recommendation to support me. By American standards it was very cheap. So I felt secure to pursue my studies.

Teaching Thai

Without a full-time job, I looked around in London for something else to do. Stuart Simmonds, in charge of Thai language and literature at the London University School of Oriental and African Studies, said, "This is the BBC's loss and our gain. Please come and help me teach Thai. I'll pay you by the hour, and we'll make sure you don't starve." At that time, interest in Thai was increasing. London University was the first real Western academic institution to train people in Eastern languages. When the foreign office wanted anybody to study Thai, they were sent there. I taught Thai and helped Simmonds translate some difficult classical Siamese poetry. He was more or less the only authority on Thai language in the United Kingdom, maybe even in the world. But he wouldn't teach; he was too lazy. He'd say, "Sulak, you can do that privately. You can earn the money yourself." So I started teaching Thai to a few people privately and through tutorial colleges.

One of my students, Joe Holmes, eventually became the Royal Air Force attaché in Bangkok. Another, Guy Micklethwaite, became director of the British Information Service in Bangkok. They both became good friends of mine. One student at the School of Oriental and African Studies, Julian Hartland-Swann, had just graduated from Oxford. He was about to be sent to Bangkok to become the third secretary. I taught him Thai in London and continued the connection when I went back home. In the foreign office, they gave you one whole year to get to know the culture. It was a kind of spying, but done in a more gentlemanly fashion. You had to be able to pass advanced Thai, which meant reading Thai handwriting, Thai newspapers, and translating.

The most interesting person who came to study with me was a young man of sixteen or seventeen, Francis Cripps. He was just finishing at Eton, one of the most prestigious public schools in England. His grandfather was a very well-known man, Sir Stafford Cripps, the Chancellor of the Exchequer during the Atlee administration after the war. Francis finished school early and had a year to wait before beginning at Cambridge. He wanted to spend it in Siam with the Voluntary Service Overseas (VSO). (President Kennedy imitated the VSO when he started the U.S. Peace Corps.) Francis contacted the School of Oriental and African Studies and came to private lessons with me. Our connection has endured over thirty years.

I also got a position teaching at St. Godrick's College in Hampstead, an English finishing school for teenage girls from all over the world. There you were trained to be an English lady. They prepared students to marry gentlemen and be good housewives, because a true gentleman of any country, whether it was Kenya, India, or Malaysia, would have an English education and would want his wife to have the same. The Thai sent their daughters as well, but since Siam had not been colonized, their English was very weak. When the college asked Simmonds to recommend somebody to teach Thai students, he recommended me.

I went once a week to teach both English and Thai at St. Godrick's to all these rich Thai girls, daughters of generals, princes, and merchants. I got on quite well with them. They thought I had one foot in the grave. I was only twenty-six years old, but even so I was seven to ten years older than they. Two or three were quite beautiful. I was attracted to one or two, but I behaved with decorum. I would always invite two at a time to dinner. As they got to know me, they trusted me. They talked to me personally: "If a boy invited me to dinner and a dance, would you object?" I said, "No, we're not living in Bangkok. When in Rome, do as the Romans do." Sometimes they would bring their boyfriends to my house. First of all, it was cheap, and secondly, by Thai custom I was a chaperon.

I was interested in one girl. I invited her to the Royal Opera House in Covent Garden—very posh. When I went alone, I would buy the cheapest ticket, but for that night, I got an expensive seat. The opera was a sad love story, and we had champagne and caviar at the intermission. When I took her home, it was raining. She touched my arm, but I didn't do anything. She was very sad. "Teacher, I had a wonderful evening. The story was sad, like my own story—very sad. I would have liked to fall in love with you, but I can't. I have fallen in love with someone else. I know that I will not be happy with him. I think if I fell in love with you, you would take great care of me, and I would be very happy." She said good-bye and ran up to her room. I felt very sad.

Years later when I went home, an American friend invited me for a swim at the Royal Sports Club in Bangkok. I saw her at the swimming pool, in a bikini. She was still beautiful. She was shocked to see me. She said, "Ah, teacher, I never expected to see you in this kind of place. I thought you were old-fashioned—you would not approve of this Western decadence." I said, "I wouldn't join a club, but somebody invited me, and I enjoy a swim. It's lovely to see you." She said, "I'm glad to see you, too. You may not recall what I said to you a long time ago in London." I said, "Yes, I remember every word you said." She said, "It was true. I married the man I loved—I thought he loved me. But he betrayed me; he treated me very badly; he jilted me; he divorced me. Now I'm married to a foreigner. I'm all right, but I'm not happy." I never met her again.

Although the government closed down the BBC Thai section, it did not want to lose its propaganda network in Siam entirely. It wanted to continue to have British interests heard and British culture respected, so it decided to have cassette tapes made for broadcast on Bangkok radio. The Thai radio stations were happy to oblige: "If it's free, why not?" They came to me, an unemployed ex-BBC man, and managed to employ me very cheaply. I was full of ideas, and by that time they trusted me. I could write, and I understood English customs and culture better than anybody else available. I traveled around the country, and they paid for my airfare or a first-class compartment on the train. I had a good time. I did a piece about the Morris car—they were small, cheap, and could be converted to taxis. The public relations officer at the Morris factory took me to a beautiful lunch, they showed me the factory, and I wrote it up. I wanted to go to the Henry Wood Philharmonic concert conducted by Sir Malcolm Sargent, the best conductor at that time. All the tickets were sold out six months ahead. When I said I wanted to tape a report on the concert, they gave me a box seat. I wrote about "My Fair Lady," "The King and I," and so on. I was supposed to be advertising England.

Because I was a little bit better off, I had moved from Barnes to a flat near Kensington High Street, a very fashionable and conve-

My flat at Stafford Terrace

nient area. I still had one room, but the room was beautiful, with chandeliers, bookcases, and so on. Sometimes I entertained there. I paid five guineas—more than double my previous rent. There were two other Thais living upstairs.

Opposite my flat in London was a Thai restaurant, the first one outside Siam. It was called "Siam Rice" and was run by a princess. Her father, Prince Boripat, had been educated in Germany and was the most prestigious prince before the 1932 coup. He was half brother to Kings Rama VI and Rama VII. He was the only person the coup leaders were afraid of, and they put him in confinement. Eventually the king won his release, but he was forced to go abroad to live in Indonesia. He had five daughters nicknamed Number 1, Number 2, Number 3, Number 4, and Number 5.

The fourth princess, HRH Princess Churairatna, opened the restaurant, and I became friendly with her. She had a strong influence on me without realizing it. Up until then, I had been very ambitious and thought I might end up as a prime minister or minister of state. Living in London, I met a lot of people—politicians, ex-ministers, and so on. This princess was the highest of the blue bloods—her grandfather was King Chulalongkorn, the greatest Thai king of modern times. She dined with King Rama VII. She was a very strong woman. She had royal style. Yet she once told me, "Sulak, do you know what my ambition is? I would like to be a charwoman, looking after public toilets. They are quite clean. I could sit there knitting and get some tips."

She was half joking, but I felt she was saying that all the status and power didn't really mean anything. What she said made sense. It really influenced me. Her father was half brother to the king, but he had to live in exile for over ten years. He died abroad and people forgot about him. Although I came from the other end of the spectrum, I had been presented to the Queen of England, I talked to Lord Mountbatten, I met all the top dignitaries passing through from Bangkok. I realized, "Good lord, these people are just like me."

A visit from the king and queen of Siam

I was still in England in 1961 when the Siamese king and queen made a state visit to the U.K. It was the king's first visit since he had come to the throne. The Thai military government kept him under tight control and did not allow him to move about freely. But things changed after Field Marshal Pibun was ousted by Sarit Thanarat in 1957. The new dictator wanted to be more friendly toward the monarch. To pacify the Americans and show the world that we were a wonderful country, they decided to allow the king to travel freely. The BBC reinstated the Thai section during his visit because they figured all the Thais would tune in. There were only two of us left in London—

Traveling with the king and queen

Kriengsak and myself, both studying law. We agreed to broadcast the state visit and were paid handsomely for three-days' work and a bit of preparation. Because we were not well-known, they hired a man from Bangkok, Kukrit Pramoj, who eventually became prime minister and my adversary. At that time, though, I admired him. He was a great writer, columnist, and MP. I had read all his books. I went to greet him at the airport and invited him to have lunch with Stuart Simmonds and the people from the foreign office.

The royal visit was a great opportunity for me. I went everywhere they went. I was invited to the Guild Hall, where the Lord Mayor of London would entertain the king and queen. I had a special pass from the Queen of England's press secretary to come and go freely at Buckingham Palace. Our king and queen were entertained there by the Queen of England and the Duke of Edinburgh. The royal carriage in which they rode from Victoria Station was beautiful, just like one in a fairy tale. I composed a poem about this, and it was printed for free distribution. The king's private secretary wrote to me and told me that His Majesty, the King of Siam, was very pleased.

Our king and queen entertained the Queen and Prince Philip at the Thai Embassy. There were only a few selected guests because the Thai Embassy was very small. I had to rent evening clothes at Moss Brothers—white tie and long tails. I looked like a penguin! The Thai officials, foreign minister, and king's counselor stood together talking; they were all afraid to talk to the English people. Princess Alexandra, the English queen's cousin, came straight to me, and I told her I was reporting for the BBC. We both knew Prince Dhani in Bangkok. She had been to Siam before, knew the king and queen, and served as a link between the two royal families. She said, "Tomorrow night your king and queen are coming to a private dance at my house, Kensington Palace. I hope you can come." I said, "But Your Royal Highness, I have not been invited." "I am inviting you now. Please come." I was very moved, but I didn't go. I did not like dancing, and I had had enough of royalty by that time. Besides, I would have had to hire another suit.

The king continued on to Switzerland, Scandinavia, Germany, and Holland. One day I got a telephone call from Holland. The Dutch didn't want to be outdone by the British for the king and queen's visit.

Since they had no broadcasting company on the scale of the BBC, they asked me to come to report. They would send the tapes to Bangkok for broadcast. They paid my airfare, all expenses, a chauffeur, and one-month's salary for less than two weeks of work. I flew to Amsterdam. They took me to see the boss of World Radio Broadcast. At the BBC I had never met the top man; at best, I met the head of the Asian section. I was curious why they had chosen me. By BBC standards, Kriengsak was my senior. It turned out that Kingsley had recommended me because, although he liked Kriengsak better, he felt I was more competent. I was more attuned to the entourage. I used the proper royal language. This is British fairness. Kingsley was a nasty man, but he was fair.

In Holland, I accompanied the king and queen to meet the Dutch royal family. At the dinner they hosted for the Dutch queen and the Prince of the Netherlands, the entourage was beautifully attired. There was a chap from the Thai Embassy—he was third secretary, a short man like me, and in the lowest position at the embassy. We stood next to each other, and he said, "Sulak, do you see all those honorific decorations? Doesn't it make you think of the chiefs of tribal people in Africa with their feathers and so on? It's the same." Among the entourage they had been fighting like mad about who would get to wear which decoration. It made me question the meaning of such status symbols.

I returned to England and took up my life teaching English by radio at the BBC, teaching Thai at the School of Oriental and African Studies, studying for the law exams, and broadcasting for the Central Office of Information. By then I had become a sort of authority on Thai affairs. The Thai Embassy had opened a public relations office. Typically for the Thai, they sent somebody who could not speak English properly to be in charge. But he was a very nice man, and I helped him. In exchange I was able to buy things like wine through the embassy without paying tax. (I continued to entertain almost every week.) He would ask me to give lectures on Thai Buddhism and culture at Oxford and Cambridge. So I was broadcasting about British culture back to my country, and I was teaching about Thai culture and Thai Buddhism to the British.

Buddhist activities

I continued helping at the London vihara, the Singhalese temple established by the Mahabodhi Society. I also remained active in the Buddhist Society and the Pali Text Society. They started a small sangha trust in London to support British monks who had been ordained in my country. The first one was Kapilavaddho, who was a controversial man. He was ordained and disrobed many times, liked to drink, and had had a sex scandal. Kapilavaddho took four British men to be ordained at Wat Paknam in Thonburi in 1957. One of them still remains a monk, Pannavaddho, whose British last name is Morgan. His grandfather was the dean of St. David's Cathedral, attached to my college, Lampeter, in Wales. After ordination he came back to London and started a group called the Buddhist Sangha Trust. Pannavaddho wanted to go back to my country for further study and meditation, so I taught him Thai once a week. We went back about the same time, in 1961. He found a teacher to his liking, perhaps the most famous meditation master in my country. He's still there and has become a great meditation master. He wants to remain unknown. He's never written anything and wants only to be devoted to his teacher Phra Maha Boowa.

After the king's visit, there was a visit from the Sangharaja, the supreme patriarch of the Siamese Sangha, sponsored by the Asia Foundation. Their idea was to fight communism through cultural, religious, and intellectual freedom, so they invited the Sangharaja to visit the United States. (I learned later that the CIA was also involved.) He stopped in England on his way to the U.S., and I took him to the Pali Text Society and the Buddhist Society and invited Bhikkhu Pannavaddho to visit him. It was a big occasion for our small group of Buddhists in England.

To stay or to go

I also continued to study law, but by that time, I had no ambition left. What could I do? A dictator was running my country. I thought perhaps I would just settle down in London and seek tenure at the London School of Oriental and African Studies. It wouldn't be a bad life. Perhaps I'd write some novels or short stories and become immortal in that way. But at the London School I met a Burmese man who taught there. I'd noticed that in one important way the Burmese were entirely different from the Siamese. We like to adapt ourselves to our surroundings, to act like Englishmen when we're in English company—drink beer, go to the pub, smoke a pipe. But the Burmese were entirely different. For however long they lived in London, they dressed in the Burmese style. They did not go to pubs, and during the Rains Retreat period they ate only one or two strictly vegetarian meals a day. Very serious. I admired them.

We didn't know each other very well; he was many years my senior. He asked me, "When will you go home?" I said, "I don't know. I like it here. Perhaps I won't go home." He said, "Mr. Sulak, if you can go home, you should go home. You should give yourself a chance to do something for your country. People with your background and education are not many. As for me, I can't go home. Since the military took over in 1962, my country's been going to the dogs. They would not let me go back. If I'd had a chance, I would have gone back. I have been nostalgic about my country all my life. Don't follow my bad example." This reminded me of my time as a novice. I didn't want to leave the novitiate, but my teacher told me, "I don't want to encour-

age you to leave, but if you ask my advice, you should go. If you want to rejoin, you can rejoin. Like you, I joined the monkhood very young. I was interested, but now I find it very boring. I can't leave now though because I am already in my fifties. I don't want you to be like me."

I then began to consider going home. I realized that first I had to take my law examination seriously, so I went to a cram school. Even though I had found that law was not my cup of tea— it's all technicalities—I took it seriously and did well. I passed

A young barrister

the examination and was called to the bar in 1961. I invited Mrs. Barrett from Bournemouth and my landlady in Kensington to attend the ceremony when I received my degree. But by then I felt my time had come to return home. If I stayed in England, I might never return to my own country.

With Phra Bhadramuni

I made one last tour of Europe. I wanted to go back to Holland first. I wrote to the World Radio at Helversum, and they invited me to broadcast again. This earned me enough money to travel freely. From Holland I went to Germany and stayed at the ambassador's residence, as Direk Jayanama had become ambassador in Bonn. I continued on to Paris, and then Rome. Prince Wongsa Devakul, formerly ambassador in London, was now ambassador in Rome, so I spent New Year's Eve in Italy. From there I traveled to Athens, where I had stopped when I first left Siam in 1953. By that time I knew Greek, and I felt very much at home there. I visited various islands and went to Delphi by bus—it was my last stop in Europe. Around this time, I learned that my teacher, Phra Bhadramuni, had died. I rushed home in order to attend his funeral in early 1962. I was twenty-nine years old.

CHAPTER **6** | *Back in Siam*

Traveling home, I wrote a personal recollection of my teacher Phra
Bhadramuni. I had been very close to him. I also worked on a sum-
mary of Arthur Waley's translation of *Yuan Tsang*. I hoped to have
it published for the cremation ceremony of my teacher, in his honor.
It's a wonderful book, the story of a famous Chinese monk who went
to India as a pilgrim. When I arrived in Bangkok, I went to see Mr.
Pierson at the Asia Foundation. I told him I had translated this book
and wanted to publish it in memory of my teacher. He was delighted. He knew our custom of distributing Dhamma books free of charge
to everyone who came to a cremation or memorial service. Within a
few months it was reprinted twice for other cremation ceremonies.

I had also written a long poem describing the king's visit to England.
It was traditional to commemorate such a visit with poetry. I thought
it would be appropriate to distribute it to the many friends who had
supported and encouraged me all these years. I published this poem
with my cousin for the cremation of his father, to whom I had been
very close. It was an honor for our small family. I even presented a
copy to the king and received special thanks from him. I became "a
little star in a naughty world."

Looking for work

It was 1962. I had been away for eight years and needed to find a job.
I certainly didn't want to be a lawyer. I didn't want to join the government. The superintendent of the Thai students in England had
recommended I join Chulalongkorn University and become a professor. The Fine Arts Department was interested in me. But I wanted to work somewhere else, perhaps in a foreign firm or international
organization, where I would make a lot of money and do as little work

as I had at the BBC. Then I would have time for my own activities, perhaps start a nonprofit organization or something else for the welfare of my people.

I went to the Shell company. The Englishman there would have offered me a job, but the Thai boss wanted to give it to someone in his family. So the Englishman referred me to the Grant Advertising firm. The manager at Grant interviewed me and offered me a job straightaway. He said, "We are not as big and influential, but within two or three years you will replace me and eventually go to Hong Kong. You won't be stuck in this country. You'll have a car and an entertainment account." But I had friends who worked for foreign companies, and they were telling me stories. "Working for the foreign companies means you have no security. You have to please them. You become a kind of colony—not nationally, but intellectually and culturally." My father had worked for a foreign firm, and although he admired many things about the Westerners, deep down he felt that they looked down on us Asians. I remembered Kingsley at the BBC. But the most decisive factor was something I had read in a book on Taoism: "If Lao Tsu were alive today, he would have said about the Americans: 'Of all the wonderful things you have done to save the free world, your worst sin is advertising.'" That struck me. I pictured myself working in advertising, telling lies, making a lot of money. I thought, "I'm quite clever with language. I would deceive people." I refused the job.

Two very senior friends helped me with my search. Mr. Direk Jayanama, now ambassador in Bonn, suggested I join the Southeast Asian Treaty Organization (SEATO—an imitation of NATO). He offered to write a letter of recommendation to the secretary general. When I was in Rome, the ambassador there also wrote recommending me. I went to SEATO, and the secretary general looked at my letter. I told him, "I want to work for SEATO. It is a prestigious organization. I will do whatever I'm asked to do. I like the pay, and perhaps I would have time to pursue some extracurricular activities to help my country." He said, "Well, if that's your dream, it won't come true. You'll have to work very hard. I'll send you to Pakistan, or the Philippines." In those days there were only three Asian members in SEATO—

Thailand, the Philippines, and Pakistan (even though Pakistan is not even in Southeast Asia). Then there were New Zealand, Australia, France, the U.K., and the U.S. He didn't give me the job.

I turned down a few interesting job offers from the government. The man in charge of public relations asked me if I would like to join the government to draft the prime minister's speeches. He asked me how much I earned, and I said, "My minimum requirement is six thousand baht." He said, "The government's top salary is 2,500, but we can employ you as a civil servant for 2,500 and give you 3,500 as a political appointment. You don't have to pay taxes, and you would be close to power." I was tempted. Perhaps I could influence the dictator, Sarit Thanarat. I went to ask the advice of the prize-winning journalist Ms. Nilwan Pinthong, editor of a woman's weekly and winner of the Magsaysay Award, the so-called Asian Nobel Prize for Literature. She had accepted a post as advisor to the prime minister. "They invited me for prestige. My job is really to help the prime minister's wife with her shopping. I also act as interpreter when foreign visitors come." Thanks to her honesty, I declined this offer. (When I wrote about this episode in the Thai edition of my memoirs, she claimed she had never made such a statement, implying that she had been happy to serve the dictator.)

Later on, when Sarit died and Field Marshal Thanom Kittikachorn became prime minister, I was offered another job in the government. It was a higher position—I would be ghostwriter of the prime minister's speeches. I was told that the prime minister liked my writing because it was very clear, that I used convincing and forceful arguments. He wanted me to write those kinds of speeches for him. I was a bit rude and arrogant in my reply. I told this man that I wrote clearly because I thought clearly, but that I could not write clear speeches for the prime minister because the prime minister did not think clearly.

Field Marshal Thanom's second man, Field Marshal Praphas Charusathira, also offered me a job. At that time, the Chinese were backing the Communist Party of Thailand, and the Thai government felt that some of their best people had been attracted by the communists. The government wanted to produce a white paper for government employees telling them how dreadful the communists were.

I was asked to draft this document. Not being a modest man, I said, "Of course, I could convince people, but I have been trained in London in the legal field. In England, if you want to represent a client, you must be convinced that your client is not guilty." They liked that. But I asked further if I would be allowed to examine their so-called ex-communists to know if their statements were genuine or had been gotten by torture. If I could interview them and become convinced that communism was bad, I could write a very strong article. They said, "We can't allow you to do that. You can use the documents we provide you and from those documents write a white paper." I said, "No, thank you. I'm not going to be a government propagandist."

For a while I earned some extra money teaching Thai to English people through the British Council. Then, finally, at a party, I ran into Guy Micklethwaite, who was now in charge of the British Information Service (BIS). He was delighted to see me and asked, "Why don't you come and work for me? I need somebody." He said, "I can offer you 3,500 baht a month." It was good pay, but I had set my standard at 6,000. "Thirty-five hundred is too little for me." So he offered, "Okay. I'll pay you for full-time work, but you can come to work at seven a.m. and leave at one. You can work at another job from one to five and easily make the other 2,500." I said okay. His office was very near my house, and I could walk there in the morning. The job was very simple, similar to the BBC. I would read all the Thai newspapers and translate whatever I felt the British Embassy should know. They also wanted me to translate some of the news from the BBC, and they would feed it into the Thai newspapers. Being an ex-broadcaster, they introduced me to various radio stations. Sometimes I was on television. It was nice to work there, but I needed some more money to fulfill my goal.

While I was working at the BIS, I was asked to teach philosophy part-time at Thammasat University. I loved philosophy, and Guy happily allowed me to teach one morning a week at the university. The class was Western philosophy at the Faculty of Social Welfare. It was more or less compulsory. I had been teaching classes of six, ten, thirty people at the most. Now, at Thammasat, I had a class of three to four hundred students! I had to use a microphone, and there were television circuits for people outside the room. I taught there for two years, from 1962 to 1964, then offered my class to a full-time teacher with a Ph.D. in philosophy. I had only studied philosophy as part of my specialization, so I thought it only fair that he replace me.

I was also asked to teach English at Chulalongkorn University. I tried to avoid it. I told them I couldn't get released from any more work, but they set the class up on Saturdays. A Thai lady whom I had met at the British Council said, "Mr. Sulak, you must realize that before you went to England you would have loved learning English from a person like yourself. Please don't think of money, think of service." "Okay, okay!" So I went to my first class. In those days the dress code was very strict—European-style jacket and necktie. I didn't even wear a jacket or necktie if I went to see a prince.

The first Saturday I dressed up properly. The second Saturday I went wearing trousers and a shirt. The lady from the British Council came to see me. "Mr. Sulak, could you at least wear a necktie?" "Who do you want to teach, me or my necktie? I told you I didn't want to teach English. I went on Saturday, my day off. I enjoy teaching, but if you want a fashion show, find somebody else." They wouldn't compromise. I went once more and then received a very nice letter: "Very kind of you to teach the English class. The students enjoyed it, but we find it's not quite convenient for you…"

Around that time I met an American named Curly Bowen. He was deputy director of University of Chicago Press and had been sent by the State Department to set up a Thai university press. The Americans were gaining more and more influence. They had a policy known as Public Law 480, which meant that whatever profit the American firms earned in Thai currency would be given to the Thai government. Up until now it had all gone to the Ministry of Defense, but by 1957 Pibun and Sarit, the new commander of the army, were fighting. Since the Ministry of Defense was divided, the Americans decided to give the money to the universities. They felt that we needed a university press and more American texts translated into Thai.

By this time, things had become deadlocked with the university press. The American ambassador, Kenneth Todd Young, asked for a report on the state of textbooks at primary and secondary schools. Curly Bowen needed a good collaborator and came to me. I said, "My dear chap, too late. I have taken employment with your rivals, the

British. Anyhow, you'll be gone in three or four months." He said, "All right, you come straight to me at one o'clock and work until five. I'll also pay you 2,500. You wanted 6,000; now you have it. How about that?" I said okay because my house, the BBC, and the U.S. Information Service were close together. I could walk everywhere.

The beginning of the Social Science Review

Within three months we produced a report on the state of textbooks and why we needed a university press. Bowen wrote up our recommendations and then went home. He said we needed textbooks, particularly in the social sciences at university level, and that a university press needed a good director with academic qualifications, experience in the literary world, and a good command of English and Thai. He went on to say, confidentially, that he'd been working in this country for six months, and I was the only person he'd met who could do the job.

Of course, the dean of the faculty of political science at Chulalongkorn University didn't like the report, but USIS and the American Embassy were very strong. They would not release any more money unless the Social Science Association appointed a full-time director and established a prestigious editorial board. The Americans were quite clever and diplomatic. The compromise was that the dean, who was vice president of the association, would be in charge of the printing press, and the publishing would be entirely separate, with the two groups sharing an office at Chulalongkorn.

The new editorial board was headed by Prince Prem, also a professor of English and foreign languages. My old teacher, Phya Anuman, was on the board, and there was one representative from each of the five universities. They interviewed several people for the job of director, and at last it was offered to me. I would report to the editorial board once a month and work very closely with the chairman, Prince Prem.

The press was called the Social Science Association Press of Thailand, also known as the University Press of Thailand. Nobody really knew what to do. In my country there was an oral tradition. Nobody wrote unless they were stirred up to write. Luckily, I was interested in publishing. I told my editorial board, "We need to start a magazine, a quarterly. I will encourage my friends to translate and to write articles and short stories." But since it was the height of the dictatorship, there was no allowance for new periodicals and very strict censorship. The board said, "If you can get it registered with the government, you have our blessing."

I wrote to Prince Wan Waithayakorn, president of the association and deputy prime minister, and explained my plan. He had been a literary man and used to have a newspaper. He was also professor of Siamese literature and had been Siamese minister to the Court of St. James's. His soft spot was coining words. The Thai words for democracy, constitution, philosophy—he coined all these. I wrote, "Your Royal Highness had a newspaper stirring people to think about democratic ideals. I also want to stir my colleagues to think and to write. I would like Your Royal Highness to name the magazine, to serve our association, and to serve academia. Since the government does not allow any new periodical to be started, I would also like you to be the owner of this new publication as president of the Social Science Association." He wrote back, "Your idea is wonderful. Let the new periodical be called the *Social Science Review*." He signed on as the owner of the publication and appointed me as editor. I went to the police department with his name and got permission straightaway.

I had the approval of the editorial board, but I had to get the approval of the whole executive committee, and I knew the dean was against me. I had to use skillful means, because I wanted autonomy. So I asked Dr. Somsak Xuto, the association's editor, to be honorary editor. He was a friend of mine. We had both been on the editorial board of the Thai Students' Association journal in England. I wrote to the board, "The magazine is owned by the Association, which appoints Mr. Sulak Sivaraksa to be the administrative editor and Dr. Somsak Xuto to be the honorary editor. These two are jointly responsible for the magazine. If the two of them disagree as to which article to print or not to print, they will refer to the formal editorial board, presided over by Prince Prem." It sounded good, but, in fact, Dr. Somsak had no say. He was honorary. I never consulted him, and since he trusted me, I never had to refer to the editorial board. I had a free hand. I didn't want to make it academic, rather I wanted it to be more intellectual, something like the *Encounter* in England or the

Atlantic Monthly in the U.S. It was a one-man show. I was the editor, director of the press, and a writer.

I went all over looking for manuscripts, but I also had to look for money. I went to the Asia Foundation and explained, "The intellectual climate is very bad. We have been under a dictatorship for so long. We need fresh ideas. I want something to prompt people to start writing, and soon we'll have really good books coming." They agreed to pay for the printing costs, and I had a thousand copies printed. I asked that writers

First issue of Social Science Review

be paid handsomely as well. They gave me a big annual grant. To insure success, I then went to the U.S. Information Service. I said, "You buy many magazines from America to give away to scholars. Why don't you buy five hundred copies of the *Social Science Review?* You can give them away, too." They said they could use Public Law 480 funds. So before the magazine was printed, I had already sold half.

The first issue was published in June 1963.

Life at the Review

At first we published three issues a year. Later on it became quarterly. I thought that my audience would be those who were educated abroad. Many were employed by the government. The Thai government is such a nice place to work that it can become too cushy. It's easy to become assimilated into the mainstream. I wanted people to remain critical, and I wanted the magazine to be controversial, to make people think and write. I felt it should be in Thai and that these people should serve Thai society. Their education should not be confined to themselves but should benefit the public.

But I had not bargained on the changes in society during my absence. Since 1947, the dictatorship had suppressed intellectual activity. I didn't know how terrible it was. A lot of people had gone to jail.

By 1957, there were no intellectuals left. There was no academic atmosphere. The universities were controlled entirely by the military. The generals were the rectors and presidents. There were no student clubs, and people were not allowed to meet on campus after five o'clock in the evening. The military was afraid of communism because the leftist movement had been strong. The dictatorship had created darkness.

Since I had been in England during much of this period, I was a bit more daring. I utilized my liberal education, writing freely. As a result, the magazine attracted current university students. The country had just started higher education outside Bangkok, and the magazine became well-known and controversial in outlying areas. Students everywhere became interested and wrote letters. Sometimes I wrote letters myself, condemning the editor. They loved it. At every university and every college I became well-known within two or three years, and I was asked to give lectures all over the country.

In the first issue, I included Prince Damrong's unpublished writings, and for the cover, I used one of Prince Naris' drawings. Prince Naris was an old aristocrat. His father was King Mongkut, the king in *The King and I*. He was a wonderful, old-style artist and architect. He had planned the Marble Temple in Bangkok. He was also a great composer of traditional Thai music and an eloquent writer. He knew all about the court customs. I mentioned Prince Naris' centenary celebration. "Prince Naris was a great man, but the celebration was a flop. The committee did not do it properly."

There had been a *khon* (masked play) performed by Kukrit Pramoj. He danced as the demon king. I wrote, "If he had taken the time to rehearse, he might have danced better. People only admired him because of his name." He was furious. Kukrit was an MP, the Deputy Minister of Finance, a bank manager, and a very popular man. He had written a book against communism called *Red Bamboo*, an imitation of Don Camillo's books about priests written in protest against communism in Italy. He was good at taking ideas from elsewhere and translating them for our country. People believed whatever he said. No one dared criticize him. The director general of the Fine Arts Department, who served on the editorial board, was also furious and wrote that he would never sit on the editorial board as long as I was director and editor of the magazine. He said that I should be sacked!

I used the best technology at that time. I got the finest poets, writers, and artists I could find, and I paid them generously. The best poet I discovered was Angkarn Kalayanapong. He was known in Silpakorn University as a Beat poet. He was admired by his contemporaries but not outside the university. I featured him in my first issue. I paid him eight hundred baht. At that time, the top people would get only one hundred baht for that sort of article. He nearly collapsed when he got the money. "You must be making a mistake!" he said. We became good friends.

During this period I was invited to America by Experiment in International Living, a project involving young "ambassadors" from each country. I stayed for two months during 1964 and visited several university presses in the U.S. On my way home I stopped at the Congress for Cultural Freedom in Paris. There I met their man Ivan Katz. He told me, "Our organization fights the Communists, but in a very meaningful way. We want to preserve cultural freedom in every country. We support magazines, we support liberal thinking, we publish books. We have friends in the Philippines, Burma, India, and Japan, but we know nothing about your country. We have no friends there. I need to come and see your operations." The Congress organized a big symposium in Kuala Lumpur, the capital of Malaysia. This was in 1965. It was the first time I was invited out of my country to attend a conference. Afterwards, Ivan Katz came to Bangkok and visited the *Review*. 1 saw their publications, and we translated one or two and made them into special issues.

I was also invited by the Peace Corps to give orientation lectures on Siam. When the volunteers first arrived in my country, I had to wear a jacket and necktie and interview them on television. The Peace Corps still invites me to give orientation lectures on popular Buddhism in modern Siam, explaining why the Buddhism they see practiced here is not the same as the Buddhism they read about. In fact, Jack Kornfield, now a well-known American Buddhist teacher, was in one of my orientation sessions. He says I was the one who introduced him to Thai Buddhism. Now he has his own meditation center, called Spirit Rock Meditation Center, in California.

Around this time, students from the seven institutes of higher learning had gotten together to publish a magazine. Since we were not allowed to publish new periodicals, they called it a book and kept on changing the name. Their first issue was *The Seven Institutes*. The next issue was called *Seven Together*. But by not having a regular publication schedule, they couldn't earn income through advertisements and had no money to pay the printers. They came to me for advice. I said that it was very simple: "My magazine is legal, and I have registered it as a monthly. So far I have only produced it quarterly. If you want, you can publish your magazine as the eight other issues. Don't worry about money. I will go back to the Asia Foundation for another grant." They liked the idea, but asked, "What about censorship?" I said, "Legally, I would be responsible. If you publish something dreadful, I will go to jail. I wouldn't censor you. Just remember that I am the one who would go to jail."

They formed a committee and called their magazine the *Social Science Review, Student Edition*. They started off with one issue per semester and took it very seriously. Two articles in particular were very controversial. One revealed for the first time the corruption in the student club—that faculty members interfered and the students had no free vote. Another article criticized the students at Chulalongkorn University, the oldest university. "The students are so superstitious. Every time they go up the stairs past the big photograph of King Rama V, they prostrate, kowtow, and ask the king to help them pass examinations. These are not really future Thai leaders. They are still in the eighteenth or nineteenth century."

Before publishing it, the students came and asked me if they should print it. I told them, "You are entirely responsible. You are not young anymore. Next year you will be graduating. Some of you are M.A. students. Some of you are even married already. Why do you ask me? Decide for yourself." They were concerned that I might go to jail if the magazine were prosecuted. I said, "You ask my opinion? Print it! Publish it!" The student edition became a big success. Every university had it reprinted, and the magazine was read around the country.

Book publishing

Once the magazine got started, I looked around for books to publish. The printing press had published the *Life of Kennedy*, but it was an awful translation. I edited it properly, and USIS said they would buy the whole press run. I went to all the universities and read theses. I found one or two good ones. They have now become classics. I continued to look for young scholars, but it was difficult. Those educated in England and America were hopeless—they could not write Thai. I wanted to encourage young people, but I really enjoyed working with old manuscripts.

Phya Anuman was an authority on Thai customs. He had written a book on Thai customs in four volumes, mostly for free distribution at cremation ceremonies. I revised the book in a scholarly way, with a new introduction and an index. It has become a standard work. He told me that he had been corresponding for many years with Prince Naris. I asked Phya Anuman if I could publish their letters and went to the prince's daughter for permission. I put the entire correspondence out in five volumes in a set entitled *Notes on Knowledge*. I was very proud that it became a work of reference. That was in April of 1963.

I got hold of Princess Jongjit Thanom's correspondence with her father, Prince Damrong, a great administrator and historian. She wanted these letters to be published at her cremation. "At your cremation, you will not be there to see it," I argued to her. She was afraid people might think that she was boasting because her father had written very nice letters to her. The first edition was published on her eighty-fourth birthday and has become a classic.

At that time, we regarded China as our archenemy, and we could not publish anything about China. The Asia Foundation had invited the authoritative Sinologist from Princeton, Fritz Mote, to come to our country. He came to advise our Ministry of Education on the development of a curriculum in Asian studies. We had always believed that the Thai people originally came from South China, but Fritz Mote went through all the Chinese documents and said this was a mistake made by missionaries who did not understand Chinese properly. The Ministry of Education did not want to have anything to do with his findings. "It is the opinion of one scholar," they said. I published it in our magazine.

At another seminar, Fritz Mote mentioned that he was very sorry nobody knew about China except to regard her as an enemy. "China is your neighbor. You must know something about her." Everyone said, "We can't do it; it's against the Thai government regulations." I told Fritz Mote to recommend three books on China written by American scholars. (I did not want any American propaganda against China, only the works of scholars.) That would not be against the law, since they were our allies. There was great admiration among the Thai for the Americans. We would translate the books, and the Asia Foundation would pay for their publication. They agreed, and we published *The Cradle of Eastern Philosophy*, on China and Japan; a history of Buddhism in China, translated by an ex-monk who worked at the Royal Institute; and a history of China, which I translated. This helped break the Thai fear of China, and these books are still in print after twenty-five years.

We were becoming more and more involved in the Vietnam War. We had American troops in our country. We had air bases in Korat Province, Udorn Province, Ubol Province, and at U Tapao near Pattaya. Yet no newspapers dared to mention that they were American air bases. The government had declared that we could not criticize our great allies. If you wrote anything to their detriment, you would be punished severely and your publication closed down forever. If you published something that the government denied to be true or against the Official Secrets Act or the security of the country, you could be punished by at least twenty years' imprisonment. No one dared to publish the fact that there were American troops in our country.

By that time, the *Social Science Review* had become very popular. We had the table of contents in English, and, in every issue, we published one or two articles in English. It had become well-known among non-Thais who were interested in our country. One day in the late 1960s, someone sent me by airmail a congressional report containing Senator Fulbright's speech condemning the U.S. government's involvement in Vietnam. It was a magnificent speech, mentioning how many troops, how many air bases, and how much they spent in Siam. I saw my opportunity. He was a U.S. Senator. They could not accuse me of writing something to the detriment of an ally. I translated and published it. It was a bombshell. The American ambassador made a speech denying Mr. Fulbright's speech. I had Mr. Fulbright's speech reprinted together with the ambassador's (a very dull one), translated by USIS. I tried to balance them and wrote my own introduction. I had it made into a small pamphlet and sold it cheaply in front of the big auditorium at Thammasat University, where the foreign minister was making a speech on Thai foreign policy. They sold like hotcakes. The foreign minister was furious with me, but he couldn't do anything. It was all legal.

Life outside the Review

When I became editor of the *Social Science Review*, my boss was Prince Prem, a grandson of Rama V. He had studied in England when he was young and was more English than Thai. He involved me in teaching English by radio. We would broadcast from the educational radio station to schools all over the country. Prince Prem used to pay us by treating us to a meal. He took us to eat at the Erawan Hotel. It was really awful food, so I proposed we start going to other restaurants. Luckily, John Blofeld, a former professor at Chulalongkorn University, was a good friend and an excellent gourmand. He would recommend restaurants to me, and a group of us formed what we called the "Wednesday Club," going to the best Chinese restaurants with reasonable prices. We enjoyed that.

Professor Sanoh Tanbunyuen and his English wife, Irene, also taught English by radio. They were both very prominent English teachers, but they got tired of teaching, and Sanoh asked me to take his class at the Military College for Junior Officers. All the young cadets had to study for several months at this college in order to be promoted. I agreed and taught once a week. I exposed them to social issues and tried to show them the value of truth and beauty. I remained friends with many of the students, some of whom later became generals and colonels. I met a few many years later, and they told me that my teaching had helped make them aware of the social dimension as they pursued their careers.

By then I knew some members of the royal family personally. Prince Dhani was the most senior member of the royal family. He used to have what they called a "salon" every Saturday. People would come—supposedly the top people, intellectuals, men of letters—for a free lunch and personal conversation with him. He had a soft spot for me because I liked to dress in the traditional Indian-style dhoti and buttoned-up jacket. He was the only other person who dressed in that style all the time. I was more or less his unofficial secretary. He asked me to do some writing for him. I would type things and send them to him to be edited.

Though Prince Damrong died before I ever met him, he had twenty-five children by his eight wives, and I had come to know his eldest daughter, Princess Jongjit, quite well, partly through having published their correspondence. She was a woman of great character. She was also a great cook. She invited me to have lunch with her every Sunday, and I would bring along various friends—English, American, anyone else. The only condition was that we enjoy her food. She was almost eighty at that time. While we ate, she would talk about King Chulalongkorn and his various queens, her father, the good old days, and life in the palaces. Princess Jongjit's sister, Princess Poon, later complained that her sister should not have told me all the family secrets. Princess Jongjit told me everything—she was very honest and sincere, and she trusted me. At first I thought I would write about all this, but she trusted me so much that I found it hard to write. I had become one of the family.

CHAPTER 7

Working with the Monks

During this period I started working with the monks, aiming to make them more aware of social issues, conservation, and peace. These included such radical monks as Buddhadasa Bhikkhu and Bhikkhu P. A. Payutto. The Sangha was acquiring a more visibly active role in the contemporary world. This work began in 1962, in collaboration with Don Sweetbaum, a Peace Corps teacher at Mahachulalongkorn Buddhist University in Bangkok. I presented his idea to the Asia Foundation for a training program to make monks more aware of social issues. But the Asia Foundation had no money and recommended another foundation. I suspected it was a CIA foundation but didn't know for sure. They gave us a lot of money to train student monks up and down the country in social work. We also invited monks to attend courses at the university dealing with social injustice. The monks asked me, "Is this CIA money?" I said, "I have no idea, but even if it is CIA money, it doesn't matter, because we are left to do whatever we want." Eventually, it was revealed to be CIA money.

There was a lot of communist activity in the countryside, so I described Buddhism as the only safeguard against communism. With this language, we got support even from the supreme commander of the armed forces, General Saiyud Kerdphol, who was in charge of the anticommunism unit. He was the most enlightened of all the generals. When I wanted to take our donors from America to visit the young graduates in the remote provinces, the army provided us with a helicopter. They sent one colonel along with us, and as we talked, he became convinced of the value of our work. He said, "You know, we've been fighting the Communists and spend too much money on weapons; instead, at least a percentage of that money should be given to you to help these monks. It would be much more effective." Later on, I got money from the government to support the monks.

I was very ambitious. I wanted all the monks to be concerned about

87

conservation, peace, and society. I felt we should teach them at the universities where they studied. I didn't want the training to be limited only to Mahachulalongkorn Buddhist University but to include Mahamakut University, belonging to a second Buddhist sect. The first time we sent the monks up to the northeast, those from both sects stayed in one temple together. They became very friendly and began to trust each other. Although these two Buddhist universities were teaching modern subjects, I thought they were too big and too much in imitation of secular institutions. I wanted to start a new college at our Wat Thongnopphakhun to teach Buddhist philosophy, Sanskrit, and Pali. We would study Mahayana Buddhism, integrate meditation with education, and help with social awareness.

A bright, young novice named Sathirapong Wannapok came to our temple. He was the first novice to complete the grade-nine Pali examination during the reign of the present king. Since 1782, only two novices before him had done so, and both eventually became Sangharaja, supreme patriarch. Grade nine is a kind of doctorate. I talked to the abbot of my temple, a great Pali scholar himself, and told him that this novice was very bright, and that we should send him abroad to study Sanskrit and get a college education in England. I argued that our monasteries had to become more modern, and our monks needed to understand the West. We can't keep Buddhism as it is. It has to change to meet the modern world. Young monks should be encouraged to study abroad. Perhaps Sathirapong can help reform the system of education and make the Sangha more active in the contemporary world. The abbot agreed, and a friend of mine secured him a place at Trinity College, Cambridge. Sathirapong became the first Siamese monk to study in Cambridge, get his degree, and return home. I told him I wanted him to help teach at our temple, but he wanted to disrobe and get married. He became a lay professor at a university in Siam and a fairly well-known journalist. He was also appointed a royal academician.

Buddhadasa Bhikkhu

At that time, Buddhadasa Bhikkhu was the most important Buddhist thinker in Siam. I had read some of his work as a student, but he was too advanced and radical for me since I had been brought up conservatively and my temple was conservative. Buddhadasa was very pro-democracy. He wanted to rewrite the history of the Buddha without using royal language. That was very progressive for the time, and for me. He shocked a lot of people. He was the first monk to stand up at a podium and use his hands when he lectured. Traditionally, monks must sit down and preach quietly without emotion. They must not try to convince people by arguments or actions but merely make the teachings available for people to take as they wish. That is the form, and I was very much for form and formality.

One of Buddhadasa Bhikkhu's lectures was a real bombshell. He said that the Buddha image could be a hindrance to the Path, to the Buddhadhamma, because a lot of people become attached to the image. He said that the Buddha discouraged images. During the time of the Buddha, there were no images at all. Images came much later, from the Greeks. To provoke people, he said that if he had absolute power, he would order all images dumped into the river! I became upset because in our temple we paid respect to the images every morning. A lot of people were attacking Buddhadasa Bhikkhu, and I didn't like him either.

After my return from England, when I was more mature, I began reading his books in a new light. His most important book was *Following the Footsteps of the Buddha.* It was very sensible and taught me a great deal. I went to visit him at Suan Mokkhabalarama, the Garden of Liberation. I was just starting the *Social Science Review* and was surprised to find that Buddhadasa Bhikkhu had read my magazine. By that time he was a very well-known and controversial monk, but he treated me as an equal. He gave me a good interview, and we had a long chat. I barely knew him, but he invited me to go with him to visit all the islands as a kind of pilgrimage. I thought he was an intellectual and provocative monk, but when I followed him, I found him to be very humble. He prostrated at all the images and said that the Buddha image could also be a help if you paid respect not to the image but to the Buddha. He also paid respect to the senior country monks, some of whom were illiterate, prostrating to them as if he were prostrating to the Buddha image. He explained to me that he did not prostrate to a monk as a man but as a representative of the Sangha.

We traveled with Khantipalo, the English monk whom I had been responsible for getting from India to Bangkok. I was asked to be the interpreter. Buddhadasa encouraged the English monk to speak, despite the fact that Buddhadasa himself was much more senior and all the people had really come to listen to him. He even allowed me to speak. He allowed everyone to participate. We went by steamer, and people came out in canoes when they saw him. It was wonder-

ful traveling with a famous monk. Everywhere we went there was a beautiful reception. People came offering food and fruit, and he would preach to them. He ate only one meal a day, of course, and he ate very little, so we ate what was left over.

Buddhadasa Bhikkhu's books, writings, and thinking became a great inspiration for me, in particular his book on Dhammic socialism. He found socialism and even communism in Buddhist teachings. Sangha

With Buddhadasa Bhikkhu in 1991

means commune or community. The monks do not own anything except one alms bowl, three robes, and one needle and thread. The rest they own jointly, or it belongs to the community. I think if we used this model for laypeople, it would be something wonderful.

Bhikkhu P. A. Payutto

Although my abbot had been disappointed in Sathirapong, his adopted son who left the order, another monk, Bhikkhu P. A. Payutto, became the second novice in the present reign to reach grade nine in Pali before his higher ordination. This monk was very humble. At the early age of twenty-five, he became deputy secretary general of Mahachulalongkorn Buddhist University. He more or less ran it. I worked closely with him from the time he was a newly ordained monk. He was very active at the university, and I realized he was very talented. I told him not to spend his time on administration but to do more creative work. Buddhadasa was then the only one doing creative work in Buddhism, and we needed more young monks to capture the minds of the younger generation.

In the sixties, Buddhadasa Bhikkhu had come to debate with the well-known writer Kukrit Pramoj. Kukrit said that Buddhist thought is a good way to cultivate personal happiness, but to develop the country, there must be greed. "Greed is a wonderful ingredient in development. In Buddhism, you say greed is bad; that is okay for monks. But in lay society, I want my bank to be bigger, my salary to be higher." They debated. Although Buddhadasa was very good, he could not outdo the wit of Kukrit, who was much more versatile. But in the seventies, this young monk Bhikkhu Payutto was even sharper than Buddhadasa, in a humble way. His remarks stirred everyone up. He used Buddhist terms to help us understand things properly. In response to a book on development by American scholars condemning Buddhism's attitude, he pointed out that they ignored the destruction that development caused to the environment. He was very eloquent, very scholarly.

In 1971, as part of Prince Wan's eightieth birthday celebration, we asked people to write articles for a book to be published in his honor. Bhikkhu Payutto wrote an article on Buddhadhamma. It was the best of them all, and we invited him to give a lecture at Thammasat University. His lecture captured the essence of the Buddha's teaching and captivated the whole audience. His article was translated into English and later expanded to ten times its original length. It could be considered the whole corpus on Theravada Buddhism. It is very scholarly and convincing, written in beautiful language. Since then Bhikkhu Payutto has become a great Buddhist writer and inspiration to many people. Years later, when I was working to organize monks around environmental and social issues, I asked him to name our group. He chose *Sekhiyadhamma*, meaning "to make the teachings of the Buddha relevant for the modern world." I got most of my own ideas from him and Buddhadasa.

Abbot Dhammacetiya

I worked with the monks via Mahachulalongkorn Buddhist University all through the 1960s when Bhikkhu Payutto was in charge, but I switched when he left the university. Phra Dhammacetiya, the abbot of Wat Thongnopphakhun, which my family has supported for five generations, was promoted to ecclesiastical governor of the Thonburi Sangha across the river from Bangkok. I followed him, moving from an academic involvement to a more practical involvement. Teaching at the university was mainly theoretical and had no real power to direct the monkhood. The abbot, in his new position, had the authority to tell the monks what to do.

I began working closely with the abbot, acting more or less as his lay secretary. I gave him a lot of ideas about administration. I told him we must look after the art in all the temples; we must use our money wisely and keep a record of our expenses; we must preserve the buildings, and any new buildings should have his approval; and we must train the monks to be aware of social issues. Monks must understand larger social issues and be involved in society. We were no longer living in villages. He agreed, so we formed lay and monks' committees that were very effective.

The 1971 coup consolidated Thonburi and Bangkok into one big city, and the abbot lost his position. He was asked to become governor general of the fourth region in the center of the country. The patriarch of the entire northern region also wanted him in charge of training and educating monks throughout this area. The abbot asked me if he should accept. I said yes, and against the advice of many other people, he did. I got money from a Christian foundation from Germany, Bread for the World, to support his work on conservation within the Buddhist Sangha. The Sangha had no conservation policy. The monks were not proud of their temples. They liked building new ones. I felt we had to teach them about architecture, art history, and preservation. We became very active. The abbot's work as a scholar and administrator was very much appreciated. Unfortunately, he worked very hard—unlike most monks—and died when he was only about seventy-one. I worked with the Sangha until his death in 1979.

CHAPTER **8** | *Forging Relations*

t was the 1960s. My country was being used as a base for doing
great harm in the name of anticommunism. But I came from a middle-class background and could afford to keep my mouth shut and
be happy while other people were suffering. In fact, British Quakers
in my country had wanted me to demonstrate against the American
bases, but when I consulted my Buddhist advisor, the English monk
Pannavaddho, he said, "Sulak, if you take Buddhism seriously, don't
get involved with these people. We Buddhists should calm ourselves."
So I didn't get involved. But my Buddha-nature eventually made me
feel that I must do something. Communists are also human beings.
I realized that for Buddhists simply to keep themselves at peace within was not sufficient.

American Friends Service Committee

Through meetings hosted by the American Friends Service Committee
(AFSC), I became exposed to the political issues. I got involved with
the AFSC through Russell Johnson, who was running their South
Asian office in India. Their idea was to arrange seminars and workshops to raise people's consciousness about peace and social justice
issues in order to cooperate internationally. He himself was not a
Quaker but an outspoken Christian minister from New England—
very pro-Mao Tse-tung. The East Asian office was run by Dewitt
Barnett, a prominent Quaker, the child of missionaries to China. He
had a small office in Tokyo but no knowledge of Southeast Asia. His
first job in our region was to call a meeting in the Philippines. It took
place in 1966, and I was the new man from Siam.

The purpose of the seminar was regional collaboration. We met
in Manila but stayed in the countryside at the headquarters of the
Philippine Rural Reconstruction Movement (PRRM). (The Thai Rural

Reconstruction Movement was later modeled after this group.) The governor of the province was Benigno Aquino. He came to talk to us, and I found that the Philippine and Thai systems were entirely different. A Thai governor behaves very properly and speaks carefully but without much substance. He has to wear a necktie and jacket or a uniform like Western colonial administrators in our neighboring countries. By contrast, Mr. Aquino was very American and very informal. He would challenge the presenters and wore just a shirt. He and another man we met both said they aspired to become president. I was quite surprised. "Good lord, I have met two persons aspiring to become president!" In our country nobody aspired to become prime minister—or if someone did, one kept one's mouth shut.

Although this was not my first time in the Philippines, it was the first time I went to the rural areas and really got to meet the Filipino people. Before the war, the Philippines was a model for democracy and higher education, a kind of window display for American activity in Asia. The Americans treated their former colony very well. We used to send our sons to be educated in the Philippines if we could not afford to send them to Europe or America. But by the time I went there in the middle sixties I was shocked. I went to Forbes Park where the superrich live. They had their own guards on big estates, their own islands, their own troops, their own private yachts. And then there were the slums. The gap between the rich and the poor was so great. My main fear was that my country would follow that model. At that time we had no big gap between the rich and the poor, and not even the king had a private yacht. We had no absentee landlords. Unfortunately, within thirty years we have become just like the Philippines.

The AFSC tended to go out of their way to develop leaders from various walks of life through their seminars or youth training camps. Many of the people who attended the meetings eventually became recognized leaders in their own countries. I met quite a few future leaders from Siam and other countries at this meeting. I also met former President Magapagal at his official residence, the Malaganyang.

After our meeting in the Philippines, the AFSC organized another meeting in Japan. It was at this meeting that I became seriously committed regarding the Vietnam War. I was already working to preserve our culture and environment—to keep the American troops from destroying our culture and creating more prostitution—but I had not been very aware of the political issues because I tried to keep myself from getting involved in politics. Not any longer.

The Southeast Asian Intellectual Exchange Program

Japan was now a nouveau riche country. They wanted to show off their riches and establish a relationship with other countries, including Southeast Asia. The International House of Japan was formed to promote internationalism and end their insularity, which America felt had been a factor in the Second World War. A year after the AFSC meeting on Vietnam, International House invited me to Japan as a cultural representative for their Southeast Asian Intellectual Exchange Program. International House had a good library on Japanese culture and history for foreign visitors, as well as accommodations and wonderful Japanese gardens in the heart of Tokyo. I stayed in Japan for a month. I wanted to know about Japanese Buddhism, so I was taken to Mt. Koya, the sacred place of the Shingon sect. I also stayed at a Zen temple. It was interesting culturally, although I was disappointed not to meet a practicing Zen master.

During my stay at International House, the Quakers were holding their own meetings on China. They didn't invite me since I knew nothing about China, but I invited myself. I found out about the situation in China. Although we didn't meet any Chinese, we talked with people who had just come back from China. They gave us firsthand reports. It was the height of the Cultural Revolution. At that time I was publishing the *Social Science Review,* so when I got back to Siam, I wrote an article arguing that we must recognize China. We should not simply follow the Americans. Of course, we should keep China—and the Americans—at arm's length. This was very controversial because we could not even import shirts, let alone books, from China. Many of those who went to China in the fifties had been arrested and were still in jail. People said I was very brave to write what I did because I could have been put in jail for it even though I was known as a royalist and anticommunist.

On my way home from Japan, I stopped in Hong Kong for the International Press Institute (IPI) meeting. I had been elected a member. The IPI, headquartered in Zurich, was supposed to be the guiding light of the free world, promoting freedom of speech and freedom of the press. They wanted to help the Thai people by training our journalists to present news in depth and commit themselves to freedom and liberty. They felt we needed an Asian who wrote well and had worked his way up from nowhere, so in 1965, they sent us Victor Anant, an Indian. He had gone to London as a boy and worked his way up from porter at the British Railways to office boy in Fleet Street and later columnist with the *Daily Telegraph*. When Anant came to Bangkok, he asked me to be his interpreter, and through him I came to know many more journalists.

In those days, to be elected a member of the IPI was very prestigious. Many Thai journalists were jealous of me because in their eyes I was not even a journalist; I was only a journal editor. I was elected partly because my magazine stood for what the international press stood for— freedom of expression. Most of the Thai newspapers of that time simply went along with the government, which was understandable because we had a dictatorship.

I wrote a book on my trip to Japan named after the Japanese classic, *A Pillow Book*. I continued working with the International House of Japan and the Quakers. In fact, many Japanese working against the Vietnam War eventually became my friends. They worked on various peace projects and later protested Japan's exportation of toxic waste to our part of the world. They also worked against the building of Narita Airport and to preserve the tram in Kyoto. I often joined them. I even bought land symbolically. Some of my friends asked, "Why do you interfere with other countries?" I said, "Some issues are universal. Trams should be preserved everywhere."

Cultural Relations for the Future

At the meeting in Japan in 1970, I met a young assistant in the AFSC named Brewster Grace. He came from a distinguished Quaker family in Philadelphia. He was selected to open a new AFSC office in Singapore. He consulted me about having seminars in my country and in other countries in Southeast Asia. We became good friends and were quite active. He was also selected to attend a meeting in New York called "Cultural Relations for the Future," funded by the

Edward Hazen Foundation. Paul Braisted of the Foundation felt that since the Americans had been all over the world educating people to develop according to the American model, it should be a two-way street. Americans should be educated by others.

A very important man at that meeting was Soedjatmoko, then the Indonesian ambassador to the U.S. He was one of the best Southeast Asian intellectuals I had come across. Soedjatmoko said, "You Americans have wonderful ideas, but you always think of America as being at the center. Why don't you think globally? Why don't you let other people think for themselves? You have the money. Set up five or six committees in different parts of the world. Ask them to meet among themselves and find out what they would like to do in their own regions, and then vis-a-vis the Americans, the Europeans, and other regions." His idea was adopted, and they set up six committees: in Southeast Asia, India, Japan, the Middle East, the U.S., and Africa. Brewster Grace represented Southeast Asia, and he proposed my name to lead the committee. Although I was fairly unknown at the time, I became chairman of the Southeast Asian study group on Cultural Relations for the Future.

With the Cultural Relations for the Future committee, I could now conduct my own seminars. Our first meeting was in Singapore in 1970. I felt that the Southeast Asian group must not be limited to the countries in the Association of Southeast Asian Nations (ASEAN), the successor to SEATO—Siam, Malaysia, Singapore, Indonesia, the Philippines, and later Brunei. I said we needed to try to bring in Laos, Burma, Cambodia, and Vietnam. (Later, Laos, Burma, and Vietnam joined ASEAN.) I managed to get some Vietnamese, and I went to Phnom Penh to get a former minister whom I had met in Manila. The idea was first of all to get to know each other within our region. We would try to understand our own cultural identity and think about our cultural relations. Nobody else was interested in these things. The military was interested only in power, and businesses only in money. Secondly, we wanted to understand our relationships vis-a-vis the other groups. We met and made an agenda for the next two years, including what we ought to learn from each other and where and when our next meeting would be.

The Hazen Foundation gave me a small amount of money to travel around that part of the world in the Quaker manner—no per diem, only airfare and expenses. We met every nine months in a different place. We had local hosts to look after us. At the end of two years, all the chairmen of the six groups met at the Villa Serbelloni in Bellagio, Italy, to compare notes and talk about what we should do in the future. Out of these meetings we produced two books. One had the very ambitious title *Reconstituting Human Society*. This was published by the Hazen Foundation and distributed free of charge to U.S. organizations and various foundations. Later on, we produced *Questioning Development in Southeast Asia*. As far as I was concerned, it had been wonderful to get to know my region of the world. I now had many good friends from each country. I got to know all sorts of people involved in alternative development and alternative education with many different religious and cultural backgrounds. With some I still keep in touch.

After a few years, the foundation money ran out. The study group wanted to stay together and carry on even though the Americans would no longer support us. We decided we had to link with another study group and contacted the Japanese. The chairman's assistant, Mr. Yoshiyuki Tsurumi at the International House of Japan, was my good friend. He secured some money from the International House to keep us going. The Southeast Asian group and the Japanese group kept meeting every year. I did not want to be the perpetual chairman, so I asked my friend William Lim from Singapore to succeed me. He is a well-known architect and intellectual in Singapore. He was succeeded by Randy David, a young, very articulate Filipino who ran the Third World Study Center at the University of the Philippines. Unfortunately, he got very involved in other work, and the study group is now more or less defunct. I feel sorry about this; however, everything that grows will eventually die.

The Pacific Ashram

My role in Southeast Asia did not end with the Cultural Relations for the Future study group. Brewster Grace, after leaving the AFSC, became the Southeast Asian representative of the American University Field Staff (AUFS). AUFS is a consortium of American universities interested in worldwide exchange. He made arrangements for students who wanted to study in the region. His predecessor in the AUFS felt that when American students came to Asia, they should also study the spiritual tradition. When Brewster took over, he was in charge of implementing these ideas.

A meeting was called by the AUFS in Singapore. The upshot of the meeting was that the group would get a small sum of money from the Danforth Foundation in the U.S. to collaborate with the AUFS to create what they called a "Pacific Ashram." The idea was to experiment with young people living together for three to four weeks to share spiritual traditions. If they were to be our future leaders, they should get to know each other beyond a purely intellectual encounter. Whereas our Cultural Relations for the Future was more or less a forum for intellectuals in their late thirties and forties who were already fairly well-known in their countries, this program was for youth under thirty. I was just giving up the chairmanship of the Southeast Asian study group on Cultural Relations for the Future and was asked to become the secretary of this project. There was no pay involved, but AUFS would take care of all my travel expenses. I accepted the challenge. It was 1973.

Being Thai, I did not want to hold the first Pacific Ashram in my own country. We found a beautiful site at Kuala Dungun on the east coast of Malaysia. At that time there were no tourists, and it was quite undeveloped. We used a small hotel—not ideal for our ashram—but there were also bungalows and campsites. We were there for three weeks in 1974. As chairman of Cultural Relations for the Future for the last four years, I had been exposed to a lot of people. We chose our participants mostly through personal contacts. These budding leaders had been recommended to me by their professors and interviewers. My job was as a kind of guru-in-residence, and Brewster was there as the coordinator-administrator. There were quite a number of leaders from all over Southeast Asia as well as some Japanese and Americans. I remember one Filipino and one Thai quarreled like mad.

We tried to combine everything, both American and Asian traditions, and not be exclusively Buddhist. We taught yoga and whatever else they wanted. Meditation was not compulsory, and people could write or work on other things. I myself translated Thomas

Merton's book on Chuang Tzu. It took me three weeks, and it became one of my bestsellers.

I thought the second Pacific Ashram should be in my own country. We held it in Chiang Mai at a beautiful monastery halfway up a mountain. This was more to my liking. I wanted to make the gathering more spiritual. Mr. Karuna Kusalasaya was the guru-in-residence. He had a deep understanding of Indian culture, he knew yoga and Buddhism, and he was a very humble man. We invited the Buddhist Thich Nhat Hanh and Swami Aganivesh from the Hindu tradition. We also invited Bhikkhu P. A. Payutto and Bob Bobilin, chair of the Department of Religion at the University of Hawaii. These four acted as senior advisors. Bob later wrote an article entitled, "Three Men on a Mountain," a very moving account of the one Hindu and two Buddhist monks at our meeting. We had a wonderful three weeks together. That was in 1975.

The third gathering was held in Japan. Unfortunately, it lasted only ten days. I didn't go. I felt that this moving ashram had no roots and wanted a more permanent ashram. I tried to get more money from the International House of Japan, but the director wanted to set up a kind of International House of Siam instead of an ashram. He put me in contact with one of his protégés, Dr. Saburo Okita, who later become Foreign Minister. Dr. Okita agreed to help me with some money. From there I went on to speak at the Smithsonian Institute and visit the Aspen Institute, a kind of American ashram. Unfortunately, my idea for an ashram had to be put on hold. The 1976 coup took place when I was on my way home.

M y work at this time generated its share of conflicts. In fact, one episode involved the king himself. It began when some of my academic colleagues and friends decided that the Social Science Association wasn't fulfilling its function by producing enough textbooks. They claimed that I was spending most of my time running the magazine when the Social Science Association was really supposed to be a university press—that I only published what I wanted, instead of representing the whole academic world. Of course, there may have been some truth in this. In fact, I argued that a university press shouldn't produce textbooks anyhow. So they went to the Rockefeller Foundation asking for money to form a rival organization, the Social Sciences and Humanities Project.

The Rockefeller Foundation representative in Bangkok was Bill Bradley, whose great-grandfather had been one of the first American missionaries to Siam. He had also been a famous doctor who introduced Western medicine to Siam, along with printing, publishing, and newspapers. Bill Bradley said, "That's a wonderful idea. If you people want to start something, the Rockefeller Foundation will help you, but none of you academics knows anything about publishing. If you want to start this new venture, you must have Sulak involved. With all his faults, he knows about publishing." They were very angry, but they had no choice. They had to take me. They also asked Dr. Puey Ungphakorn, who was a very honest man, an able technocrat, and the governor of the Bank of Thailand, to help with the project. Dr. Puey talked to me, and I agreed, adding, "But I'll just help. I'll give you what advice you want. All I want is one vote in a committee." They quite liked that.

The brain behind this whole idea was Dr. Neon Snidvong. She was also a member of the royal family. She had been my contemporary in England, and we had a love-hate relationship. She said, "We must get a royal blessing for this new project," and she arranged for us to see the king. We all dressed up—I even wore a jacket and necktie because I didn't want to be the odd man out by going in our national dress. Of course, we didn't crawl to the king, we just bowed and sat on chairs with him.

I think the king is a very shy man. Shy men never listen to people; they always talk. He gave us a long lecture on how to publish books. Unfortunately, I am a man of very bad manners, so I said, "Your Majesty, what you say is excellent. Only Your Majesty can do it; I can't do it." He became very angry with me and said, "You think because I am the king I will do it?" I said, "Yes, Your Majesty." He replied, "No! I am a man of good intentions, but my people must help me." We left the audience in a very uncomfortable atmosphere. Poor Dr. Puey could have attacked me afterwards but instead spoke very personably and consoled me. He drove me home and said jokingly, "Many of us would have liked to argue with the king, Sulak, but we didn't know how to use royal language. You knew how to use the right language." I felt that, meaning well, I must speak my mind to the king. If you're not honest, to me it means you have no respect. To show the forms of respect is not real respect. Anyhow, from then on I was not seen anywhere near the palace.

On another occasion, when I was involved with Prince Sitthiporn Kridakara on an agricultural project, he asked the king for help. In his letter he mentioned that I was helping him. The king responded, "If Sulak is helping you, I won't help you." The prince was very disturbed and asked me, "What happened? Why this personal vendetta?" I told him everything. He wrote again to the king, saying, "Sulak has an independent mind, but as far as I know he's a man of loyalty. I beg Your Majesty to understand." The king supported his project. On the whole, I feel that the king is quite fair. From what I gather, he usually reads my articles and books. Once I heard that he even said, "Sulak regards himself as my friend. He always wants to teach me." I don't know whether he meant it sarcastically or jokingly.

Kukrit Pramoj

When I started the *Social Science Review*, there was very little freedom of speech or freedom of the press. Most progressive journalists were in jail or living in exile in China and Russia. The only well-known journalist at liberty at the time was Kukrit Pramoj. In the first issue of the *Social Science Review*, I had criticized his dance performance in a masked play. I wrote about what a wonderful writer he was, but that he looked down on others and always wanted to be number one. That article, published in 1966, became the talk of the town. At the time, I truly admired him. We had something in common. Deep down I'm a conservative, intellectually trained in Britain just as he was. However, I felt that he should be open to criticism and to the younger generation. He never replied to my article but was privately furious. I learned later that he had vowed to destroy me one day. Now I felt I must be careful.

In 1967, I thought we should do something to commemorate the destruction of our old capital, Ayuthaya, by the Burmese two hundred years ago. In the *Social Science Review*, I published an editorial asking, "What can we learn from Ayuthaya? Why did we lose the kingdom to the Burmese?" I quoted a passage written by King Chulalongkorn sixty years before. He said that during his time Siam was nearly lost to foreign colonialists because the people were not united. They distrusted each other. They were selfish, corrupt, and valued form above essence. His reign had been very similar to the period of the fall of Ayuthaya. He felt so ashamed he became sick. He wrote a poem to his friends, saying that he would fast unto death because he could not save his country. Prince Damrong, Chulalongkorn's half brother and right-hand man, wrote another poem, urging him, "Please be our captain. If the captain will steer, even if the boat sinks, let it sink mindfully, and let us be together." Because of this poem, King Chulalongkorn recovered and came back and faced the storm bravely. He gave away four provinces but saved the country. He survived colonialism because he learned from Ayuthaya. He was mindful.

I felt we were now in the same state—we squandered our money, destroyed the environment, filled in the canals, cut down the trees. We were mindless. Our leaders quarreled among themselves. Indeed, there was no leadership. We did not even know we were under a dictatorship. We had lost our roots. I wrote that we must also learn from

Ayuthaya as Chulalongkorn had. I said, "Today, likewise, we have no leader; we have no captain. We regard formality as important, not essence. The only captain we have now is captain of a sailboat." At

that time the king was an avid sailor. I knew this was a controversial editorial, and I asked a lawyer to read it. He said, "Nobody can sue you."

I went to Phya Anuman and talked with him about my plans to commemorate the anniversary of Ayuthaya's fall. He felt that it was a good idea, but said that I must be careful. I went to Prince Dhani and received his support, and again the Asia Foundation gave me money. We created an Ayuthaya exhibition that traveled from campus to campus. The project also involved a series of lectures in the National Library. As a way to recon-

Kukrit Pramoj at Ayuthaya

cile with Kukrit Pramoj, I invited him as keynote speaker for the closing ceremony among the ruins of the old capital in Ayuthaya, and he accepted.

People had warned me that Kukrit sometimes accepted an invitation but would not show up, so our whole committee went to his house. He was shocked to see me in person. We had quarreled only on paper. He lived in a beautiful Siamese-style house, big and old-fashioned, full of treasures. I felt a bit sorry for the man. I thought he must be lonely. He had divorced his wife. He did not get on very well with his children. He was almost sixty years old, and his only friends were dogs.

He embraced me, "Mr. Sulak, how good of you to come to my house." (I was told later by his son that he was in a very bad mood that day. He was even nasty to the dogs.) "What can I do for you?" he asked. I said, "I want you to be the keynote speaker at our commemoration of the two-hundredth anniversary of Ayuthaya. We need to look to the future. Tell the people, tell the nation what we should do." He replied, "That is a very difficult and important lecture. Why don't you do it yourself?" I said no. "I organized this commemoration and have been criticized by all sorts of people saying, 'Why should we commemorate an event in which we lost our country?'" Finally he agreed to come. I added, "On this day, I want every one of us to dress in the traditional Siamese style, not in European style." He agreed, and then confided, "Mr. Sulak, I will tell you a secret. I'm afraid of only two persons in this country—the Princess Chumpot and you! If you asked me to speak in Ayuthaya naked, I would do it."

When I went to see Kukrit Pramoj, he said nothing about my editorial, but the next day, he wrote in his daily newspaper column, "There is a magazine called the *Social Science Review* financed by the American imperialists. The editor is paid by the American dogs. His editorial said that our king is no good and does not lead; that he only plays with sailboats every day." He said that I should be punished for lèse-majesté, criticizing the king and tantamount to treason. I found out later that he had sent his private secretary to the chief of police saying I must be put in jail. In fact, when he accepted my invitation, he had already spoken to the authorities and expected me to be put in jail soon. That's why he accepted the invitation. When he came to give the lecture, he would have said, "Mr. Sulak—I love him; he is wonderful. But, poor chap, he wasn't careful enough. I feel so sorry for him in jail."

Kukrit had done a similar thing in 1961. When he was in England during our king's visit, I had organized a lecture for him at the Thai Students' Association. He told of an episode with Mr. Chote Gunakasem, his senior in the finance ministry. They quarreled, and Kukrit was thrown out of the ministry. This man became the governor of the Bank of Thailand and minister of finance at the same time, which was not quite proper. Eventually, he was arrested for corrupt dealings and put in jail. Kukrit Pramoj was the one who had informed on him to the dictator, Sarit Thanarat. Kukrit told us, "This man, Mr. Chote, I loved him; I respected him. Poor chap, he fell into such corruption. I had no choice but to go to the prime minister. As a patriot, I felt I must go and tell him, and he cheered me for my patriotism. I did not realize poor Mr. Chote would go to jail."

As for my case, I learned later on that Kukrit had even brought it to a Cabinet meeting. The secretary-general of the Cabinet, a senior military man said, "If Mr. Kukrit has a quarrel with Mr. Sulak, he should not use the Cabinet to punish his adversary. Let bygones be bygones!" Prince Wan, my boss at the *Social Science Review*, said, "Well, I'm the owner of the magazine. I will talk to Mr. Sulak. I will have all the magazines withdrawn, not by the state, but by ourselves. I will ask Prince Dhani to lecture Mr. Sulak that he must behave in the future." I was asked to see Prince Dhani. He said, "You should not have written something like that. You don't know the king personally. You should go to see him, get to know him. He is a very nice, lovely man." I heard that Prince Dhani also remarked, "I have known Sulak for some years now, and I have never known him to be a liar or to use his pen destructively. He may not be wise, but he's honest." The whole thing was resolved. It was done very beautifully in the Siamese way. Of course, the editorial was probably very bad taste on my part and perhaps implied that I didn't really respect the king.

Kukrit was furious that I wasn't punished. On the day of the Ayuthaya lecture, he came dressed in the European fashion, wearing a necktie. I went to say hello to him, but he would not talk to me. I said, "Your Excellency, I thought you had agreed to dress in the traditional Siamese style?" He replied, "I can't stand to dress in the damn Siamese style! I'll dress the way I like!" He sat down in a very bad mood.

The plan was that he would be the last speaker, speaking until dusk. Then, we would burn torches, and all two or three thousand of us would march with them as an offering to the most important Buddha image in the city. We would all pay respects and then have traditional drama, dance, and fireworks. But when Kukrit Pramoj finished, it was not yet dusk. He said, "Well, I was to speak until dusk, but I can't go on any more. Please, Mr. Governor, declare it dusk and let them light the torches!" The governor said, "We have heard Phya Anuman Rajadhon, from our grandfathers' generation. You have heard an excellent speech by Mr. Kukrit Pramoj, the leading intellectual of our fathers' generation. Since it is not yet dusk, may I call on Mr. Sulak Sivaraksa, the leading intellectual of our generation, to speak!"

Kukrit Pramoj became very annoyed. He felt that I had betrayed him since he was to be the last speaker. I was not supposed to be in the show; I was supposed to stay in the background. I wasn't prepared, but I had to speak. The people of Ayuthaya booed me because I had criticized them in an editorial two weeks before, saying they hadn't been interested in our exhibition. It was just like an election. Of course, when they booed me, Kukrit loved it. We never met again.

With Phya Anuman (left) and Prince Wan (right) at the National Library

D ue to the popularity of the *Social Science Review,* I had become well-known very quickly, and I think I was too proud. I was known by high officials and nobility. Even the king read my magazine. One day Prince Sitthiporn Kridakara came to my office. He was considered the father of modern Thai agriculture. In his younger days he had been director general of the government's biggest department—the Department of Opium at that time. When he left office around the age of forty, he became a farmer because he was unhappy that educated people had all become bureaucrats. He introduced modern farming to our country.

When Prince Sitthiporn visited me, he said, "Sulak, what are you doing? Yes, this country needs an intellectual magazine, but don't let it become intellectual masturbation. Do you know anything about the farmers? Eighty-five percent of our people are farmers. The government has pushed the price of rice down in order to make you middle-class people happy at the expense of the farmers. They suffer, and you know nothing about it." I realized he was right. Up until then, with my English education and privileged background, I felt that to remain in one's class was proper. You must be kind and fair to people, but the lower class should remain where they are. At his urging, I went to visit farmers and grow rice. I saw that the structures making the middle class so content and happy were at the farmers' expense. Through this experience, my ideas changed, and with my magazine, I decided to organize students.

Beginning the Paritat Sevana

There was a Protestant youth organization called the Student Christian Center, run by Kosol Srisang. Kosol had noticed that the *Social Science Review* was the only magazine that really appealed to the students, so in 1966 he asked me to help him organize a seminar for young students on "Youth's Social and Ethical Responsibility for Siam." We asked Professor Sanya Dharmasakti, the Lord Chief Justice and president of the Buddhist Association of Thailand, to give a presentation from the Buddhist point of view and a senior Thai Christian to speak from the Christian point of view. Dr. Puey Ungphakorn, then the governor of the Bank of Thailand, spoke as a layperson. After the plenary we divided into small workshops. There was an essay contest in which students wrote about their concerns for the country, and the best essay was published in our magazine. It was a two-day seminar and had tremendous impact. It was the first time students were brought together from many universities, teachers' colleges, and technical colleges. Almost two hundred came.

After this meeting, several students came to me and said, "If the Christians do all this, what about us Buddhists? We should do something." I said, "Good. Social responsibility means that we must care for those who suffer more than we do. We can visit people in jail, in the slums, in homes for juvenile delinquents." We formed a small nucleus. Some I had known before at the magazine, some I met for the first time at the seminar. But they said this was not enough. "We need our own place, our own club."

I went to the university to ask permission to use the office of the Press. The vice president of Student Affairs said, "It's a good idea, but you must realize that we're still under martial law—if more than five people meet together, the police can raid the place at any time." I thought next of Wat Bowornives. This monastery was a royal temple. King Mongkut had been abbot there for fourteen years before he disrobed and came to the throne. If I had the abbot's permission to use the temple, no police would dare raid us. I went to him and explained, "I have been to the Student Christian Center. They don't preach Christianity at all, but they attract young people. If we don't do something, all our young people will go there. Buddhism is no longer relevant to these young people. Your lordship has a beautiful temple with many unused buildings. Can I have one building? I don't want you to preach Buddhism, but I want the youth to have a Buddhist atmosphere. Would you allow this?" He said, "Yes, good idea." His secretary took me around, and we found one lovely old house in very bad shape.

We formed a committee, all young people, and called the committee *Paritat Sevana*, meaning "the group on reviewing society," or, "we look around and discuss what to do." We met three times a week. They wanted to learn English, so I went to Bhikkhu Khantipalo, an English monk, and suggested, "Teach them English. That's the way you can propagate your Dhamma." We had free English classes once a week. I made arrangements for them to meet anybody they wanted to meet—the chief justice, the governor of the Bank of Thailand, the dean, the rector of the university, even the abbot. They enjoyed themselves, and the club became lively. After graduation, they didn't want to lose the comradeship, so we started another club for graduates. These two clubs would meet—the older would support the younger, the younger would challenge the older, and we continued to grow.

Since we met within the temple, we kept a low profile and didn't attract much attention from the government, except on one occasion when I was planning to give a talk. I wanted to give it a provocative title and chose, "The Danger of Western Civilization." After several years we had become rather daring. The building we were using was the old consecrated assembly hall, but in the newspaper advertisement, they left out the word "old" and said, "in the consecrated assembly hall of Wat Bowornives." This is the most prestigious consecrated assembly hall in the whole kingdom, and I was going to give a talk on the dangers of Western civilization! There was an uproar, but the abbot remained very calm and nothing bad happened.

Working with a volunteer group to improve living conditions in the rural provinces

Teaching ethics

When we held the first national workshop for Thai students at the Student Christian Center in 1966, quite a number of progressive and concerned professors had come. The topic was how to get students to develop moral concern for national development. I argued that students hadn't been taught to be aware of ethical issues and that the Buddhist morality they were taught was outdated. Teachers simply gave sermons to the students, and they fell asleep because they didn't want to listen. I said we must teach our students moral ethics so they could argue and make decisions about what should be done.

Professor Saengarun Ratakasikorn in the Faculty of Architecture at Chulalongkorn University thought this was a wonderful idea. He asked if I would like to teach ethics on his faculty. I could introduce a modern approach to ethics that need not be entirely Buddhist. I accepted and taught there for two years. The class was compulsory, and quite a number of professors also attended because it was rather innovative for them.

The rector at the time was General Praphas Charusathira, the dictator who was also deputy prime minister. His daughter happened to be studying in my class. Unfortunately, she did not do well on her examinations, so I gave her an "F." The faculty didn't know what to do. They could not tell me to change my mark, but they couldn't fail her either, so they decided that just for that year, anybody who got an "F" would receive a passing mark.

But I didn't really enjoy teaching compulsory subjects. I felt that people should come to my class out of enjoyment, not because they were forced to. After two years, I stopped teaching ethics. Dr. Vid Viddhayavet, head of the new Department of Philosophy at Chulalongkorn, asked me to teach an elective subject called "Western Political Thought." I taught there for eight years until 1976. The class was for third- and fourth-year students—mostly women—and I enjoyed working with them. Some of them became close friends. I translated a book for the course which has become a standard work, Maurice Cranston's *Political Dialogue*. In fact, every time I taught a course, I produced at least one book to use as material. I translated some of Plato's work, and it became a standard book on Socratic dialogues. I wrote a long article that became a booklet on ethics. Later on, when

I was invited to teach in the Faculty of Economics at Thammasat University, I produced a book on the philosophy of education.

Starting the Sathirakoses-Nagapradipa Foundation

As the *Social Science Review* became well-known, writers began coming to us—writers who were poor or in difficulty. I tried to help these writers with my own money and by raising money from other successful writers. Among them, I went to Phya Anuman. I reminded him that while he had been an author almost all his life, he was also employed by the government and had a salary and pension. Many other writers were not so lucky. Their works were being lost, their names forgotten. He agreed, asking, "What should I do?" I said, "I would like to use the royalties from your books to set up a foundation named after you. The interest from this money will help suffering authors and young would-be authors and artists. They want to be themselves; they do not want to sell their souls. We can help them." He said, "It's a very good idea, but my royalties aren't much." I estimated they were worth more than 100,000 baht, or about $5,000. So we started the Sathirakoses Foundation—using his pen name—on his eightieth birthday. I told everyone, "Don't give him any flowers, don't give him any presents. Give money to the foundation!"

I collected only small amounts of money here and there from his publishers, so I had my lawyer write to all of them, saying, "We now have a foundation that owns the rights to Phya Anuman's works. Those who publish or reprint without our authority will be sued." I collected even more money. I employed someone to edit his work and do proper indexing. Phya Anuman had a coauthor and translator named Phra Saraprasert. His *nom de plume* was Nagapradipa. He was a great Pali and Sanskrit scholar who had died many years ago. I went to his children and asked for permission to have their copyrights signed over to me. We amended the name of the foundation to include both names, the Sathirakoses-Nagapradipa Foundation. It is still in existence today.

When the foundation began in 1968, it took ownership of a new magazine called *Pajarayasara*. Originally, it had been the magazine of the alumni association of Prasanmit College, a teacher's college in Bangkok. Bibhob Dhongchai, one of my assistants, had become editor of the magazine and enjoyed it so much that he had expanded it to include all teachers' colleges around the country. He introduced new and innovative ideas in education from people like Paulo Freire and Ivan Illich. Bibhob asked me to choose a new name for it, and I suggested *Pajarayasara*—"Teacher of Teachers." When the magazine changed its name, Prasanmit College cut it off, and the Sathirakoses-Nagapradipa Foundation took it over. Later, when the *Social Science Review* closed down, *Pajarayasara* succeeded it in a way, with its alternative ecological, environmental, Buddhist, and sometimes even Marxist, approach. My idea all along had been to give young people a chance to experiment, to give them a platform to explore new ideas and be creative. There have been many young editors, and it's still being published.

In 1969, before his eighty-first birthday, Phya Anuman died suddenly. When he was critically ill, his wife called me. "Your teacher informed me that when he died, he wished you to organize his funeral." This was a great honor for me. I consulted with his nine children, and they all agreed. I went to Princess Jongjit, who was an expert on funeral services, and arranged everything. In our custom, the deceased lie in state at home for one hundred days. We had chanting almost every night and sermons every week. Monks chanted in the Thai manner, the Cambodian manner, the Laotian manner, the Mon manner, and the Chinese manner. Phya Anuman had written a book on other religions, so we included Hindu and Catholic rites. The old man would have loved it. After his cremation, his remains were placed in a royal urn befitting nobility. He was a Phya, which is a kind of knight. The king and queen came to light the funeral pyre at the royal crematorium. We published beautiful memorial volumes and collected money for the foundation.

Starting a bookshop

All this time I really wanted a proper bookshop like the one I had seen in the Philippines, Solidaridat, run by my friend Frankie José and his wife. I presented my idea for a bookshop to my editorial board, but they wouldn't agree. They would allow a small shop to sell books, but they would not let me have a place for meetings on the university grounds. I said, "All right, I'll do it on my own." I began to plan the bookstore with an old friend, Sudjai Jermsiriwat. Sudjai's father had been a very rich man before the war and had run a large import company called Siam Architect. His son was my classmate at Assumption College and went to England at the same time I did. His wife had married him for his money, but she jilted him. He nearly went crazy. I introduced him to Buddhism, and I believe the Dhamma saved him.

The two of us went to another former classmate who was general manager of a construction company that had built a development of shops near Chulalongkorn University. The shops were all rented, except for one. It was exactly opposite a temple known for its crematorium. According to Chinese belief, placing a building opposite a temple gate allows ghosts to walk straight in. Nobody would take it. I didn't care about superstition, so we took it. Our friend reduced the price for us. He was happy to be rid of it. We opened our small bookshop on April 20, 1967, at 1715 Rama IV Road.

We had a big argument over the name of the bookshop. My Thai and English friends said the name should be short and easy for Westerners to pronounce. It must have a good historical connection. I was given the task of finding a name. I looked up names in the dictionary and historical encyclopedias, and I selected a few. Nobody liked them. Finally, we came across a poem written by a famous Thai poet. "Suksit," which means "educated" or "intellectual," was the poem's title. Everyone agreed on this name. Suksit was short enough for the foreigners, and even if they mispronounced it, it still had a good meaning. But I thought Suksit was too short and that we needed to include the word "Siam." Suksit Siam was the best compromise.

My friend Sudjai was the manager. Friends became shareholders. Curly Bowen helped me open an account in Cambridge, Massachusetts, so we had an American account to make it easier to order books from America. I also had an account in England. Some said ours was the best bookshop for books on Buddhism, Southeast Asia, and Siam—our three specialties. Apart from being a bookstore and a place where intellectuals could meet, the bookshop became a kind of center for social, cultural, spiritual, and educational activities. Suksit Siam was on the ground floor, and exhibitions and meetings were held on the second. The young students still went to the temple, but the graduates would come to the bookshop. Technically, we could have been in trouble with the government for hosting these meetings, but by that time things had relaxed a bit.

Joining the Thai Wattanapanich Publishing Company

After editing the *Social Science Review* for six years, I left. I had been invited by the biggest private publishing house in the country, Thai Wattanapanich, to become their chief editor. Thai Wattanapanich had started out as a small family business in the thirties and had become the biggest private publisher of textbooks. Thai Chinese families have been very successful at starting something from nothing. But after a few generations, it typically all disappears because success breeds mindlessness. The eldest son asked me to help. He was my contemporary from Assumption College and knew that I had connections with some leading intellectuals and artists. I think the idea came from his mother, Mrs. Boonpring T. Suwan. She is one of the cleverest women I have ever come across—Thai Chinese, hardworking, aggressive. I told them that with the Japanese and the Americans, if the family business is having trouble, they look elsewhere and invite bright, able people to run it. The family said, "Okay, we want you to be our new management. You set it up in the Western style."

My experience was with university textbooks, and I recommended we get into the universities. Their numbers were increasing. When I was born, there was only one university. When I went to England, there were only four or five. Now we had universities all over, and eventually we would have private universities and colleges. I also said, "You must publish research work; you must have archives. You are rich, so you can do it." Finally, I urged, "You must give up matriarchal power. We must have a new committee to make decisions." They liked all these proposals. At Thai Wattanapanich, I think my dream more or less came true. With my previous publishing house I had no money, but this was a real company. It could develop into something great.

I employed all the best people. I asked one of my friends, a former classmate and top artist, Uab Sanasen, to join me as the chief art director. He brought other good artists to work there. I was interested in conservation, so I asked photographers to take pictures of old buildings. I felt that a company like this could make a great contribution to future generations by at least documenting this history on film. I put all my ideas into that publishing house.

But when I tried to implement my ideas, the family didn't like it at all. They thought my ideas were too grand. Perhaps I was too ambitious, too impatient, too political. They were afraid of me because of my political stance. I made many enemies within the company. The company was run by the matriarch, and eventually the reorganization upset her, because it eroded her power. People gossiped, "You have to be careful. This man Sulak is new, and he is ambitious. He's going to take away your company."

So I was reduced from being chief editor to editor of their magazine. This magazine imitated our *Social Science Review*, but it was for the young people. Mrs. Boonpring came to me and said, "Since you have magazine experience, why don't you continue it?" This was new for me—a fortnightly magazine for the young. Again, I wrote some controversial editorials, and they eventually asked me to leave. Unfortunately, when I left, what I had built was lost, and the whole company went back to the way it had been. I'm afraid, even now, that once the old lady dies, the company will disappear. The three children have no interest in their future together.

After I got the sack, I went back to the bookshop. I had no other job.

The Komol Keemthong Foundation

There was an exceptional young man in the group that met at our bookshop, Mr. Komol Keemthong. He was a student at Chulalongkorn University, very bright, and everybody loved him. He was involved in all kinds of club activities. Supported by the Americans, we had started what we called the work camps. For three or four weeks during vacation, students would go upcountry to build something for poor people. Students from Bangkok had a chance to see the suffering in the countryside and learn about the rural society. They usually ended up building something and not learning very much, but it was still a useful program. Through the work camps, Komol became interested in working in the countryside.

After graduation, he was offered a lectureship at his university, but he refused. He wanted to become a school teacher in a region heavily influenced by the Communists. I was concerned. "Someone like you is very difficult to come by. I don't want to lose you." He said, "I'll be all right. I shall be skillful." He became interested in local arts and crafts and started a community school. He was so active that the Communists thought he was a government agent, and at the same time the army thought he was a Communist agent. In 1971, he was tragically killed. We brought his body back to Bangkok to lie for one hundred days. I had all of his articles and letters published for his cremation.

People wanted to keep his spirit and name alive. They talked with me about starting a foundation in honor of Komol. They wanted to encourage young people to be full of idealism. The new foundation would promote activities for social welfare and social justice. Since our two clubs and our *Review* had been involved with that already, they felt I was the right man to do it. I was close to Professor Sanya Dharmasakti, the president of the Buddhist Association, who had now become the privy counselor to the king, and I asked him to be the president of our new foundation. He readily agreed. We formed the Komol Keemthong Foundation. Professor Sanya informed the king, and the king sent the royal fire to light the cremation. In our tradition, this is a great honor.

Money for the foundation came initially from the book we published for Komol's cremation. It was paid for by his former employer, who had helped young Komol to start the community school. Instead of giving copies of the big volume away, we sold them, and those who could afford to pay more did so. But we needed one hundred thousand baht to incorporate legally. I went to the Asia Foundation with our proposal to help youth involved in various activities, and they supported us. This foundation and the Sathirakoses-Nagapradipa Foundation had their offices on the third floor of our bookshop.

We also started a series of annual Komol Keemthong lectures, featuring exemplary speakers who had something new to inspire the young people. These lectures attracted a lot of attention. We started the Komol Keemthong publishing house, publishing all of Thich Nhat Hanh's works in Thai, *One Straw Revolution* by Masanobu Fukuoka, and many other wonderful books by international and Thai authors. Over the years it has become an inspiring publishing house, sponsoring lectures and many other activities for young people.

The Siam Society

At this time I also became active in the Siam Society, a prestigious association founded in 1904 by expatriates. Many scholars participated along with members of the royal family. After Prince Dhani retired from the presidency, it lost its prestige and became little more than a club. It was run by a Dutchman who thought it was his own society. I arranged a coup in 1969. Of course, we took over democratically. I put Phya Anuman forward as president, and, with his election, I was more or less in control.

I felt the Siam Society must now work more for the public. A younger generation of Thais should be in control. It had never been open to the common people, only to the expatriates and aristocrats. I wanted to open it to all and have the lectures and seminars in Thai. I became program chairman for the society. Instead of the former three or four lectures a year, I scheduled three or four lectures a month in Thai and English. We organized trips to Laos, China, India, and Sri Lanka. After every trip abroad, we offered one scholarship to a Thai student from the extra money we collected. I also became editor of the *Journal of the Siam Society* and made it more relevant for the modern world.

During my first year, we hosted a big seminar on Buddhism in Society. It was the first time we spoke openly, criticizing the Sangha and discussing their role, saying how we thought they had failed, and what they should do. At times there was very heated argument, but it was all open. Bhikkhu Payutto, Abbot Dhammacetiya, and a number of high ranking monks attended. Among the leading laity were the president of the Buddhist Association and the minister of education. The abbot of Wat Bowornives came and closed the meeting in a very beautiful way. But the next day, there were posters denouncing me at his temple: "A Communist has infiltrated Wat Bowornives. This Communist is now denouncing Buddhism!" The abbot told the monks to remove the posters and not to let me know about it, but I learned about it later on. This abbot is now our Sangharaja, the supreme patriarch.

SCONTE

Some of my friends were then in control of the Siamese Architectural Association. They were concerned about the conservation of national treasures and the environment, trying to preserve trees and old buildings. Bangkok was on a fast track to development, and developers wanted to fill in the canals and cut down the trees. I wanted to resist what was happening in my city. I had already become interested in conservation partly because of my English education—the English are very good at preserving old buildings—and partly because of my Buddhist education—Buddhists are concerned about the environment. So I joined my friends, and we formed an association called the Society for the Conservation of National Treasures and the Environment (SCONTE). They asked me to become the editor of their magazine, which I called *Future*. We got money from the Ford Foundation.

As one of our projects, we asked Princess Ubolratana, the king's eldest daughter, to help us plant trees. (She was very young then. Unfortunately, we lost her—she eventually went to study in Boston and married an American. I think she was one of the best brains in the royal family.) We got all the big companies, including Shell, to agree to look after the trees. That was in the early sixties. No young progressives were interested in environmental conservation at that time; they only wanted to work for social justice, and they thought I was mad.

At one point, I spoke with the minister of national development. When I suggested he pass a law requiring one-third of all new development projects be devoted to public parks, he laughed. He said that this might be fine in England since all the people lived in flats, but we in Bangkok live in big houses with lawns and gardens. Why do we need public parks? When I asked about the poor, he said they could go to seaside resorts to enjoy open spaces! (Of course, nowadays, all the beautiful lawns and gardens have been developed by the rich into condominiums—a modern, concrete jungle.)

On November 17, 1971, since Field Marshal Thanom, the prime minister, could no longer handle Parliament, he staged a coup against himself. He dissolved Parliament and the constitution. My friends at SCONTE said, "This is our chance. There's no Parliament, only one group of people running the country. They want input from intellectuals. We can simply go tell them to implement new policies on environmental conservation, and they will listen." I said, "No. I don't want to work with people who destroyed Parliament and the constitution, and you cannot bring SCONTE along. The society is registered as a nonpolitical entity. What we should do as intellectuals is be watchdogs. We can sell them ideas; we can write articles in our journal; we can even write them letters. But in no way should we be near them. If we come near them, we will be corrupted by power or become their lackeys."

They agreed with me, but when I was away in Japan for three weeks, they changed their minds. Without recording anything, they all went to talk to the government in the name of the society. They were made very welcome by the dictator. Some of my friends said, "This is the first time in our life that we shall realize our dream. The members of Parliament didn't understand—they were stupid, country people." I made a big scene because they had betrayed me, but they wouldn't argue with me. Instead, when I wrote an editorial attacking the government, they said I was too political and asked me to leave. Of course, the real reason they asked me to leave was not because of my editorial. This was simply the last straw.

Being sacked for speaking my mind was not an unusual thing for me. The same had happened earlier at the Siam Society because of an editorial I had written, criticizing some members for speaking about Thai culture and values without really knowing anything about these things. I have a reputation for either resigning or being asked to leave. I have learned very well to understand the Buddhist teaching of impermanence.

CHAPTER **11** | *Getting Married*

I did not have any real girlfriends in my youth. I had been in love with my cousin, but eventually she married somebody else. When I was in England, I had occasional dates, but we exchanged nothing more than a few kisses and embraces. I liked a Canadian girl once. We met on a bus tour to Germany and Denmark. When she went back to Canada, we corresponded, and I was tempted to emigrate to Canada. The Canadian government wrote me a wonderful letter encouraging me to go because I already had a degree and they wouldn't have to invest anything. But I didn't want to marry a Western woman.

When I went home and started working, there was not much time for girls. I was not really pursuing a love life. Most of my time I spent working. I was living with my stepmother, sister, and brother. My mother was living on the other side of the river, so I went to see her every weekend and stayed with her one night a week. In my spare time, I taught English to the monks. There wasn't much time for wine, women, and song.

The Thai custom at the time I was growing up was that boys had to visit prostitutes, otherwise they were not considered men. Luckily, I went to England and escaped all that. When I came back home briefly in 1958, a friend of mine who ran a massage parlor invited me for a free bath. The massage parlor was supposedly a Turkish bath. In fact, it was just a normal bath, but a hot bath in a tub was still something new for us in the fifties. We usually took a cold bath, dipping water from a big urn. At the massage parlor, you get in the bath naked, and a girl comes to rub you down. If you want to have sexual dealings with her, you pay her extra or take her out. I never thought I was a smart-looking boy because I didn't know how to dress. When I had this so-called Turkish bath, the girl said, "The way you dress, you look awful. But without clothes, you are quite a good-looking chap." I thought it was a beautiful compliment.

Becoming engaged

When I came home for good in 1962, I didn't court anybody. I was constantly considering whether I should be ordained as a monk. Meanwhile, my younger brother had been courting a girl since he was very young. He was now a naval officer and wanted to get married. I had a little bit of money at the time, since I was working at the BBC and teaching, but not that much. My stepmother said I should sponsor the wedding. This is a great compliment. Usually the father would do it, or an uncle. My stepmother felt I was the closest, so I sponsored it. I bought the engagement ring and more or less arranged the wedding festivities. I gave them a small amount of money to build a modest house in his mother-in-law's compound.

At their wedding, I met my future wife Nilchawee. She and my new sister-in-law attended the same college, a kind of vocational college for girls, taking home economics. When I told my sister-in-law that I was interested in Nilchawee, she discouraged me. "She's not for you. She's a difficult woman. She's not interested in boys; and to anybody who comes after her, she just says no." I didn't know that my sister-in-law had somebody else in mind for me. I didn't know that my own sister had somebody in mind for me as well. They both very much disapproved of Nilchawee. Anyhow, I asked my sister-in-law to arrange a meeting. She invited her candidate, also. In the typical Thai manner, you don't meet a girl alone. I borrowed a jeep, and we drove just outside Bangkok on an evening outing. That was the first time I went out with Nilchawee and talked with her.

I thought we liked each other, so I asked for another meeting. We have a kite ceremony every summer, flying kites in a contest just outside the Grand Palace. We watch the kites, drink beer, and eat snacks. I said, "Next Sunday, why don't we go to the kite contest?" This time only two or three others came. After having a few drinks—Nilchawee and her girlfriends didn't drink beer, of course—the others all excused themselves, and I took Nilchawee to a Chinese restaurant. We started talking very quickly. We got on well, but I didn't think of marrying her yet.

She came from Uthaithani, a country town where people live in traditional floating houses. I said I would like to go and see her family. If the girl allows you to meet the family, you know she's serious about you. She said okay. I met her mother, her father—an ex-monk and Pali scholar—and her grandmother, who was blind and a great lady of that area. She supported the Buddhist temple next door. I fell in love with her family. They lived in the traditional style on the river. This had always been my dream. In my younger days we had floating houses in Bangkok, but when the country changed its name to Thailand, they were no longer allowed because they were supposedly decadent. Uthaithani, being off the main track, kept their floating houses. I thought, this is for me. Since my own mother and father didn't get on, I felt I had a broken family, but her family was very much a real community. When I had informally asked for her daughter's hand, my mother-in-law-to-be wanted to find out about me. She was a country lady—very honest, very direct. She said, "I just want to ask you directly: have you been married before? Do you have a wife or mistress somewhere? How much do you earn?" I told her everything.

My mother insisted on going to see Nilchawee's family. She approved of them, so we arranged for the engagement ceremony. I had already introduced Nilchawee to Princess Jongjit at a Sunday lunch, and the princess liked her. I told the princess, "I want you to select the ring." She liked that. "All right, I will perform the engagement ceremony to ask for the bride's hand," she said, "but Uthaithani is too far, and I am too old." Traditionally, you must go to the bride's home for the ceremony. But in those days there was no bridge across the river. You had to go by ferry and over very rough roads, and you had to spend the night. So she told me to have the ceremony in Bangkok, and I agreed.

I told Princess Jongjit that we could have the engagement ceremony any time. She said, "No, no, no. If something goes wrong, you'll blame me. I will consult my brother-in-law. He is a good astrologer." She found out a good day for the engagement. The bride's mother and father came to Bangkok, and we went to Nilchawee's cousin's house for the engagement ceremony. It was very simple. Afterwards, the princess took us—Nilchawee, her two brothers and sister, and my mother and me—to a Chinese restaurant.

I followed the English custom of having a stag party before the wedding. It was at my home, and all my male friends came. I sent cards to my friends in England who had not yet married because I was thinking of them, too. We had a good time together.

On the eve of my wedding, I met the king and queen. Though I had already met the royal couple abroad, I did not know them personally. I was helping with the Second Asian Writers' Conference in Bangkok, organized by my boss, Prince Prem, and, on the eve of my wedding, we all went to the Grand Palace to have an audience with the king and queen. The queen in particular showed me her royal favor. She talked to me at length, saying that she was very pleased with my writing. I was very flattered.

Our wedding

Traditionally in our country, we go to astrologers before our wedding. They give you two dates—one day for the wedding, the other day for moving to your new home. When they select the dates, they also look at your horoscopes. If you don't work well together, they don't even give you a date. Some of them are very firm. Since Princess Jongjit's brother-in-law was ill, I said we didn't need an astrologer. She again said, "No, no, no." To please her, I went to a friend of mine who is a fairly well-known astrologer. Weddings have to be in an even-numbered month. I was getting married in November, the twelfth month by the Siamese system. I got two dates, and the princess took me to see Prince Dhani. The wedding was to take place at his palace, and he would preside. I asked His Highness to choose the date that suited him. It was November 27, 1964.

We had a Buddhist wedding first, although there's no Buddhist wedding ceremony as such. Theravada Buddhist monks are not allowed to be involved with weddings, but they can be invited to give blessings to the couple. In the old days, when you had a wedding, you also had a new house built. The monks would bless the new house and the new couple. We invited to our house the monks from Wat Thongnopphakhun, headed by Abbot Dhammacetiya. They recited a prayer and gave us blessings; we gave them food; and they went home. They

My wedding (Phya Anuman is second from right)

finished by nine o'clock in the morning. We served breakfast to all the people who came.

Afterwards, both of us walked to the district office to sign our registration for the official wedding. Normally, you would invite the district officer to come to your house—you pay about five dollars as a kind of tip. But I wanted to do it simply by walking to the district office. In this case they charge you twenty satang, about one cent. I did not realize that if you go to the office, they think you are a nobody. They gave us a hard time. Nilchawee still had to go to the hairdresser, but they couldn't care less. I became very irritated and impatient. I banged on the desk. Then I dropped the name of somebody I knew high up in the Ministry of the Interior. The district officer himself came out and apologized. He signed and gave us the wedding certificate. I gave him one baht, which is five cents, and I insisted on my change. "I want my eighty satang back. It is my right." He was shocked.

We went to Prince Dhani's beautiful house. By that time, people liked having weddings at big hotels, but I didn't want to spend so much money. Everything was planned very carefully. We invited only the people that we respected. I didn't want to invite social big shots. I selected our relatives. In our custom they had to be older, and they had to be married. If they were not married, how would they know how to bless us? If you were divorced, you were not invited. Quite a few members of the royal family came. Dr. Puey Ungphakorn came, too.

It was a small ceremony, but very nice. We all dressed up in the traditional Siamese style. Most important is the person who puts the two circles of white thread, each attached to the other, on the heads of the bride and groom. You are bound together symbolically with these threads. You must choose a person you respect very much to do this, because they touch your head. Princess Jongjit refused to perform this. "I am a woman. I don't want to touch a man's head." I barely managed to get her to pour the water in the traditional ritual of blessing. If the guest is very senior, they pour the water on your head, anointing you. Otherwise, they pour it on your palms. Phya Anuman and his wife removed the thread and then asked us to stand up. Traditionally, whoever stands up first will become the dominant one, so many people rush to get up first. But Phya Anuman said, "Nowadays, we believe in equality. Get up at the same time." We rose and stood together.

After the wedding we had a very simple tea with the senior people we respected. In the evening we had a big reception for our friends. I insisted on traveling in an old Austin open car that belonged to Princess Jongjit's sister, Princess Marayart. She very kindly decorated the car with fresh flowers, just like in the movies. We went to the house of my friends Tula and Chanchaem Bunnag. I knew them both when they were in England. When I first saw their beautiful Siamese house, I thought, "This is the place for my wedding party." Chanchaem was delighted. It was a cocktail party. Chanchaem was working at SEATO, so she had diplomatic privileges and could buy liquor without tax. She made it her contribution to our wedding. My mother arranged to have a traditional Thai orchestra. I asked my stepmother to buy some food, and we asked a friend to do a saté, similar to a barbecue, on an open fire. We had duck, and Princess Jongjit contributed some homemade dishes. People seemed to enjoy themselves, but some of my Thai friends complained. They expected it to be a sumptuous meal. As I said, I didn't want to spend too much money. In fact, my wedding cost me about one hundred dollars.

But it was not over yet. The wedding is not complete until the bride is presented to the groom in his bedroom. That is the last ceremony. We had Phya Anuman and his wife perform it. They prepare your marriage bed for you—put on the sheets and the pillowcase. Both of them lie down on the bed, say a prayer, and pay their respects to the Buddha, the Dhamma, and the Sangha. They pronounce a blessing while you are sitting there in front of them. Phya Anuman and his wife said, "This is a wonderful bed, and anybody who sleeps on it will be happy and joyful." They put some flowers, some coins, a cucumber, and a mortar on the bed. In a marriage, you must be cool to each other like a cucumber and firm with each other like a mortar. The coins symbolize the money you need to raise your family.

Before you lie down on the bed yourselves, you have to pay respects to your parents. Next, the bride pays respects to the groom's parents, and the groom to the bride's. Then the bride pays respects to the groom, and the groom gives the wedding ring to the bride in return. Princess Jongjit had said that a plain gold ring was not enough, so she had had my signature inscribed on the inside. The princess said, "This ring is from me. It's your wedding present." In the old days, in a traditional middle-class family, the bride and the groom often did not meet each other until the engagement day or even the wedding day, and they never touched each other before the wedding.

After the wedding, you must pay respects to your elders and ask for their blessings. Usually, they will give you a sum of money. The idea of bringing presents to a wedding was something new, only for friends; your seniors do not bring presents. Of course, we had to go to Uthaithani to pay respects to Nilchawee's grandmother. This was the first time we went there without spending the night because we wanted to rush to our honeymoon. My wife's grandmother gave us ten thousand baht, about five hundred dollars. In those days, this was a good sum of money, enough to pay for our honeymoon.

After the bedroom presentation ceremony, traditionally the bride and groom stay at home together. But because I'd been abroad, I wanted to take my wife somewhere on a honeymoon. As it happened, my friend Anek Tiphayom was having his wedding about the same time as we were. So we said, "Why don't we take our honeymoon together?" This was very unusual, but we did it anyhow. We went to Songkhla, the southernmost seaside resort at that time, because they knew some-one who had a big, empty house not far from the sea. In those days I had to be very economical, and we could stay there free of charge. We took the second-class sleeper train. We met a friend of the other bride's mother, who was a local millionaire. Her husband had a pri-vate clinic and some patients in Malaysia, just next to Songkhla. He said, "Why don't you go to Penang for your honeymoon? You don't need passports—just get a border pass. Take my car. Nobody will stop you because they all know me at the border." So we went to Penang. At the border we had to bribe the officers a little bit. I was surprised because when I first went to Malaysia, it was all very honest. It was still a British colony at that time. Corruption had crept in within just a few years after independence.

Becoming a family

In the Siamese tradition, the groom lives with the bride and her fam-ily, but both of us were working in Bangkok. Nilchawee was teach-ing home economics at a finishing college, and I was working with the press, so it was difficult to go back to Uthaithani. My mother-in-law got enough money to build us a house—in those days you could still build a house cheaply. I said, "You don't need to. We could live in my house in Bangkok." She agreed. So we came back to live with my stepmother, my sister, and a servant to my uncle who even-tually became his mistress.

The neighborhood kept developing all the time. A small canal was filled, and the street became bigger, with more traffic. Eventually it became a through street, which brought more noise and traffic. Land became expensive, so people sold and moved out to live near the fields, without realizing that within five or ten years all the fields would become housing estates and development projects. When other people sold their land, the developers built it up into shops. We kept our house's architecture and all the trees—coconut, banana, and mango. We built a little bit within its original structure but didn't add to the height, so even today our house retains a certain charm.

We had our first child, our son Chim, in 1966, not quite two years after we were married. My stepmother was very fond of him. He became very much attached to her, and she became like his mother, since my wife was working. Four years after my son's birth, my daughter Khwankhao was born. Na Kam, one of my uncle's wives, became more or less her mother, and they became very close. We had our last child ten years afterwards, our daughter Mingmanas. This time my wife felt that it was her turn to be a mother and look after her own child. So Ming became very attached to her. Along with their grandmother and aunts, there was always somebody to look after the children. In our custom, the baby sleeps with grown-ups. Generally, my son would sleep with his grandmother, my daughter Khwan would sleep with Na Kam, and Ming used to sleep with my wife. Sometimes, we would all sleep together—papa, mama, and children—in a kind of big, family-size mosquito net. We continue to live as an extended family with my stepmother. She spoils me, and I like to be spoiled. An extended family is wonderful.

My children

Sometimes I was involved with so many activities that I hardly spent any time with the family. I would have to go abroad or upcountry. My son Chim would often go with me. He got to know all the lead-

Chim and Khwan with me at the bookstore

ing intellectuals of the time. On one hand, this was good, but on the other hand, his "peers" were ten to fifteen years older than he. He felt that his friends at school were inferior and that the teachers on the whole were second-rate.

Chim had begun his education at a Buddhist school named after the monk Venerable Ajahn Maha Boowa, the most famous meditation master in the northeast. It was very far from our house. One day, while riding to school, the car caught fire and Chim nearly died. I wasn't happy with this situation. Later, when giving a lecture at Assumption College, the director of the school asked if I wanted to send my son to the same school both my father and I had attended. He said I wouldn't even have to pay the usual "tea money" to enroll Chim, a sum at times as much as one hundred thousand baht! So I enrolled him at Assumption College. It caused a scandal because we didn't pay the tea money and we didn't have to wait in the long queue to get in. But Chim was not very happy there. He had no friends his own age and thought of his peers at school as too young to talk to. Also, the school was too conservative and reactionary for him.

In later years while I was abroad, Chim went to school in the U.S. and Canada. On one occasion, he had to fly home ahead of me because his airline ticket was about to expire. He was very brave and went alone. I was worried because he was so young. In fact, he had a small accident in Toronto, and they had to give him an injection. I fainted when I heard. We were very attached to each other.

After his experiences abroad, Chim could not readjust to school in Siam. My Quaker friends were instrumental in getting him into Westtown High School, a Quaker school on the south side of Philadelphia. He went on to Swarthmore College. This was unfortunate in a way, because he was uprooted very early from his culture. At least we had made sure he was ordained as a novice before he went abroad, like me. I was ordained for eighteen months, but he stayed for only five weeks. Times had changed.

When he came back home after college, I offered him the chance to work with our social activities, but he didn't want to do that. He wanted to join our publishing house, but it turned out he didn't like the way that I ran it. He wanted to run it his way. We had a disagreement and parted company, not in a very friendly way. I feel a little bit sorry because, although he was in the company of the Quakers, whom I know to be very radical, he prefers the establishment. He's thirty-one now. He sells big machinery—mega technology—which is not quite my line of operation. At the same time, I feel that I respect him. If he wants to go that way, then it's up to him. I understand that he wants to be independent. Sometimes it's difficult to have a famous father.

When my daughter Khwan was young, she also followed me around on my travels. At that time, twenty-five or so years ago, many schools were interested in democracy. They allowed the students to run their own students' congress or students' forum, imitating the Parliament. We were experimenting with the idea of parliamentary rule, so various schools invited me to talk. One was run by a Catholic convent called Mater Dei, mother of God. The nuns asked me why I didn't send my daughter to their school. Again, I told them I was not willing to pay tea money; it's against my principles. The nuns said, "Oh, no, no. For you we will not charge tea money. Please bring your daughter." She was admitted to what is supposed to be the most famous private school in Siam. She graduated and is very proud to have gone there. Later, she graduated from Thammasat University and then earned an M.A. in telecommunications from the University of Colorado. Like her brother, she joined the establishment, working for the multinational corporations. But I respect her, and she is on good terms with my wife and me. She is now twenty-seven.

Ming is ten years younger, a big gap. I thought that she should follow in her sister's footsteps by attending the Catholic school. I was in trouble with the government at that time, however, and the nuns were not happy to have her. I wrote to them very angrily, saying, "You are supposed to be a Christian school. When I was famous, you invited my older daughter to enroll. Now I am being oppressed as the victim of an unjust law, and you make a distinction. Christ stood for the oppressed. Why make an unjust case against my daughter." They replied that she was rejected simply because she was not good enough. Eventually, they invited her, but I said, "No, I don't accept your charity in this way."

My wife decided to enroll Ming at the demonstration school of Chulalongkorn University. I had nothing to do with it because I know

With my wife Nilchawee on my fiftieth birthday

many people at the university and didn't want others to think I had used my connections. I heard that there was a big debate at the university about whether or not to accept my daughter. They said, "If we don't accept her, he will write something nasty about us. If we do, he may write something nasty anyway." I guess they thought they'd be better off accepting her, and that once my daughter was in their hands, I would not be too hard on them. She is now in her last year there and hopes to attend Chulalongkorn next year. She plans to become a civil engineer.

None of my children has followed in my footsteps. They pretend not to admire me, and they make jokes about me, but I believe that deep down they appreciate what I am doing. My youngest wrote an essay about me for school, and she won first prize. Khwan pretends that she doesn't read my writings, but I think that she does. In fact, she asked to inherit some of my books. Whether or not they appreciate my work, at least I understand them and love them. I haven't devoted all my energy to making money for my children. For me, that's wrong. I feel my children are privileged already to have schooling and knowledge. Even if I should die tomorrow, I'm sure somebody will look after them.

Throughout our life together, my wife has been very devoted to me, and I feel indebted to her. Without her, I could not carry on my work. She really sustains me. She is an honest woman with a very good, solid character. She is not ambitious and is very devoted to her family, to me, to her mother, to all her relatives, and even to my relatives. We are entirely different. She is a quiet person but works very hard behind the scenes. Among other things, she has served as treasurer and cashier of our bookstore.

Most wives would not tolerate the way I live. People come to our house all the time—Thai, foreigners, grassroots, upper-class, lower-class. She makes them all feel welcome. At the same time, she has her own life, her own privacy. She can go upstairs to be away from it all. That is the understanding we have. Nilchawee is also devoted to the children. She's attached to them but doesn't spoil them. I'm very grateful for my wife and family.

My family (with my brother Sajja) in front of my mother's coffin

CHAPTER 12 | *Political Unrest*

The 1971 coup

Nineteen seventy-one was a very bad year for me. The coup d'état came at the end of the year. The prime minister, Field Marshal Thanom Kittikachorn, had succeeded Sarit Thanarat as dictator in 1963. He had experimented with democracy in 1967, but by 1971 he was fed up with the constitution and fed up with Parliament. He had to put up with their questions and bribe them to get his work done. He'd had enough. He dissolved Parliament and declared a state of emergency and martial law on November 17.

I had just returned from Italy, the U.S., and Mexico, but had planned a big conference before I left. The Komol Keemthong Foundation was bringing together young people from all over the country to meet in Chiang Mai. The coup occurred one week before our meeting. What could I do? I called one of our board members who worked in the Prime Minister's Office: "We have been planning this meeting for months. To cancel it will be very difficult. Can we go ahead?" He said, "Let me check with my boss." Eventually, we were allowed to go ahead—it was educational, nothing revolutionary. I had planned a meeting of the Cultural Relations for the Future study group to be held in Chiang Mai simultaneously. I wanted the Thai students and the older people from Southeast Asia to meet each other.

While these meetings were taking place, Chiang Mai University had invited me to speak. Unfortunately, I lost my temper—I never liked coups or dictators. I made a speech denouncing the coup leaders. I said, "These people treat the soldiers as if they were in the zoo, giving them fruit. (The Field Marshal himself had brought fruit and drinks to the troops.) What is this coup? You staged a coup against yourself!" The tape was sent straight to Thanom. He was furious.

The Special Branch of the Police was sent to our meetings. When one speaker referred to credit unions, they thought we were Communists. The next day, forty-five armed policemen showed up. Had any of our boys run, they would have been shot. I went to talk with them. "What's going on here? Why are we surrounded?" They said, "You need special permission to call a meeting of more than five people. You cannot talk politics."

"What do you mean by 'politics'? If we came to plan to overthrow the coup leaders, I would call that politics. Talk like this I wouldn't call politics. If so, all the words in my vocabulary would have to be considered political, except what people say in bed while making love." They didn't know what to say. "Anyhow, you need special permission," they repeated. "I have permission from the Prime Minister's Office," I said. "If you don't trust me, call them. Besides, do you think all the principals, rectors, and presidents of the government colleges would allow their students to be here had I not gotten permission?" Again, he didn't know what to say. Finally, a major or colonel came: "I'm very sorry. This young chap made a mistake. We came to ask the students to return to their hostel since there is a curfew at ten p.m." They didn't dare to call the Prime Minister's Office. They even offered to take all the boys to the prostitutes to make up for it! I couldn't believe how they made such a serious thing into a joke.

I continued to write articles and speak out against the coup. I was invited to speak at colleges, my articles appeared everywhere, and we had meetings at our bookshop every week. The Field Marshal didn't know what to do with me. One day, the chief of the Special Branch of the Police came to see me. I was sitting in the office of the foundation, on the floor, as is our custom. The chief sat down with me. He was very polite. He said, "Professor Sulak, you know we have a state of emergency. The last Parliament was full of bad MPs. That's why Field Marshal Thanom dissolved it. He wants to have a new Parliament with good, clean MPs. If one's house is in need of repair, we must all help to repair it. But if unruly children are running about and shouting, it's bad for the people to see. Mr. Sulak, if you keep quiet and collaborate with us, we can repair the house much more quickly. If you like, I can arrange for you to meet the leader of the coup. He would love to listen to you. If you're interested, we would like you to become a senator and help draft the new constitution."

I replied, "I don't like your analogy. We are not children. The house belongs to all of us. We are not misbehaving. We are shouting that you do not do the right thing. I don't want to see him—I don't want to be bribed or bought."

"I know you are a man of principle. I ask you not to write articles attacking the coup leaders."

"My articles are published by colleges, and those colleges belong to the government. If I write anything illegal, you can put me in jail."

"You are too clever. You are a lawyer. We can't put you in jail. Your writing hurts him—you are always punching hard. Can't you stop speaking out?"

"How can I? I don't like speaking, but nobody else will do it. Mr. Kukrit Pramoj has put a notice up in front of his office: 'State of Emergency. I don't accept any invitations to speak.' This leaves only me. Besides, it would be very easy for you to stop me from speaking. Send a circular to all the colleges saying, 'Mr. Sulak is a dreadful man. He should not be invited, and none of his articles should be published.'"

"We can't do that. We want to show that we respect freedom of speech. I must ask you, however, to discontinue your weekly meetings here at the bookshop. You know it is illegal. We can put you in jail anytime."

"You can put me in jail anytime, but my meeting is not illegal. 'Political' to me means that I am planning to overthrow you. But in our meetings we discuss situations like traffic jams and pollution. We discuss the wrong goals of development and propose alternatives. We discuss the conservation of trees and buildings. I don't think that's political."

"Well, in that case, may I have one of my boys come to listen to you?"

"Certainly, we advertise in the newspaper. You're most welcome to come." They were very fair. When they came, they announced that they were from the Special Branch of the Police. Our boys enjoyed attacking the police department.

Dr. Puey Ungphakorn's letter

Dr. Puey was in England when the coup occurred. He had left the governorship of the Bank of Thailand, but he was still dean of the Faculty of Economics at Thammasat University. Thanom and Puey knew each other well and trusted one another, but when Thanom staged the coup, Puey could not restrain himself. He wrote a famous letter called the "Letter from Mr. Kem Yen Ying." (When Puey was in the Free Thai movement during the Second World War, he used the nickname Kem Yen Ying.) He wrote as a humble man would write to the headman of the village, instead of the former governor of the central bank writing to the prime minister.

It was a very simple letter saying, "You, headman, are wonderful, good, and honest. You have rules and regulations for our village. After the long absence of a constitution, you even gave us a new constitution. It is not perfect, but it's better than having none. At least there's the rule of law. We have a parliament. It's not great, but it's better than having none. Unfortunately, only one year after the elections, you abolished it all, as if trampling on something with your foot that you wrote with your own hand. It's a shame. Please be sensible. Restore law and order, return the constitution as soon as you can, hold elections. Keeping power within your clique is very bad for the country. However good your intentions, abuse of power can take place anytime." The letter created a big response, and people circulated it. Though it was a humble, polite letter, Thanom was furious. His son, Colonel Narong, said Puey was Enemy Number One. "Puey can legally come back, but I will not be responsible if he is run over by a ten-wheel truck!"

The coup leaders used all kinds of psychological warfare. Colonel Narong said about me, "Mr. Sulak is very clever. What's white he says is black, and people believe him." My wife was afraid for my life. When the postman came to our house, her knees were trembling. She thought the police had come to arrest me. They told my cousin Sala, then first secretary at the Embassy in Tokyo, "You must talk to Sulak. He should kowtow to the powers that be or at least shut up for the time being." Even my father-in-law became very angry with me. He said, "You brought difficulty to my daughter. You have been very well educated, and you have refused everything that has been

offered to you. You have no security. In ten years you have not risen—
you still make only six thousand baht a month." But my wife,
Nilchawee, was very supportive.

The 1973 uprising

By 1973, the students were becoming a powerful force. They were
upset about a case in which three MPs were jailed as traitors merely
because they took a case to court charging that the prime minister's
actions were unconstitutional. Scandals emerged among the leaders
of the universities. The rector of Ramkamhaeng University was
Thanom's lackey; the students attacked him. The vice rector at
Chulalongkorn University was involved in corruption; the students
demonstrated against him. They also demonstrated against Japanese
goods. The *Social Science Review* became even more political, attacking the Americans. (I was no longer the editor of the *Social Science
Review*, although I served as a member of the editorial board.) The
dictatorship wanted to preserve its benevolent image, so they did not
act.

The students demanded democracy within six months. They consulted with me, and I said, "This is silly. They won't give it to you."
They said, "Never mind, we want to make a point." At first they
planned to teach democracy at the Reporters' Association, but the
association was afraid of the dictator. The students said, "Okay. We'll
use the bookshop." They created a big flyer: "Anybody that wants to
learn about democracy, come to the Suksit Siam Bookshop."

The vital incident of the '73 uprising is still a mystery. On October
6, eleven people started distributing a leaflet asking for democracy, a
constitution, and elections. Some were students, some professors.
They were arrested on charges of obstructing traffic. Within two
hours the charges had changed to treason for Communist activities.
The sentence for Communist activities can be life imprisonment.
That's why people protested. This was during the university examinations period. Protesters at Thammasat University refused to take
their exams. They all demonstrated. The whole university voted to
demand that their friends be released. One of them was the secretary
of the Komol Keemthong Foundation. Many were former members
of our club. All were close friends of mine.

The government refused. Field Marshal Praphas Charusathira, the second man, minister of the interior and former commander-in-chief of the army, consulted an astrologer, who advised the government not to yield to the students. If the government stood firm for two weeks, they would win triumphantly. The thing dragged on for a week.

The students started a big campaign, and many people joined. Much of the country was fed up with the government because it had been a dictatorship since '47. There had been no real elections since '57. The same group of people—three generals and two field marshals—had been running the country one after the other. The rich became richer, and the poor poorer. More and more people—half a million—joined the demonstration. The poor people fed the demonstrators and the students. Shopkeepers and fruit vendors gave them free food. The shop next door to my bookshop toasted bananas and gave them away. There was a wonderful spirit in the air.

One of the student leaders, a friend from our club, Mr. Seksan Prasertkul, made a speech: "We want to walk peacefully to the palace with a picture of the Buddha, the national flag, and photographs of the king and queen. We want to demand that our friends be released and that we return to democracy within six months." Supposedly, the government agreed to release the thirteen people in jail and grant a constitution within six months. Everything was settled.

But on October 14, something went wrong. The king's words are still with me: "This is the darkest day, the most sorry day in our history, because our own people were killed." Some demonstrators had been attacked in front of the palace. First they were shot with tear gas, then with real bullets. Some of them fled into the palace. Of course, the king, the queen, and the king's mother were very nice, looking after them. We don't know who started the incident—whether the demonstrators had incited anything or whether it was a ploy by the army. It was said that Colonel Narong had wanted to kill all of the demonstrators. Nobody has yet told the truth.

I was at a meeting in Singapore at the time. When I arrived home, things were very tense. I couldn't stay at my house—people told me that it wasn't safe. My friends took me to my mother's home. Nobody would know where I was, and there was no telephone. They said I must pack and leave the next day, but by then things had calmed down. The king announced that Professor Sanya Dharmasakti, then rector of Thammasat University and president of the Komol Keemthong Foundation, would become the new prime minister. The king had persuaded the three strong men—Field Marshal Thanom, his son Narong, and the deputy prime minister Field Marshal Praphas—to leave the country. The prime minister went to Boston, his son went to Germany, and the deputy prime minister went to Taiwan. It was announced that they had fled the country.

Aftermath of the 1973 uprising

People had died, and the dictator was gone, yet the army was still in power. In fact, the army was delighted. These three men had wanted to control the whole army. Narong was very arrogant and thought he had all the power. He was known to be corrupt and outspoken in a bad way. He treated the generals very badly. They all hated him and would not cooperate with him.

Of course, the students thought that they had won. I told them that they hadn't really won. "This is not your victory. Only three oppressive leaders are gone, and the army is still a state within the state. Nothing has changed. The structure is still oppressive to the people." I told them that we had been used as a kind of convenience. I said, "Be careful, they will come back against you." They didn't believe me.

Before '73 I had been a very popular speaker. I was the only one speaking out against the coup. But now I became very unpopular because they said I only wanted the Buddhist way, the Middle Way, the weak way. I had told them, "You must study our roots. The Buddha's teachings are very radical—the Buddha left the palace to become a beggar—but you have to change yourself first. Then you can change society." They said we had followed the Buddha for 2,500 years, but it hadn't changed anything for the better. We had also followed the Americans for thirty years, and things had gotten much worse. Now we must march the Marxist way. We must rebel against both Buddhism and the Americans. The students became drawn to communism. They studied all the Marxist terms and imported the red book of Mao Tse-tung. We got rid of the Americans, and we recognized China for the first time. We also recognized Vietnam.

The king held a "royal and people's assembly." He dissolved the old House of Assembly appointed by the former premier to make way for a new Parliament. He selected people from every profession—ten farmers from all over the country, ten labor leaders, civil servants, and people from the military, journalism, whatever. They met at the Royal Turf Club—a horse racing club next to his palace—so I called it the "Race Horse Parliament." I was excluded. So was our national hero, Seni Pramoj, Kukrit's elder brother. He was our minister in Washington, D.C., before the Second World War; he led the Free Thai movement in America all through the war; and he was prime minister a few times. Of course, the thirteen people who had been in jail weren't invited either, although some of them were invited later on.

There were over two thousand people at the first meeting. Two hundred sixty people were elected to the "constitutional assembly." Some of them would draft a constitution; the rest would act as a kind of interim Parliament, with Mr. Sanya as the prime minister, until we had elections and a new constitution. The country was supposed to be a wonderful country now.

Unfortunately, the king's good intentions were exploited. Kukrit Pramoj was elected number one. He got the most votes partly because the people who came all knew him. He had been outspoken until Thanom staged the coup against himself in 1971, but then he shut his mouth right away. Again, at the October 14 event, he had been with the people, but when he felt that the demonstration might be crushed, he said he was ill and went to the hospital. I had been active and outspoken throughout, but Kukrit was a man who was very slippery—what we call an "eel." Eventually he became very unpopular. Dr. Puey Ungphakorn was elected the second man.

There was much turmoil during this time. The Communist Party of Thailand had recruited quite a number of leading students. They felt that we had to revolutionize everything in reaction against overly traditional approaches. On the other hand, the civil servants who ran the provinces didn't want any interference by nongovernmental organizations (NGOs) or universities who would challenge their authority. The system was very corrupt, from the top down and the bottom up.

Poor Dr. Puey was caught between these two poles. He was a national hero. But the students felt he was too liberal and too Western. Although he managed to keep everything that he directed clean of corruption, his projects always helped the rich. He saw to it that the first Friendship Highway outside of Bangkok was not corrupt, but once the road was built, elite land owners on both sides of the road sold out for profits, and the farmers became landless laborers. Dr. Puey felt that was wrong, and that he had failed in working with the government. He turned to the NGOs, but then he was accused of being pro-Communist.

I got involved with Dr. Puey around this time. I introduced him to Mr. Alec Dickson, founder of the British VSO. He was impressed by Mr. Dickson and said he wanted to do something similar in our country. He said the Thai equivalent should be recognized by the government—otherwise they would regard it as a Communist orga- nization—but it should be run autonomously by the university. He started what he called the Graduate Volunteer Service. He asked me and a few others for help. This program sends middle-class univer- sity students to care for the poor and oppressed, helping to broaden their awareness. It is still going on.

Beginning a book distribution network

Around that time, Klett Verlag, the biggest German textbook pub- lishing house in Stuttgart, was interested in Siam. They wanted to do something for the Third World and had started a sister company in Indonesia. Now they wanted to start one in Siam. They became partners with someone who had no experience in printing or pub- lishing. They gave a lot of money to him and started a big printing plant, second only to my former employer, Thai Wattanapanich. Eventually, the Germans found out that their partner was a swindler, and somebody recommended me to replace him. I told them that they didn't need a printing house, because in Bangkok we had over two hundred printing houses, and they were all very cheap. "If you want me, start small—only me, my secretary, and an office."

They liked my proposal, and we started a small office called Klett

Thai—a kind of sister company to Klett Verlag. I was the managing director, and I asked one of my former colleagues to become secretary—Mr. Anant Viriyapinit, who is now very close to me. I wanted high-quality books. I repeated my experience from the Social Science Press, but made it even freer. I was the boss. I formed my own editorial board. This was just before the '73 student uprising.

It had been over ten years since I had started the *Social Science Review,* and I knew that publishing was not easy. I had enough connections, and the Germans would supply me with the money, but the difficulty lay in selling the books. It was easy to send books to the bookshops, but it was very difficult to collect the money. Hitherto there had been only five distributors, known as the "five tigers." These "five tigers" distributed only books that were within their control, only bestsellers, and they charged for it. It was difficult for a small publishing house like mine to make money when we only had one or two books to send to the bookshops. If they couldn't sell our books, they wouldn't pay us. But after the '73 uprising, there were many new publishing houses, particularly left-wing publishers. They could not find anybody to distribute their books, so they came to us. I thought we should put all our resources together, and then the books could go out regularly through a distributor, and we could collect the money. If bookstores refused to pay, we wouldn't supply them anymore. So I started a distribution network.

The Pha Mong Dam

Another project I got involved with was the Pha Mong Dam. During the Vietnam War, the Americans had spent a lot of money on bombing, and many people had died. Kenneth Boulding, a prominent Quaker, wrote to President Kennedy suggesting the Americans spend money on development instead of war, that they use their resources for peaceful purposes and build a dam on the Mekhong River. The Mekhong is an enormous river, and the dam would have to be bigger than the Aswan Dam in Egypt. Four countries benefit from the Mekhong—Siam, Laos, Vietnam, and Cambodia—all with Communist infiltration. The president acknowledged that Boulding's idea was wonderful, and set up a Mekhong Committee.

Another American Quaker, Stuart Meecham, with the AFSC office in Singapore, came to my office in Bangkok. He said to me, "You know, if this big dam is built, one province of your country will be entirely flooded. Hundreds of thousands of people will have to be evacuated, and they have never even been consulted. What can we do?" I said, "The least we can do is ask the people. We can have a small seminar in the Quaker manner." He liked the idea. The AFSC tried to encourage people to think differently—to work for peace and nonviolence rather than war. This was in '75.

We planned the seminar to take place in the area where the dam would be built. We'd meet on the Thai side, and then we'd cross over to the Laotian side. The Laotians would come to join us, and we would go to join them. It was all planned, but the American Embassy objected. They said, "No, you don't need to do that. The decision has already been made. Why do you want to interfere? We don't need your seminar. It will make no contribution." They thought it was a crazy idea. Stuart told me, "Without the Embassy's blessing, I would find it very difficult to work." I replied, "Well, then, you can work with me. We'll do it through the Komol Keemthong Foundation."

Dr. Puey, the president of Thammasat University, and Professor Saneh Chamarik, the vice president, were involved in this seminar. So were many academics, specialists, and ministry officials. Of course, we also invited farmers. It was the first time farmers met with top officials. The first day of the seminar we met a farmer named Thongpan. He had been affected by an earlier dam. He lost his farm and was now a landless laborer. He and his wife were employed to spread chemical pesticides containing DDT. We were shocked when his wife died the second day of the seminar. We all contributed to her funeral. A very talented man named Mike Morrow, a writer for the *Far Eastern Economic Review*, felt we must document this, so we made a film called *Thongpan*, describing this man's life and the seminar. The film has now become a classic.

At the end of the seminar, we had a group photograph taken. The police got hold of this photo, and it was published in a right-wing newspaper and in the *Bangkok Post* (a mouthpiece of the military at that time). The Thai paper *Dao Siam* said that this had been a meeting of the Communist Party of Thailand, whose chairman was Dr. Puey. They circled his face on the photo. They also circled my face,

The so-called Communist Party meeting (Dr. Puey is standing to the far right)

saying that I was a leading member of the Communist Party. Circling Stuart Meecham's face, the Quaker organizer, they said he was a Russian KGB agent. Stuart wrote a very strong protest to the Embassy and the paper, but he got no acknowledgment. This photograph became a classic.

The 1976 coup

By this time, the three exiled leaders from the '73 coup all wanted to come home. Thanom, who now lived in Singapore, said his father was very ill, and he had to see him on humanitarian grounds. The prime minister, Seni Pramoj, said, "We can't stop him from coming; any Thai who wants to come home has the right to do so. There is no case against him." Thanom's return made the unstable situation worse. He had been ordained as a novice monk in Singapore, returning home in yellow robes, and he wanted to have higher ordination as a fully ordained monk, a bhikkhu. People put up posters against him saying that this man was using religion and the sacred robes as a pretext. Two young workers in nearby Nakhorn Pathom who put up one of these posters were found hanged. People were very angry, and demonstrations took place.

The military had been lying low for three years. With the current state of unrest, they wanted to bring the country back to the "good old days" of military rule. They felt the students were too Marxist. Dr. Puey had already been accused of being a Communist. These things gave the military a good excuse to have a coup. It came on October 6. Thousands of students were jailed; hundreds were killed. Thousands more left for the jungle and joined the Communist Party of Thailand. The right wing wanted to lynch Dr. Puey. He had to leave the country and has lived in England ever since.

When the bloody coup took place, I was not at home. The police came to my house, to my bookshop, and to the office of the Komol Keemthong Foundation. The police who came to my house were very nice. They talked to my wife, and they only took four books away. In my bookshop the police were also very nice and only took a few books. But at the Komol Keemthong Foundation, across the street from my house, they were much more dramatic. They blocked off our small lane with two tanks. A television crew climbed up to film the office, and they said: "This is the national headquarters of the Communist Party of Thailand." It affected a lot of my people. The police asked who was in charge. Everyone was afraid, but my wife very bravely stepped forward and said she was in charge. They took her to the police station and interrogated her. Luckily, we knew somebody who knew somebody, so she was not put in jail. They took three or four truckloads of books published by the Komol Keemthong Foundation and Sathirakoses-Nagapradipa Foundation. They even confiscated poetry books. Anything that had a red cover was taken away to be burnt. I lost quite a bit. I wrote to the United Nations Educational, Scientific, and Cultural Organization (UNESCO), giving them all the details, telling them my rights had been abused. UNESCO sent my letter to the Thai government. They never replied.

But that was not the only place where my books were taken. At that time I was working at Klett Thai. Afraid of the Communists, when Laos fell, Klett Verlag, our German parent company, withdrew, and I bought the company from them. By '76, most of the books we distributed were leftist books. The police confiscated all of them. The company went bankrupt as a direct consequence. Luckily, I was not there myself. Otherwise, I think they would have tortured or killed me. The military thought I was a Communist, and most leftist students thought I was a CIA agent.

Stranded in England

When the bloody coup of 1976 took place, I was out of the country. I had been invited to Washington, D.C., on the occasion of the American bicentennial for a symposium called "The American Contribution to the World." I think I was the only one invited from Southeast Asia. The American ambassador in Bangkok objected very strongly. I was not educated in America, nor was I a man who flew American flags. My host was delighted. He said he had never before gotten an objection from an embassy concerning any participants, so he must have selected the right one.

Since they were paying my fare, I thought I might as well use the chance to visit several places. I left a few months early, at the end of July. I went to Mexico to meet Ivan Illich. I also visited the Aspen Institute because I was interested in the idea of an ashram. Once in Washington, I did some lobbying with the Senate and Congress. Because our democracy was very fragile and the right wing was trying to destroy it, I told the Americans that they must be patient with us and support our democratic elements.

After my speech at the Smithsonian Institute, I headed home via Europe. I always like to stop in England, my old home. My brother Sajja was working in England, and I decided to stay there a few nights before continuing to Paris to meet the Buddhist monk Thich Nhat Hanh. My last night in England was October 6. I invited my Thai and English friends to dinner at an English pub overlooking Hampstead Heath, a very beautiful area. On the way to dinner that night, I picked up the *London Evening News* and saw a photograph of Thai people being hanged. It was treacherous. Something bloody had taken place in my country. I was shocked.

Of course, there had already been turmoil in Siam while I was in

America. The newly ordained monk and former dictator Thanom Kittikachorn had returned to Siam to get his higher ordination. The prime minister had resigned, and things were very chaotic. I had gotten all the news and had some idea of what could happen, but I was pretty sure they would resolve everything. I knew we had to be patient to set the democratic institution in order. It had only been a three-year experiment so far.

When my brother arrived at our dinner, he came with a telegram from my wife asking me not to return home. She didn't even mention my name, just: "Please inform your brother." She sent it in my brother's name since he is my half brother and has a different surname. The next day I found out in the *Times* that I was arrested, obviously in absentia. There was a long report, and my name was included. At that time they published the photograph I mentioned earlier, claiming I was a leader in the Communist Party. I was the bad guy, along with Dr. Puey. He was Public Enemy Number One, and I was Number Two.

I learned that Dr. Puey had left the country for England, so I called his home. His sons said their father was safe in Germany waiting for his British visa. We met soon after that. I told Dr. Puey we had to do something, and we founded the Mitra Thai Trust, *mitra* meaning friend, "Friends of the Thai." He became president of the trust, while I was the active trustee. He was much better known than I and was invited to speak all over Europe, Japan, Australia, and America. He was invited by the U.S. Congress to give a briefing condemning the atrocities and the disregard for human rights. I was invited to speak here and there, but not nearly as much. Wherever we went to speak, we collected money to help people in our country, those who fled abroad, and those who went to the jungle. We knew they were fighting, but we would not help them with arms—just with medicine. We also started a magazine, since nothing could be published at home. There was very strict censorship. Our *Mitra Thai* magazine became well-known and was regarded as a real opposition to the government.

The household of my brother's girlfriend was very helpful. They allowed me to extend my stay at their home much longer. I didn't know them that well, but they were very kind. I also reconnected with all my friends from Lampeter. Since I hadn't expected to stay so long,

I had no money. Fortunately, my many friends offered me free lodging, food, and even telephone calls. Bob McCloy, from my Lampeter days, put me up at his family's home for many months. Quite a number of Thai friends stayed there, too, on their way to the U.S. or other parts of Europe. My Indian friend Victor Anant's wife, Zuelika, was working for the telephone exchange, so she connected me free of charge. My friend Ted Shotter was a leading member of the Reform Club and arranged to make me an honorary member, so I also had a place to go to read or entertain friends. The International Association of Cultural Freedom helped with a little money passed on to help people who were stranded in London or Paris.

In North America

My wife came to see me while I was in England. Things were very tense. She didn't dare buy a ticket directly to England but traveled through Rome. She stayed briefly and then returned home. Soon thereafter, Herb Phillips, a professor of anthropology at the University of California at Berkeley, called me to say he had managed to persuade the Ford Foundation, the Rockefeller Foundation, and a few other universities, to ask me to come teach in America for a year. Happy to have a job for one year, I moved from England to Berkeley. In April 1977, my wife brought the children to join me there. My son was eleven, and my daughter was seven. They went to school in Berkeley for one term, and my son stayed on with me in the United States.

At Berkeley I taught two courses—"Buddhism in Southeast Asia" and "History of Intellectual Development in Siam." There were quite a number of young people who were interested, but they were apprehensive about signing up for the course because they had heard that people with an English education such as myself tend to be harsh on marking examinations. When they came to me to ask about the class, I said, "You must make a distinction between being educated and getting high marks. If you are worried about your education, come take my class. If you are worried about your marks, tell me what you want, and I'll give you that mark in advance." They were quite good. They said they wanted only a "B" or "B+." I gave it to them, and they didn't have to worry.

The students enjoyed my classes. We went out to meditate in the redwood forest; we visited a Zen monastery; and they came to my house for my wife's cooking. For one dinner, they brought crabs and lobster. Herb was very jealous. He said, "I've been teaching here twenty years, and my students never brought anything for me." I replied, "You never invited them. Your wife never cooked for them. In our tradition, teaching is in the family. The teacher and student are like parents and children."

From Berkeley I moved to Cornell for one semester. At Cornell they were much more politically active because the university was linked directly with Siam and Southeast Asia. My house during that time became the headquarters of political maneuvering. We started to push the government. Quite a few of my former Cornell students have come to live in Siam. I remember one chap in particular. At first, he hated Siam—too much noise and pollution. Then he went to Singapore and wrote back, "It's wonderful. Very clean. The people are very well behaved." But he returned after one month saying it was dreadful and dictatorial. Next he went to Indonesia, but he came back saying it was very dangerous there. Next was Hong Kong: "At least everybody speaks English." Again, after two months, he hated it because the British oppressors were behind the scenes. He was a very clever boy, so he's still here in my country.

Bob Bobilin invited me to give three lectures at the University of Hawaii to celebrate their seventieth anniversary. I met David Chappell, who was about to become a professor at the University of Toronto. He asked me to come and teach there. By then, the tensions at home in Siam had eased, so I went home for Christmas and New Year's at the end of 1977. Since I had already accepted the invitation to Toronto, I returned there until the end of the semester in April 1978.

Before I left, I gave a keynote lecture to sum up my ideas. Out of this and all the other lectures I gave in North America during this time, I put together a book entitled *A Buddhist Vision for Renewing Society*. After I returned to Siam, I published *Siam in Crisis*. It contains all the articles from my time as editor of the *Social Science Review*. The English version of my 1976 lecture in Chiang Mai, *Religion and Development*, also came out. These were my first three titles in English.

Finally, I visited Michigan State University. By then I had become an "expert," and they wanted me to help reform their curriculum on Southeast Asia. I stayed there for three more weeks before returning home.

With (left to right) Herb Phillips, Ven. Dr. Chum, and David Chappell in Berkeley

CHAPTER **14** | *Back to Work*

After October 6, 1976, people stopped thinking politically. The military encouraged students to think only of their careers and not about political issues. The student clubs, the student parliament, the assembly hall, the free debates were gone. The military created right-wing organizations and the communist suppression unit. This unit trained all the lecturers, professors, and teachers to be anticommunist. Thanin Kraivichien, my contemporary in England, became prime minister in 1976. He was a real dictator—too strict and too narrow. Even the military found him uncompromising, so they staged a coup against him. General Kriengsak Chomanand, the coup leader, became prime minister, and the political and social climate in Siam improved somewhat. That's how I could go home.

Kriengsak was a nice man. He liked to drink brandy and to cook curry, so he was known as Mr. Brandy and Curry. He was much more relaxed and wanted to pave the way for democracy. He granted a general amnesty to all the student leaders in jail. Hundreds of people had been put in jail, and the key ones had been there for two years until Kriengsak released them. Rumor had it that if he did not grant them an amnesty, student leaders would reveal all the facts behind the intrigues of October 6. Even after being released, one chap wrote a book on that event; it was banned. Unfortunately, Kriengsak was also corrupt.

A curtailed teaching role

When I returned, many of my former students were still in the jungle. I had to be very careful. They came to contact me and even invited me to join them in the jungle. I said very clearly, "No. I don't believe in communism; I don't believe in violence. I do believe in humanitarian aid, and since I know most of you, I will send medicine and books." But I would have nothing else to do with them. Even so, due to the post-October 6 climate, I was rarely invited to teach at any schools or colleges. Many people felt that wherever I spoke, I aroused a division of opinion. When democratic ideals had prevailed, the schools, temples, and other institutions invited me. But now, with the democratic element in the country squelched, most educational institutions were afraid to invite me to speak.

One military colonel and medical man whom I'd known for some years did invite me to teach Western philosophy at the army medical school. In Siam, the military is a state within a state. They have their own bank, their own hospital, their own school, their own colleges, and now they were going to start their own medical school. I agreed to teach, but I warned my friend, "You know, I still have the stigma. I'm supposed to be a Communist. Don't you think it will affect your career?" He said, "No. I think you are a good teacher and a good Buddhist."

Sure enough, they said, "This colonel invited a Communist to teach." Everything that I taught at the school was reported. My first remark was very simple. I said, "Western philosophy has a strength that is also a weakness—it relies entirely on the rational approach. For example, for us Buddhists, the Buddha was enlightened under the bodhi tree. Depending on your faith, you believe the Buddha, or not. But for the Western philosopher, everything has got to be proved by Aristotelian logic. Or course, spiritual enlightenment cannot be proved." They recorded this and sent it to the commander-in-chief, claiming that I was a Communist: "He said, 'The Buddha was a liar, sitting under a bodhi tree boasting.' He's antireligion, he's a godless person." My friend was removed from his position, and he was not promoted for almost ten years.

Another time, I was invited by the director general of the teacher training department in the Ministry of Education. I had been invited to speak at the Food and Agriculture Organization of the United Nations, and all the leading professors came from colleges of education and teachers' colleges. They said "Oh, you gave a wonderful talk on ethical responsibility. How do you teach ethics to young people?"

I argued that you can only teach ethics to young people if you allow them to argue with you, allow them to be themselves. You can't brainwash them.

Teachers from three of these colleges asked me to lecture at their schools. One college was in Lampang, in the north; one was in Nakhorn Sawan, in the central plains; and one was in Korat, in the northeast. I said, "You be careful, my name is not good. I'm on the blacklist." They said, "No, no, no. The director general invited you; we all feel okay." Of course, these teachers had to get clearance from their principals. All three of them declined. They gave various reasons: one said they were not ready; one said they had a sports event; and the other said they had to postpone it.

Restarting our book distribution network

While I was in America during my exile, all my work at home was severed. Two years away, and I had to start everything anew. My former colleagues, now unemployed, came to me and said they wanted to start our book distribution network again. Our bookstore, which was still in existence, also needed a network, so we decided to start a company. I revived the old name Kled Thai, spelling it "Kled," not "Klett," to avoid duplicating the name of the German firm. My wife said she didn't mind, so we mortgaged our house to start this new company. We rented the old Komol Keemthong Foundation office just opposite our house, because the foundation had moved out to set up a new office on the other side of the Chao Phya River. We had had good publishing connections before '76, so a lot of people came to us when we started.

It was difficult to begin with. We had to distribute books up and down the country using motorcycles as well as trucks and cars. Eventually, we also started a monthly book magazine called *Literary Road*. What started as a distribution network soon expanded into publishing, because that was my interest. Eventually, we moved to a new place when the lease ran out in the mid-eighties, a very large, three-story building in old Bangkok, near Wat Bowornives. The place had belonged to the *Matichon* daily, at that time the most influential newspaper. Mr. Khanchai Bunpan, the publisher, and I had been good friends since his student days at Silpakorn University, and he was

The bookshop

helpful in starting us there. In 1987, we moved our bookshop Suksit Siam to join us at this new location. So we had the Kled Thai distribution network, Suksit Siam bookshop, and some other publications all together in the same place—at 117 Fuang Nakhorn Road, opposite Wat Rajabopit.

Organizing the Thai Interreligious Commission for Development (TICD)

I had resumed working with quite a number of activities that I had been involved with before I left. However, a lot of my friends felt that I needed something substantial to do as a full-time job. My teaching career had almost ended. I had a one-year grant from the Social Science Research Council in New York to research Prince Damrong's contribution to our indigenous Thai culture, but this work required only a minimal time commitment. The other organizations I was involved with were managing all right by themselves—the Siam Society, the Komol Keemthong Foundation, the Sathirakoses-Nagapradipa Foundation.

I felt that I had to work on creating models for development as alternatives to the government model. Instead of making the rich richer, we should be empowering the grassroots, using a nonviolent approach. I thought that the government and NGOs had failed because they did not work closely enough with the Buddhist monks. I wanted the monks to be aware of their power, to work with the grassroots, and not to obey the central Buddhist hierarchy, because it had become hopelessly corrupt. We needed a new organization, with a new name, that would not cause any confrontation with the government. It would be concerned entirely with development. We should work together with the Christians and Muslims. I talked to my Christian friends, and they agreed. "If you start something, we will find you the money." So I founded the TICD in 1979. We started a magazine in Thai, and I had several young people working on it. They eventually began a magazine in English, *Seeds of Peace*, a phrase given to me by Thich Nhat Hanh.

Many of my students went on to become leaders. In 1979, Bibhob Dhongchai and his wife Rajani started an alternative school called the Village School, in Kanchanaburi, near the Bridge on the River Kwai, of Second World War fame. Bibhob was a product of our student group. He was interested in education, and when he had been a student at the teachers' college, he imitated me and started his own magazine for the college. Bibhob had also been my secretary when I was at the Thai Wattanapanich publishing house. My role in their school was as a mentor. The school was free of authoritarian regulations. It was a real demonstration school. When I took my former French teacher from Assumption College to visit years later, he remarked, "Though your name did not appear anywhere in the place, your spirit was everywhere."

Another former student of mine at Thammasat University, Sanpasit Kumprapan, worked on children's rights. He is now recognized worldwide for his determination to fight against child prostitution and child labor.

Asian Cultural Forum on Development

In the mid-seventies, I had been instrumental in creating an organization called the Asian Cultural Forum on Development (ACFOD). The idea was not my own. It came from a Singhalese named Chandra de Fonseka. He wanted to work on alternative development, and I happened to be thinking the same thing. It was fashionable to have walkathons to raise money and consciousness, and I was popular with the young students, so Chandra came to me. I helped him organize a walk. Eventually, we organized a conference in Sri Lanka, Chandra's home country. We met outside Kandy at a Catholic place, with leading religious people from all over Asia. With this kind of development, you must also get involved with culture, and culture means religion. It was agreed that we ought to have an organization to get Buddhists, Christians, Muslims, and Hindus involved.

The World Council of Churches and the Vatican had a joint council called Sodapax to do development—not missionary work but real development—and they were willing to work with those of other faiths. Chandra got money from this council to start an organization in Bangkok, and he wanted me to run it. I worked free of charge for one year as a coordinator. This was in 1975. Then I was away for two years in exile. There was a lot of tension during this time. When I came home in 1978, they asked me to attend their council. I agreed, since I had no job. In 1981 I again became coordinator. There was just enough money to pay my salary and for one or two staff. I built up the funding and changed things to make it really work. We developed programs for the poor—small fishermen, landless laborers, working women. I managed to gain United Nations (UN) recognition for ACFOD—we joined the Roster of the UN Economic and Social Council (ECOSOC); gained Consultative Status with the UN Children's Fund (UNICEF); and gained Liaison Status with the UN Food and Agriculture Organization (FAO).

Unfortunately, ACFOD was beset by problems, and I made some major mistakes. I didn't get along with my associate coordinator, Bamrung Bunpanya. I found a Bangladeshi named Sabur to succeed him. Sabur was a wonderful number two and eventually succeeded me after seven years. Some corruption set in after I left. I had brought in a lot of money for ACFOD, and people became too interested in the money. There were so many programs. ACFOD not only became too big, it became fragmented. The fishermen dealt only with fishing issues, the women only with women's issues. The Japanese were all Marxists and didn't have time for any cultural or religious issues. When I left, I felt my role at ACFOD had been a failure. Even so, I remain grateful to the friends I made from many quarters—people like Bishop Labayan of the Philippines, Fr. John Curnow of New Zealand, Abdulrahman Wahid of Indonesia, Swami Agnives, Vikas Bai and Surendra Chakrapani of India. They always encouraged me spiritually.

CHAPTER 15

Interfaith Connections

had been educated in a Catholic secondary school, and although I was never tempted to convert to Christianity, I was very much influenced by the good teachers at the school. At Lampeter, I was interested in the Christian way of thinking. I read St. Thomas Aquinas, St. Augustine, and all the church fathers in philosophy courses. I was also fascinated by the intellectual endeavors of Anglican theologians like Richard Hooker and John Henry Newman.

Later, I became interested in the ideas of some leading Catholics such as Paulo Freire of Brazil. I was deeply affected by his idea of consciousness raising through a literacy campaign empowering the poor. Ivan Illich was another. Eventually, I got to know him personally. He came to see me at my bookshop in Bangkok, and I visited him twice in Mexico. I was instrumental in getting his book translated into Thai, and he became popular in my country. I like Thomas Merton's books and ideas on contemplation and action—that religious people should take a social stand on issues of war and peace and on social justice. I came to admire Dorothy Day and felt that she was working not only for social welfare, but for social revolution. I also admired the Berrigan brothers, two leading American Jesuits. I came to feel close to Hans Kung because of our similar predicaments— accusations against me of lèse-majesté and against him of *lèse popery*. My Singhalese friend Tissa Bulsuriya was also outspoken against the Vatican.

These are the people I feel close to. Though we come from different religious traditions, we take a similar stand on social issues and our work for peace. We are committed to our own tradition, but we are on the fringe and want to radicalize the tradition.

Projects with Catholics

After Pope John XXIII's Second Vatican Council, the Catholic Church in Asia became more open, particularly the Jesuits, with their head-quarters in the Philippines. The church wanted to change people through education, so they held a big workshop called the Educators' Social Action Workshop (ESAW) in Kyoto, Japan, in 1971. About fifteen educators were invited from each country in Asia and the Pacific, both Catholics and non-Catholics. These included officials in the Ministry of Education and people from Catholic and government schools. They happened to select me. I was not really in the schools, but I suppose they thought of me as somebody useful.

I went to Kyoto for three weeks. In the workshops, it was the first time I came across so-called group dynamics and group process to change people's outlooks. It was fascinating. I learned a lot about Asia and the Catholic way of thinking. One of the organizers, Father Bulatao, a Filipino Jesuit, said, "We apologize to all you non-Catholics. We have been haughty, on our high horse all these years, and we must now ask for forgiveness from our brothers and sisters." That had a profound effect on me. It helped me to see the Catholics in a much better light. When I had been a student, Catholics were not allowed to attend Buddhist ceremonies. All their rites were in Latin, and the priests and nuns always wore their habits. Now, Mass was being said in the vernacular, and many priests and nuns dressed like everyone else. I felt that the Catholics had become more broad-minded and were willing to listen to people of other religions.

At this meeting I got to know the Thai Catholics and educators. When we came back, we wanted to change things at home, so I formed a sort of Thai ESAW group. I got to know the Thai priest Father Boonluan Mansap, who was very active with credit unions in Catholic circles. I had never heard about credit unions—a kind of savings scheme empowering the poor to run their own affairs. I helped him try to move the credit union movement beyond the Catholic pale to include the Buddhists.

Through my development work in Siam, I was involved with quite a number of Catholic development organizations. The Asian Partnership for Human Development is a consortium of Catholic organizations, mostly in Europe, Asia, and the Pacific. They asked me to give one or two keynote addresses from a Buddhist perspective to challenge them on their development. Through the Catholic Comité Contre la Famine et pour le Développement (CCFD), from France, I came to know quite a few French Catholics and became fairly well known in France. I became a partner of Misserior, a Catholic development organization in Germany.

More connections

My dealings with Catholics and Anglicans are understandable given my early schooling and years in Britain, but I hadn't had much connection with Protestantism. In my country, there are only about thirty thousand Protestants out of 56 million people, and they have been there for only 150 years. Through the *Social Science Review*, I met Dr. Kosol Srisang, who eventually became secretary-general of the Church of Christ in Thailand. My relationship with the World Council of Churches (WCC) began through Kosol's predecessor, Ray Downs, and he introduced me to many leading Christians. I was invited to their interfaith meeting in Sri Lanka in 1974—in those days it was still called Ceylon. The meeting didn't inspire me, but I met a lot of religious leaders—Protestants, Hindus, Jews, and Muslims.

Strangely enough, it had been at this meeting that I first met the Vietnamese Buddhist leader Thich Nhat Hanh. He has since become a good friend. His work and thought have influenced me a great deal and expanded my outlook on engaged Buddhism. My concern about the suffering in Vietnam became more real and intense when I met him. Vietnam was then in turmoil, and Thich Nhat Hanh wanted the Singhalese bhikkhus to issue a statement supporting peace in his country. He was from the Mahayana tradition, and he hoped to get all the Buddhist traditions to join together. But they refused. They were awful, very insular. Thich Nhat Hanh was very disappointed, since he was desperately in need of international support. I have had all his works translated into Thai. Some appeared in Thai first, notably *The Miracle of Mindfulness*. The first English edition was also published in Bangkok.

When my own society was facing a lot of violence between the right wing and left wing in 1976, I proposed to the general secretary of the Church of Christ in Thailand that we of different religions come together to appeal for nonviolence. Women's foundations got together and put up posters everywhere: "In the name of mothers, wives, and daughters, we ask you not to use violence." It was very effective. I called a meeting in Bangkok at the women's department of the Church of Christ in Thailand. The Buddhist abbots, Catholics, Muslims, and Protestants all got together. I said that students and women were leading, and we religious people were far behind. We should come together and issue a statement. This was my commitment. Eventually, it became the Coordinating Group for Religion and Society (CGRS). This became the only viable group actively doing reconciliation work. After the '76 coup, they were the only ones brave enough to visit the students in jail. Even the students' own parents were afraid to visit them, because all the students were supposed to be traitors. They also gave flowers to the soldiers who killed the students.

Buddhist–Christian dialogue

After the World Assembly of the WCC that I attended in Vancouver, we felt we needed more Buddhist-Christian dialogue. I was often involved with this at Bad Boll Academy in Germany. I was invited by an organization called Diakonia, "dealing with neighbors," to attend meetings in Crete and Cyprus. I traveled to Spain to prepare catechism for youth in the postmodern age. The first American-organized Buddhist-Christian dialogue that I attended was at the University of Hawaii in 1980. These meetings brought me many friends, friends who call themselves both Buddhist and Christian. They were genuine and very concerned about social justice. We treated each other as equals and had a lively intellectual exchange, challenging one another like friends. In our Buddhist-Christian dialogue, the idea that one religion is better than the other simply doesn't exist, at least among these groups.

One of the most significant events for me took place in 1989. I was at a meeting of the Buddhist-Christian Theological Encounter at Hsi Lai Temple near Los Angeles. This group is known as the "Cobb-Abe" because it was started by John Cobb, a leading Christian theologian from Claremont College, and Masao Abe, a leading Zen scholar and chief disciple of D.T. Suzuki. It is a group of only about twenty-five "hard-core" people. One has to be invited. I must have been the first to join from the Theravada tradition in Southeast Asia. On Palm Sunday, during our meeting, Hans Kung celebrated Mass for us. He made it so informal and welcoming. He invited all of us to take the bread and wine with him if we wanted to be Christ's friends and remember Christ. This was the first time that I ever took Holy Communion. When I was at the Catholic school and Anglican college, if you were not baptized and confirmed, you could not take the bread and wine. There was a sense of separation. But when Hans Kung invited us to take the bread and wine, we were so pleased. For me, it was wonderful.

Among the Christians closest to the Buddhists are the Quakers. We both regard friendship as very important. They call themselves the Religious Society of Friends. Similarly, the Buddha said the most important element outside each of us is a good friend, *kalayanamitra,* a voice of conscience to develop critical awareness. We Buddhists can learn from the Quakers' social awareness, commitment to change, and nonviolence. My encounter with them has helped me to reexamine my own Buddhist upbringing. They don't make their beliefs compulsory, not even for their own children. A person must himself be convinced. For me, this is great. The simplicity of their worship— no ceremony, very Zen—also appeals to me.

Two people who stand out are George and Lillian Willoughby. George is a real pacifist. During the Vietnam War, anyone who wanted to resist the draft would go to George, and he helped them with all the technical details. He challenges his country by refusing to pay taxes. He was once arrested for taking a boat out into the Pacific where they were going to test a bomb. He walked all the way from New Delhi to the Chinese border on a peace march. (He wanted to march to Beijing, but the Chinese would not allow him.) George and Lillian were helpful in creating ACFOD. We have become good friends. They are instrumental even today in helping our young people with training in nonviolence. Their lifestyle is so simple. They don't live for money or fame, but for peace, for principles. They have a rebellious spirit similar to mine.

World Conference on Religion and Peace

In 1989, I attended the World Conference on Religion and Peace (WCRP) at Monash University outside Melbourne, Australia. John Taylor, then secretary of the WCRP, invited me as one of the keynote speakers. A lot of people suggested His Holiness the Dalai Lama also be invited, but the Chinese said no. Of course, if the Chinese say no, the Japanese usually say no, and the WCRP funding came mostly from the Japanese religious organization, Rissho Koseikai.

The local Australian chapter pressed the issue, so as a compromise, His Holiness was invited to send an observer. He sent a senior monk, Amchak Rinpoche—a very learned and humble man. Amchak Rinpoche brought a brief written message of goodwill from His Holiness, but the Chinese objected to his reading the message because he had been invited simply as an observer. The Buddhists and local people were unhappy because they wanted to hear His Holiness' message. Some of them asked my advice. I said, "Give the message to me. I will read it before my own speech."

Mr. Chao Pu Chao, president of the Buddhist Association of China, was furious when I read the statement. He walked out. When he walked out, Mr. Niwano, president of Rissho Koseikai, walked out, too. John Taylor, the secretary of the conference, reprimanded me. He said, "Sulak, you must know that at this kind of international gathering, we must behave and not divert from the text." I said, "I have been to many international gatherings, and nobody has ever censored me. I speak my mind, and I'm willing to go to jail for what I say. If you don't like it, then don't invite me again." Later on, John Taylor apologized to me. He said he had no choice but to reprimand me because he was pressured by the Japanese and their money.

Afterwards, I tried to talk to Mr. Chao. During an earlier visit of his to Bangkok, I had arranged a private meeting for him with the president of the World Fellowship of Buddhists, even though they recognized Taiwan instead of China. I said to him, "I helped you when you came to Bangkok even though no one recognized China. That's what Buddhists should do for each other. His Holiness may be condemned by your government, but as a Buddhist you should not tow your government's line." He didn't reply and walked away. I felt very sad. We Buddhists compromise too much; we often put our national interests above Buddhist principles.

CHAPTER **16** | *Lèse-majesté*

In 1984 I found myself under arrest and behind bars for an alleged case of lèse-majesté—criticizing the king. My troubles with the king began in 1982. It was the bicentennial of Bangkok and the Chakri Dynasty. I spoke at Thammasat University and said that all the celebrations were a waste of money and too hastily arranged. In fact, the government had asked Mr. Fua Haripitak, the famous artist, to help reconstruct a mural at the Grand Palace for the occasion, but he walked out in disgust because they weren't serious about the time and care needed to do the job. I criticized the celebrations and ceremonies as having too much political significance. I said that even graduation ceremonies were political. Everyone has their photo taken with the king as he hands them their diplomas, and that photo hangs in every household. It is very good advertising for the king. He knows that I'm very much a loyalist and monarchist, but he remarked, "Sulak is not fair to me." The king felt he was being magnanimous, not political, and that I had misinterpreted his actions. Maybe I did, but for me as a social scientist, his actions had obvious political impact whether he intended it or not.

Reconciling with Pridi

The next break with the king came when I tried to reconcile him with Mr. Pridi Banomyong. Pridi had been prime minister when the late King Ananda, the present king's brother, was found dead in the royal bedchamber in 1946. It was suspected that the king had committed suicide; but in order to save the throne and the monarchy, Pridi agreed with the royal family to issue a common statement that it had been an accidental death. The Opposition Party was against Pridi because he was a socialist. They thought he wanted to make our country a republic, so they accused him of plotting to kill the late king. During the 1947 coup, he was sent out of the country. He tried to stage a counter-coup in 1949 but was defeated, and he lived in exile in China and France for many years. A myth was created that Pridi must have been a Communist. Since I had been brought up to be conservative and was very connected with the royal family, I believed in that myth. I wrote many articles attacking him, and he also attacked me—not by name, but by implication.

Later on, it was proved that Kukrit Pramoj had started the allegation of regicide against Pridi. Kukrit had even hired a man to shout in a cinema that Pridi had plotted to have the king killed. I came to realize that Mr. Pridi, after all, was innocent. I felt badly that he was treated like a criminal and had to live his life in exile. As I became more sympathetic toward him, a lot of friends tried to link us. Dr. Puey, one of his supporters, said, "Sulak, I respect you, and I respect Mr. Pridi, but I know you are both stubborn men. I could bring the two of you together." Another supporter, Mr. Supar Sirimanon, a kind Marxist and an excellent journalist, wrote to Mr. Pridi saying that his attacks on me were wrong since he was much more senior and mature. My attacks were not right either, but I was younger and inexperienced. Even his children told their father that he should meet me as a fellow traveler, not as his enemy.

So the old man calmed down. On his eightieth birthday in 1981, he sent me a book summarizing the regicide case and criticizing the way it was handled. It had not been addressed by the rule of law, despite the fact that it went to three courts. He claimed that the whole judgment was void. My eyes were opened, and I felt terrible that I had been harsh towards Mr. Pridi. I wrote him a letter asking for his forgiveness. He wrote back, asking for my forgiveness. It was very Buddhist, although we didn't say so. The next year I was going to Paris, so he invited me to come see him. I looked forward to undoing what I had done.

I decided to set up a new project on Pridi Banomyong and Thai society. I wanted to publish his complete works. I also wanted young people to research his ideas for social reform and start discussions on whether they were feasible for Thai society. Pridi was a great leader. He brought democracy to Siam in 1932. He founded Thammasat University—then called the University of Moral and Political

Sciences—in 1934. During the Second World War, he organized the Free Thai Movement and became a hero. He had not wanted us to join the war and believed we should solve things nonviolently, through diplomacy.

Mr. Pridi was very pleased that I was doing this, but at the same time he cautioned me to be careful because his name was still very much disliked by the ruling powers, the military, and even the royal family. Unfortunately, he died soon after our meeting. I wrote a long letter to the supreme patriarch, the Sangharaja, asking him to recommend to the king that, in the Buddhist spirit of reconciliation, he send three monk's robes and invite monks to go and meditate on Mr. Pridi's ashes in Paris. This is our custom. His ashes should then be brought back to Bangkok under a royal sponsor. Then, the king should hold a state ceremony for one week at one of the royal temples. This would reconcile members of the royal family and monarchists with the promoters of the coup of 1932. The continuing split was not good. The king may not have liked Mr. Pridi personally, but he must acknowledge that he is a national hero.

I never heard a response. Perhaps the king was angry with me, or perhaps he didn't get my letter. Anyhow, we missed the opportunity for royal reconciliation. I think we should all confess and reconcile. We can't be right all the time. I became more and more vocal as I sided with the losing cause on Mr. Pridi's behalf. He was a patriot and a royalist. Like him, I feel that the monarchy must be constitutional. The monarch must be, in Buddhist terms, a *dhammaraja*, or righteous ruler, not a *devaraja*, or god-king. But even though our monarchy is not absolute, the military and people treat it as if it were— kowtowing, crawling on the ground, even worshipping the king. This is wrong. I argued that the king should separate himself and the royal family from the military and from any economic base such as the crown properties. To preserve the monarchy, the king must be entirely separate and beyond reproach. I considered it my role to offer this constructive criticism. Unfortunately, I was too vocal about it, and said it perhaps too often.

The charge of lèse-majesté

The final straw resulting in my jailing came in 1984. I had been interviewed about Thai education for a book to be published to celebrate the sixtieth anniversary of a teachers' college in Udornthani. I criticized our education, saying, "What went wrong is that many of us were educated abroad from the time we were young, and when we returned home we thought we knew everything. We looked down on our indigenous culture and tried to imitate the West." I said that King Rama VI, the uncle of the present king, had gone to England when very young and become a dandy. Instead of building a temple to commemorate his reign, as was the tradition, he built a public school in the English manner. On top of that, he spent much of the government's money on his courtiers.

The former minister of education, who had been one of King Rama VI's courtiers, read my interview before it was published and became very angry. He wanted the ministry to sue me for lèse-majesté. Of course, you can't sue someone for defaming a dead king—if you do that, you cannot teach history—but I had also mentioned the present king in my criticism of royalty who were educated in the West. The matter was resolved through the usual Thai compromise—the college pulled out my interview and interviewed somebody else instead. The case was not pursued. Since the government couldn't publish my article—that would have meant they agreed with or at least thought my views were legitimate—I had it printed by the Komol Keemthong Foundation instead in a book called *Unmasking Thai Society*. The book also included an interview concerning the end of the absolute monarchy and democracy. I spoke very candidly, and the interview contained some remarks that were not very polite.

Artit Kamlang-ek, Supreme Commander of the armed forces and commander-in-chief of the army, decided to use my articles to foment political unrest and stage a coup against Prime Minister Prem Tinsulanonda. The prime minister was very weak physically, psychologically, and politically, and Artit wanted to take over. He thought I was very popular and wanted to charge me with lèse-majesté, so he asked Prem to issue a warrant for my arrest. My book had not even been published yet—it was still at the printing press. Artit must have sent his men to the printing press and taken some copies. Prem, being a very cautious man, consulted with the Department of the Public Prosecutor, the Special Branch of the Police, and the Central Investi-

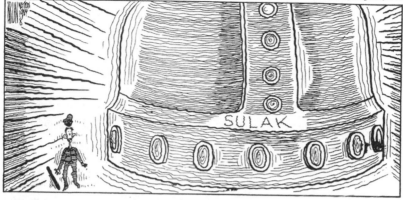

Wednesday, August 8, 1984

Reverberations in the press from my 1984 lèse-majesté case

gation Department. All three advised him not to have me arrested. Politically, it would be most unwise, and it would unnecessarily make me a national hero. Prem sat on it and didn't order my arrest.

Around this time, I went to China and Tibet to lead a Siam Society tour. On the way home I stopped in Japan for a Pacific Youth Forum. There I received a telegram from my wife: "Please return home to prove your innocence." Michio Kato, the program director of International House, joked, "Ah, Sulak, what happened? Have you been playing around? Your wife says you have to come back to prove your innocence." I didn't really know what had happened, but that evening, as I was giving a lecture just outside Tokyo, someone in the audience held up the newspaper and said, "Did you know that your book has been confiscated and quite a number of people have been arrested?" I called my wife, and she told me the story. *Dao Siam*, a very right-wing Thai newspaper—in 1976 they had circled my face as being a member of the Communist Party—printed a headline claiming I had fled to the U.S. to escape arrest.

The arrest

I took the next flight home. Nothing happened when I arrived; there were only rumors that I would be arrested. I gave two lectures at Thammasat University. At the first lecture, the house was packed; people had come to see whether or not I would be arrested. During the second lecture a few days later, somebody slipped me a piece of paper saying that the police had just come to my house with an arrest warrant. I announced to the crowd, "I'm sorry, but I have to cut short the question and answer period. I have to go home to be arrested." The police were at the lecture, but they said later that they didn't arrest me in public out of respect.

From the lecture, some of my friends took me up to the Faculty Club to discuss whether or not I should turn myself in. I wanted to take precautions, so I asked my colleague, Mr. Anant Viriyapinit, to call Mr. Khanchai Bunpan, the publisher of the *Matichon* daily, because he was very close to the military. Khanchai called General Suchinda Kraprayoon, who said that on no account must I be arrested. He asked Khanchai to look after me for a few days, so Khanchai took me into hiding in his offices. I moved around two or three times. At one o'clock one morning, he came to tell me to be ready by four o'clock, that a Royal Air Force plane would fly me from Ta Klee Airport to Kuala Lumpur, Malaysia. I waited until eight o'clock when Khanchai came and very sadly told me that the plan was off. The Royal Air Force had been told that if they flew me out of the country, that would be the end of the air force—the army would crush it. Khanchai did-

n't know what to do. He had revealed my hiding place to his friend in the air force and felt that if Artit pressed hard, he would learn where I was hiding.

Meanwhile, other friends had contacted me regarding another plan, so I moved from Khanchai's protection. They arranged to smuggle me to Malaysia on a fishing boat. I left to rendezvous with the fishing boat after five days in hiding, but I was arrested in the car on the way. The chap who had done the arranging told me afterwards that a taxi

My first trip to jail

cab that supposedly had engine troubles had been parked in front of his house almost all night. He thought perhaps it had been the police. In fact, it had been the Ministry of the Interior.

I was taken to the office of the Special Branch of the Police. I was treated very nicely—I had a special, air-conditioned room and telephone privileges—but they denied me bail. They arrested three of us—myself, the chap who interviewed me from Udornthani College, and the printer of the book. They wanted to make a show of it. In fact, they could have arrested the whole of the Komol Keemthong Foundation, which was the publisher. The chap from Udornthani College, being a civil servant, was also well-treated, but the printer, being Chinese, was put in the police station. This is the Siamese hierarchy at work. By law, the police can only detain you for one week, so after a week I was taken to court very early one morning. My lawyer and family were there. The court sent me straight to prison without bail. I was taken in a jail car with bars.

I had only one day's experience in jail. It was very crowded—a small room with thirteen people and a toilet. Most of the jailers and other prisoners sided with me. They said, "We all know you. You are a man of loyalty." They asked me to share their meal with them. One chap—he said he was being prosecuted without any grounds—asked me to look after his son and his daughter. In fact, I later asked them to work for me at TICD. I also met a fortune-teller in jail. He said, "You are somebody. Your nose is like a garuda; your ears are like the Buddha; and your eyes are very powerful. You are not an ordinary person." He looked at my palm and said, "I can't tell you whether you're going to be released today, but you have far to go. This case will make you very famous." Normally, I don't care for fortune-telling, but when you are down, it's good to have some kind of encouragement.

The court case

Mr. Thongbai Thongpao, my lawyer, arranged with the chief justice of the criminal court to allow me bail. I think it was one million baht. I felt very good that the court was not taking sides with the government. Dr. Prawase Wasi, a famous royal physician, went straight to the Special Branch of the Police to bail me out. It made headlines.

A lot of right-wing people asked him, "Why are you helping Sulak?" He replied, "He's an honest man, a man loyal to the king."

The police and the prosecutor had seven weeks to prepare their case against me, otherwise I would be free. During this time, I had to check in with the court every week. Meanwhile, foreign friends and lobby groups sent petitions to the king. Two hundred French children organized by the Catholic group CCFD sent petitions. There was a lot of public attention. Amnesty International took an active role on my behalf. It was the first time they had acted before the accused person was pronounced a prisoner of conscience. I was employed by the UN university, so the secretary general of the UN sent a very strong protest. The International Commission of Jurists, the World Council of Churches, the German churches, and the Japanese all tried to send observers to court.

My former secretary, Mr. Anant, was friendly with the king's deputy private secretary, Mr. Pawas Bunnag. Anant wrote to him privately, saying, "Everyone knows Ajahn Sulak is very loyal to the throne. The longer the case goes on, the worse it is for the Crown." Pawas sent the letter to the king. Supposedly, the king said, "Yes, what this man says is true." Soon after, my cousin Sala, a personal friend of the king's secretary, called to say that the secretary had asked to see me privately. When we met, he said, "The best thing is for you to write to the king yourself. Ask for a royal pardon. It will be resolved. The other two will also get amnesty." I thanked him, came home, and worked with my lawyer to draft a letter—not to show that I'd made any mistake but simply to ask for the king's clemency and good virtue. We sent it, but we heard no reply.

Many of my family and friends were quite worried. My sister asked various deities to protect me, and my wife visited several fortune-tellers. One, a blind Chinese astrologer, predicted my case would end within one week from that day. During this time I was officially prohibited from leaving the country. Luckily, my wife's cousin was the number two in charge of the Port Authority of Bangkok, and, with his help, I was able to attend the World Council of Churches meeting in Singapore. As it was also our twentieth wedding anniversary, I took my wife and youngest daughter Ming along with me. On the eve of our anniversary, my lawyer called to say I should return home immediately because the case was about to end. I replied, "Tomorrow is my wedding anniversary, and my hosts have arranged a party. The court can wait." So we enjoyed the party with some old friends and returned home the following day. The court invited the public prosecutors, the lawyers, and myself, and informed me that the public prosecutors would like to withdraw the case. If I had no objection, I could simply sign my name, and that would be the end. It turned out that General Prem was very angry with General Artit for having me arrested. Not that he liked me, but he felt it was bad for his government, that he had lost face. He wanted to free me in order to show his power over Artit. He consulted with the king and arranged for the case to be withdrawn.

So my case was dropped. It had been four months to the day from the date of the arrest warrant until the day I was freed—and seven days since the astrologer's prediction.

With my lawyers and codefendants at the criminal court

CHAPTER **17** | *Traveling*

China and Tibet

My country eventually recognized China after the 1973 student uprising. But the Chinese government had almost no friends in Siam. Since I was one of the very few who had espoused recognizing China, they kindly invited me to visit their country. Unfortunately, I was in exile at the time, so I could not go. When I returned home in '78, they renewed their invitation. By that time I was the program and travel chairman of the Siam Society, which is under royal patronage. They probably felt that I could promote tourism for them by bringing the rich, powerful Thais and expatriates from Siam to visit China. I conducted tours, partly because I could go for free. Altogether I went to China six times.

On my many trips to China, I made connections with the University of Beijing, Zhongshan University in Guangzhou, and the Institute of Southeast Asian Studies in Kunming. They told me about their difficulties in buying books. Under their centralized system, they had to apply for approval from their university, then write to the Ministry of Finance in Beijing to release the foreign exchange money. It took eighteen months for them to get the money, and by then the books were often out of print. I said that if they didn't mind the involvement of the "red-haired devils"—their term for Europeans and Americans—I could help them. I got funding for books from the Ford Foundation—not only for China but also for Indochina—and kept the money in Bangkok so that it didn't have to be converted into Chinese currency. My wife sent a circular from our bookshop every month listing the new books on Southeast Asia in various languages. The universities would order whatever they wanted, and we would send the books and keep their account until the money was gone. We did that for two or three years.

Visiting Tibet was the climax of all my visits to China, despite the difficulties we had. I had always dreamed of going to Tibet. In 1984, the Chinese government gave my group from the Siam Society special permission. This was before Tibet was open to tourists. It was a wonderful experience for me, though I felt very sad to see the Chinese occupation. We saw Lhasa, the Potala Palace, the Jokhang Temple, and the town of Xigatze, the former seat of the Panchen Lama. It was a superficial tour, but I met a lot of people, even though I spoke neither Chinese nor Tibetan. The Nepalese vice consul said he had attended my lecture at the Institute of Social Studies in the Hague and gave us special treatment. From him we learned a lot about the atrocities the Chinese had committed. At that time, the Chinese were apologizing for being so harsh on the Tibetans. They blamed everything on the Gang of Four for having destroyed so many Tibetan temples during the Cultural Revolution. They wanted to reconcile with the Tibetans, even to invite His Holiness the Dalai Lama to return. I had brought with me two thousand color photos of His Holiness and could have made a fortune selling them. People would have paid five yuan each (almost five dollars), but I gave them away free. The Chinese guide became very upset and told me I had not

My visit to Lhasa

acted in a way befitting a guest. I replied, "You said you wanted to invite His Holiness back." In the end, they were not happy with me.

On the night before our return, heavy rains caused a big flood. The road to the airport from Lhasa was extremely bad. We had to leave at three or four o'clock in the morning. A big jeep convoy— about twenty in all—took us through the floods. We got to dry land, but we still had some distance to go. In the middle of the road was a huge boulder. It completely blocked our way. I thought there was nothing we could do, but then I saw Mao Tse-tung's great Little Red Book in action. The Chinese, using just their hands, gathered stones from beside the road and piled them up handful by handful until they formed a roadway up and over the boulder. Within half an hour we were on our way to the airport.

Every time I went to China I had admiration on the one hand and criticism on the other. I admired socialist countries because there was no big gap between the rich and poor, and the government aspired to help the multitudes. But I hate dictatorship and oppression. The worst thing about China was its destruction of culture and cultural diversity. Generally, I kept my mouth shut, but after several trips I thought I should write a book on my real impressions of China. In those days, all the Thai books written about China were positive. Most of my countrymen went to China without knowing the language and having very negative expectations. But once they arrived, they were pampered by the Chinese. Of course, they didn't know it was all propaganda. Furthermore, many of us are part Chinese, so deep down we tend to be pro-China and feel a bit guilty about condemning them. So visitors came back to write how impressed they were with China, and this was more good propaganda for the Chinese.

In my book, I said that Mao Tse-tung had destroyed Chinese culture, that Tibet was treated like filth, and that all the Chinese propaganda about Tibet was a lie. I acknowledged that the communist revolution made some positive contributions, uniting the country and making the people proud to be Chinese. The people were no longer starving. But China was not a free country. I questioned China's arms development and role in the world, its support for the Khmer Rouge and the Burmese military. Of course, my book was condemned by the Chinese. On top of that, soon after the book came out, there was an uprising in Lhasa, and I stood with the Tibetans in condemning the Chinese government and Deng Xiao Ping. I organized a Buddhist ceremony at the Chinese temple in Bangkok during the Tiananmen Square uprising. I also tried to invite the Dalai Lama to my country. With all this, my special connection with the Chinese Embassy came to an end. In fact, when a Sino-Thai friend was compiling my biography for a Chinese encyclopedia listing ten important Thais with Chinese ancestry, the Chinese authorities told my friend that perhaps nine biographies would be enough. Obviously, I will not become immortal in China. In a way, though, I felt proud to be persona non grata with a wretched government that kills their minorities.

Indochina

In the early eighties I was one of the first from my country to visit the Indochinese states of Laos, Cambodia, Burma, and Vietnam. Nobody wanted to go because they were supposed to be our enemies, but I felt it was important to build friendships with these people.

In Laos, I loved Luang Phrabang, the old capital. Even after the royalty left, the palace was preserved. Without royalty, it was a bit dead, but even so I felt some calm and beauty. It reminded me of Chiang Mai forty-five years ago when I first went there—very few cars and many bicycles. Unfortunately, I'm sure we will spoil the new capital Vientiene with the Friendship Bridge we built across the Mekhong River.

I visited Cambodia when it was still under Vietnamese hegemony. In those days Cambodia was still closed, and they didn't allow anybody in. Of all the places in Indochina, the most impressive in my opinion is this country's gigantic Angkor Wat and Angkor Thom. Nothing can compare. The first time I went to Angkor Wat I had the whole place to myself. It is less than two hundred miles from Phnom Penh, but it took eleven hours just to drive there. The road was very bad, full of mines, and the bridges were down. We had to drive on the dry canal beds and bamboo bridges. On the way, we spent one night in Battambang and the rest in Siem Reap. In Siem Reap I stayed in the Grand Hotel built by the French. It was a beautiful hotel, but there was no electricity or water. I had to bathe next door in the canal. Even so, it was wonderful. The people were very kind, but they charged me sixty U.S. dollars a night! That's the cost of an air-conditioned room in a Bangkok hotel.

Once at Angkor, I stayed for three days. I admired the craftsmanship, size, and beauty of the buildings, but at the same time I felt sad. It was all built with the labor of many Thai slaves, some of whom were my ancestors. The stone in the beautiful Bayong building came from Korat in my country. I visualized the Thai slaves as they hauled it all the way to Angkor Thom. There were many atrocities, yet it is beautiful. I had a photographer and interpreter with me, and the guide and I became very friendly. He hated the Vietnamese, so he told me about all the atrocities they committed.

My experience in Burma was similar. I am very fond of Rangoon and Mandalay, the old capital. Pagan is beautiful—one of the most beautiful Buddhist ruins in the whole world—with its miles and miles of pagodas. We have nothing like that in my country. I love the friendly Burmese people. I made many Burmese friends during the uprising in Burma when I sided with the students and condemned the military junta. With the current dictatorship, of course, I have become persona non grata.

India and Bhutan

During my travels in India, the most spiritually fulfilling stop for me was in Dharamsala to meet His Holiness the Dalai Lama. I have felt very close to His Holiness for many years. I was working with the BBC and reported on his situation when he fled from Tibet. At that time, I was often with Tibetans, and I translated into Thai his first autobiography, *My Land, My People*. I met His Holiness on his first visit to Bangkok. I produced a special booklet in Thai to welcome him and to explain Tibetan Buddhism to the Thai people. I consider myself a small link between him and my country's people.

When I went to India, I visited him with a Thai journalist and a television man. We had a long interview and a very cordial visit. Every time I meet him I feel inspired by his compassion, his nonviolence, and his exemplary life of humility and genuine sincerity. I feel the same with the Vietnamese monk Thich Nhat Hanh. They have both been oppressed and cannot return to their countries, but they are wonderful, helping those in psychological turmoil as well as their peo-

Meeting His Holiness the Dalai Lama in Bangkok in 1964

ple living abroad. Although I remain Theravadin, I've come to respect Tibetan and Mahayana Buddhism through these monks. They inspire Buddhists all over the world, and their inspiration has been very real for me.

The most impressive place I visited in India was Ladakh. The people are very poor, yet their Buddhist practice is quite genuine. It is the only place where Buddhism is still very much alive, despite the fact that it is surrounded by Muslims, and the people are treated very badly by the local government. Tibetans have lived in Ladakh for the last eight hundred years. In my country we have been changing and modernizing unmindfully during the past one hundred years, and we are in a dreadful predicament. It would be wonderful if we could help the Ladakhis to preserve their traditions.

I visited Ladakh on the invitation of Venerable Sanghasena, a Ladakhi monk ordained in the Theravada tradition. He decided to start a Buddhist education institution for the Tibetans and asked me to lay a foundation stone for the Buddhist library. This was in 1991. Since the following year would be the centenary of Prince Mahidol, the current Thai king's father, I felt the gift of this Buddhist library would be an appropriate way to honor him. In Buddhism, the best gift is the gift of the Dhamma. Prince Mahidol's daughter Princess Kalayani agreed to give one million baht (US $40,000) to start building. I reminded other Thais, Europeans, and Americans that Prince Mahidol's children had been born abroad—our king in America, his elder brother in Germany, and his eldest sister in England—and everyone contributed a small amount of money. This Buddhist library was something I could do for Buddhism in Ladakh and for the Ladakhi people. It was also a way to honor my king's father despite the fact that to some I am known as a man who defamed the king.

Earlier, in 1989, I visited Bhutan with my wife. I was invited by the Bhutanese king's sister, whose husband admired my books *Socially Engaged Buddhism* and *A Buddhist Vision for Renewing Society*. He had hoped I could speak to the youth of his country, describing how Buddhism can bring both personal and societal transformation. Unfortunately, his relationship with the king was not good, and he couldn't arrange for any public lectures. Instead, we visited various towns and beautiful temples and attended many Buddhist ceremonies. I felt sad to realize that Bhutan may well commit the same mistakes in modernization that my country had over the past one hundred years.

18 | *More Organizing*

Pacific Youth Forum

After my visit to Tibet in 1984 we held the first Pacific Youth Forum in Japan. I had renewed my relationship with the International House of Japan. Mr. Michio Kato was director of programs there and agreed to help me financially to create a permanent youth ashram based on our earlier Pacific Ashram, as I had begun to do back in 1976. It would be primarily for Japanese and Southeast Asian youth. Since Mr. Kato felt the word "ashram" was a problem for the Japanese, we changed the name from Pacific Ashram to Pacific Youth Forum. He wanted me to run it from Bangkok because of all my connections in the region, but he felt it would be easier to hold our meetings in Japan.

Our first meeting was at Kiyosato Village, not far from Tokyo, and it was beautiful to see young people of so many backgrounds— Japanese, American, Southeast Asian. We discussed social and economic development in Asia and the Pacific. They liked it, so they invited me to do it again the next year. In 1985, we went to Morioka City and Takizawa Village and met around the theme "Participation, Development, and Peace." During our third meeting in 1987, we gathered in Hiroshima in connection with the fortieth anniversary of the Second World War bombing of that city. Soedjatmoko, my old friend and the rector of U.N. University, attended. My whole family was invited, and it was wonderful to have my wife and two daughters join me. My son was studying in America at the time.

We organized one more youth forum in Japan in 1991. Our theme was "Asia-Pacific Community in the Twenty-first Century: Challenges and Opportunities for Youth." In the end, the Japanese changed the name to Asian Cultural Forum so they could include people beside youth. They wanted to invite young entrepreneurs to encourage them to develop a more holistic view of life. They asked Soedjatmoko to become chairman of this group. Wang Kang Wu, the vice chancellor of the University of Hong Kong and Frankie José from the Philippines also got involved, together with Yeneo Ishii from Kyoto University. They planned to meet in Japan every year or two. They thought a week was enough for the young people, and for more senior people one long weekend would be enough. I did not think it would work, and I stayed with the idea of starting an ashram.

Wongsanit Ashram

This idea of establishing a permanent ashram had been with me since beginning the Pacific Youth Forum in 1973. My vision was to provide a place for social activists to take time to read, think, write, and reflect on their work for as long as they wanted—a place for people to synchronize their head with their heart and develop themselves in a serious, spiritual way. It would be a new kind of temple run by laypeople.

I'm sure my ideas were influenced by my own life. With my many activities taking so much time and energy, I needed to go on retreats every now and again. I would go to temples. Unfortunately, these traditional Thai spiritual centers were disappearing. Those still remaining taught traditional meditation concerned only with the heart, not the head. They had so many rules and regulations and preserved only the Buddhist tradition. Many have not adapted to the modern world and don't serve the people who use them. Religions have to adapt their wonderful teachings to the modern world.

I wanted a place where people could opt to live an alternative lifestyle, grow their own food, weave their own clothes. The idea was to live in community, both for personal growth and social commitment. "Work locally, think globally," because we are all interconnected. The ashram would contribute meaningfully to society. It would offer training and meditation for social activists to help them gain skills and understand the structural problems in society. It would be a kind of international, alternative training center to empower people through practical and spiritual training. I wanted to get scholarships to support people to come, particularly people from our neighboring countries of Vietnam, Laos, Cambodia, and Burma.

I saw many different types of centers to prepare for starting our own ashram. My German friend Michael Baumann took me to see German "ashrams" in the Black Forest run by Karfield Graf von Durkheim. I also went to see Christian academies in Germany and Italy. The German Christians started these academies after the Second World War because they felt that ministers and priests had been too weak to resist Hitler and stop the Nazis from killing Jews. The idea was to make the priests and the lay church leaders more aware of social injustice and learn ways to confront it through Christian ethics and theology. Practicing Christians could develop the moral courage to challenge the government and society. But I thought that the Protestants stressed too much the head and not the heart. At the Catholic monasteries I visited, it was the other way around—too much prayer and not enough social concern. I thought it was out of balance.

In India I saw the Gandhian ashrams. Unfortunately, these have become a kind of religious institution, and Gandhi has become something like a god. The ashrams were a nice place to do a little bit of spinning, to weave your own clothes, and to eat simple food. Many of these ashrams are subsidized by the government. They have become just like some of my country's Buddhist temples—wholly irrelevant to the larger society. Thich Nhat Hanh's Plum Village in France, on the other hand, was much more to my liking than any of these places. He enlivened traditional Buddhist teachings to be relevant to the modern world, stressing our interconnectedness with one another and our environment. He teaches mindfulness as the basis for non-violent social change.

I had been looking for land and money for some years. When the karma was right, I thought, someone would give me a plot of land. It finally happened in 1984. The land I ended up getting was just a rice field on a canal, seventy kilometers from Bangkok. One hundred years ago there had been elephants living there. It was cleared by Dr. Yai Sanidvong, the first Siamese medical man to be trained in Europe. It was passed down through his family to Princess Samur and her husband Prince Subhasvati Wongsanit. Samur wanted the land to be used for something spiritual, a Buddhist contribution to world peace and personal growth. When she died, her daughter Saisawadi persuaded all her sisters to give this land to the Sathirakoses-Nagapradipa

Foundation. Saisawadi was a good friend of mine. We founded the Mitra Thai Trust together in 1976. The S-N Foundation's board agreed to take charge of the property and use it for an ashram. We called it Ashram Wongsanit in honor of her parents, Prince and Princess Wongsanit.

Wongsanit Ashram is only about ten or fifteen acres, but this is fairly large by Bangkok standards. Unfortunately, the land was not very good, and things did not grow well. Two or three people came at the start to try it out. We assigned them a plot of land to see if they could grow something. Although it was difficult to grow rice, they did grow some vegetables and caught enough fish to live on. One family lived on part of the land for a few years. In another area, a group of young people formed a small project to look after street children from Bangkok. Our land was an ideal place for them—not too far from Bangkok and with a nice, country atmosphere. The children stayed from two or three days to a few weeks or months. They learned how to fish, raise chickens, and grow tobacco.

The center of the ashram, I felt, should be a hall where we could run seminars and retreats. It was through our activities for the Phya Anuman centenary celebrations in 1988 that we raised enough money to build this hall, which we located in a special area named for my

The main hall at Ashram Wongsanit

teacher, Phya Anuman. In the time of the Buddha, this kind of multi-purpose hall was called a *santhagara,* a meeting hall. You could dine or sleep there, and monks could preach there. I tried to embrace the whole tradition and put it in the modern context. The santhagara became our main building.

For improving the grounds I used the old custom of *"Thot Pha Pa."* In our Buddhist tradition, forest monks typically do not take robes offered to them by anyone directly. Instead, people leave robes in the jungle, hanging them on trees and letting the monks find them. Nowadays, we use this tradition to raise money for building or repairing a temple. I adapted the tradition into a big celebration and asked for trees to reforest the ashram. The ashram had only rice fields. People gave trees, or if they didn't have trees, they gave money to buy trees.

As we continued to grow, many other people supported us. The Green Party in Germany agreed to fund buildings and programs through the Heinrich Böll Foundation, which supported our concern for environmental issues, spiritual and intellectual growth, and social justice in a nonviolent and ecumenical way. A German friend, Reinhard Schlagintweit, who had been a counselor at the German Embassy in Bangkok back in 1967, helped us gain this support. We were able to build the library, and we had money for publications and programs for the next three years. We received a little help from a Protestant organization in Sweden called Diakonia. Although we didn't get any official Buddhist money, some Japanese and Thai Buddhists also helped.

The ashram has contributed at the local, national, and international levels. We have used it for International Network of Engaged Buddhists meetings and many workshops and training programs. Out of our training for Khmers, we planned a peace march from the Thai border to Phnom Penh in 1992. Venerable Maha Ghosananda, the leading Cambodian monk, started off the march by circling our santhagara three times. They began the march on the traditional Cambodian, Siamese, Burmese, and Laotian New Year of April 13. They went slowly, and along the way people came offering food and talking with the marchers. They planted bodhi trees along the road. It started out as a small group but ended up with thousands. With these sorts of things happening, I think my dream for the ashram has finally come true.

Buddhist connections around the world

The term "engaged Buddhism" was coined by Thich Nhat Hanh in the 1950s. The idea is that Buddhism is for social as well as personal liberation. This was in direct contrast to the Buddhism I encountered at the Buddhist Society in London in the 1950s. I was told that Buddhism was for meditation, and that Buddhists had nothing to do with society. That shocked me. It seemed very selfish, as if Buddhism were being used solely for one's own ends. Meditation alone may have been relevant for the British Buddhists at that time, but I felt it was not quite right. It entirely contradicted my upbringing in traditional Buddhist society.

Even so, I also encountered this attitude back home. The World Fellowship of Buddhists (WFB) had established their headquarters in Bangkok. Dr. Malalasekera, their founder, wanted it to be an organization in which Buddhists could develop a social and ethical message. I attended one or two of their meetings, and I found that it had become a sort of club for Buddhists from around the world to come together to pat each other on the back and say, "We Buddhists are wonderful people." But they did nothing. When it was proposed that we discuss the Buddhist stand on military conscription, many members said, "That's a political issue. We can't talk about it." "What about capital punishment?" They said, "Ah, that's political, too." It reminded me of the Buddhist Society in England. Again, I felt there was something wrong.

By the time I came home from England, Buddhism was being destroyed in the villages in my country. In South and Southeast Asia, the heart of Buddhism is the village temple, and the present model of development was destroying villages. I felt my role was to restore Buddhism at the rural level. Those of us who had been educated abroad could help people understand the larger social realities and how they relate to the villages. A few friends and I began working with village people, helping them at the grassroots level to preserve the environment, to make them feel proud, to empower them nonviolently.

We have been working with the villagers for the last twenty years, joining not only with Buddhists, but also with non-Buddhists who work with the poor for their liberation. We formed the Thai Interreligious Commission for Development, the Coordinating Group for Religion in Society, and other groups, all at the local and national levels. But we saw that our work at the national level was not sufficient and began trying to work with our neighbors, the Burmese, Laotians, and Khmers, while working with the grassroots people in our own country. This was an important step, since we Thai tend to look down on our neighbors for having been colonized. We regard the Laotian people as very backward, the Burmese as very poor, the Khmers as nobodies. The Buddha taught that we are all equal, and that we must respect each individual and each culture. That is how our international network started to grow.

Many more connections were developed together with a friend named Pracha Hutanuwatra. He had spent eleven years as a monk, and, when he left the monkhood in 1986, I sent him to live among the poor Buddhists and non-Buddhists in India, Nepal, and Sri Lanka. In India, he met a group of newly converted Buddhists. They really wanted to understand Buddhism, but many didn't know even the basic Buddhist precepts. We started a program to bring these Buddhists from India to be trained in Siam. Pracha also talked with Buddhists among the tribal people in the north of Nepal. They had been Buddhists since the time of their ancestors, but as a minority in Hindu society, they were in a desperate situation. We tried to find some concrete ways to work together in the future. In Sri Lanka, he was involved in a peace mission to Jaffna, a Tamil area, with another interreligious group. This was the first time that Buddhist monks from the south had come to visit Jaffna. We tried to provide them with international encouragement and support.

In 1987, I sent Pracha to Japan as a visiting scholar at the Institute for Religion and Culture at Nanzan University. I had talked to the Japanese before, but I didn't get very far until Pracha went there. He was much better than I at making connections. He spent a lot of time with radical priests, many of whom were former Marxists like himself. He brought them to talk with me. They also saw the need for some kind of international group so that we could work together. Our main concern was not only for those of us in Asia and the Third World but to make people in the First World aware of people's suffering as well.

Back in the late seventies I had heard about the Buddhist Peace Fellowship (BPF) from Nelson Foster, who had helped found it with the American Zen teacher, Robert Aitken Roshi. I felt that BPF could help us form a link between Western and Asian Buddhists. We made links with the Japanese, Americans, English, and Germans. I also became involved in Mongolia and the former Soviet Union. We had other connections in Asia and the Pacific through ACFOD. It was a large network.

International Network of Engaged Buddhists

When the chapter of the Buddhist Peace Fellowship in Britain contacted us, we felt it was appropriate to formalize this international network. That's how the International Network of Engaged Buddhists (INEB) came into being. Although I am supposedly the founder of INEB, it was really more Pracha Hutanuwatra's work than my own. We organized our first INEB meeting in 1989. It was held in Siam, in the town of Uthaithani, my wife's birthplace. We met on a houseboat owned by a temple that had been headquarters for Buddhist education at the time of King Rama V. The supreme patriarch during the reign of King Rama VI was also very active here. It was a very auspicious meeting place to begin INEB.

Two men almost prevented INEB from getting off the ground. A German fellow wanted INEB membership to be very strict: no smoking, no drinking, no superstition, no, no, no. I told him, "It is wonderful if you yourself want to take these precepts seriously, but the strength—and weakness—of Buddhism is that we do not place prohibitions on such things." He didn't like it, but he remained. A British man was even worse. He wanted things his way. He insisted we use voting, while the rest of us wanted to use consensus in the Buddhist manner. This caused a leading Japanese man to suggest to me, "Sulak-san, let's not make this an international network but simply an Asian network. Western people will never understand us." I had to tell my English friend, "Please, shut up." He was very nice, he shut up, and INEB came to be.

All along, we have received a lot of help from the Japanese chapter of INEB. They have provided much of the funding to run the office and INEB activities. We have very little structure, and, as I learned from my experience with ACFOD, it is best not to have too much money or power. I also learned that we need a strong spiritual element, and so we include meditation and spiritual practice at INEB meetings. We started very small. Pracha was paid as a part-time executive secretary, and a volunteer helped him. We couldn't take on very much and had to work on things one by one.

First, we organized a human rights campaign for the Buddhist minority in the Chittagong Hill tracts in Bangladesh. These tribal people were being killed or forceably relocated to India. The Japanese took this issue quite seriously and invited the Bangladeshi representative, Venerable Bimal, to speak all over Japan. Japan was a major source of foreign aid for Bangladesh, so our efforts had a great impact.

Next on our agenda was to work with the students and minority groups living along the Burmese border. This was just after the 1988 uprising in Burma, in which a lot of people had been killed. They had been fighting in the jungle, generation after generation, for forty years and had very little communication with the outside world. This was our first chance to get to know them. Since other organizations were already helping with clothes and medicine, we concentrated on the students' requests for education and training. We arranged basic health and medical training because many of them were dying from malaria. Our most important work was to expose them to the world outside Burma. With our help, they set up a "jungle university" right across the border. We arranged for teachers from Bangkok and the international community to visit the university and run training sessions for a period of time. The Buddhist Peace Fellowship and Greenpeace helped arrange a communication system for the border.

After the third annual INEB conference, we focused on Sri Lanka. Historically, there's a very close link between Sri Lanka and Siam. Buddhism had been imported to Siam from Sri Lanka eight or nine hundred years ago and exported back to Sri Lanka during the eighteenth century after the monkhood had disappeared there. On their request, we arranged a six-week conflict resolution training for thirty Sri Lankan monks. The trainers were the American Quakers George

Lakey and George Willoughby and Tord Hovick from the International Peace Research Institute in Oslo, Norway. The whole approach was very Western—how to solve conflicts from the viewpoint of modern sociology and political theory.

When we were invited to do a similar reconciliation training with the Khmer monks and lay community in Cambodia, we used a Buddhist approach. All the factions involved in the Cambodian conflict came except the Khmer Rouge. We tried to understand their country's situation within a Buddhist framework using the concepts of *upadana* (attachment or clinging), right speech, and so on. At the end of the training, one of the Cambodian patriarchs, a faction leader, noted, "All the factions in this conflict are under the illusion of upadana." It was a very good experience for us all.

INEB has worked closely with the International Fellowship of Reconciliation, War Resisters International, and Peace Brigades International. We also work on more theoretical issues such as Buddhist social analysis and women in Buddhism. Our annual INEB conferences have been an inspiration to everyone. These conferences are only possible because our members in the First World often pay double so that members from the poorer countries can be invited. We have received donations from friends in the U.S. to help us continue our work. After much initial support from Christian organizations, INEB decided that for the organization to survive meaningfully it must be supported by Buddhists. From then on, we have received support from Buddhists throughout the greater international community. Rev. Teruo Maruyama, INEB's cofounder, said of our group, "We must do everything possible to maintain the international network. It is the only really viable network we have in the Buddhist world." I am very proud of INEB. It does wonderful work.

Reviving our democracy

In 1988, I founded the Santi Pracha Dhamma Institute. The name came from Dr. Puey's well-known book, *Santi Pracha Dhamma* (Peace, People, Righteousness) that I had published at Klett Thai in 1973. This name and the book's ideas had become well-known among many progressives during the 1970s. With this organization, I wanted to carry on both Dr. Puey's and Dr. Pridi's ideas for democracy and social justice. I began it with Dr. Puey's blessings. The institute does research and arranges public forums on social justice and Buddhism under the umbrella of the Sathirakoses-Nagapradipa Foundation.

In the early 1990s, some of us worked to have August 16, 1995, recognized as the fiftieth anniversary of Peace Day. The first Peace Day had been declared by Mr. Pridi, then regent of King Ananda Mahidol, on this same date in 1945. It signified the end of the state of war between Siam and the Allies. As the military is still a state within the state in Siam, the civilian government did not want to tread on the military's toes. They were reluctant to commemorate Peace Day because it celebrates the power of nonviolence and the wartime Free Thai Movement, the clandestine but popular freedom movement headed by the regent himself.

Nonetheless, we managed to gain approval from HRH Princess Maha Chakri Sirindhorn. She agreed to preside over a Peace Day ceremony at Thammasat University. We arranged a big gathering. Adam Curle, the Buddhist Quaker from London, delivered an opening address before Her Royal Highness. We named Dr. Puey Ungphakorn the "Man of Peace." In the evening, Lady Phoonsuk Banomyong led a peace march from Thammasat to the Democracy Monument on Rajadamnern Avenue. There, hundreds of people joined us. We had a minute of silence amidst the Bangkok traffic to honor all who had died for peace. We prayed that there would be no more war, that justice and peace would prevail in the world. Two years later on this date, the City of Bangkok dedicated a large, beautiful park—Suan Seri Thai—to the Free Thai Movement. This has become a significant day for all of us, a reminder of the meaning of nonviolence.

The 1991 coup

On February 23, 1991, I was at the third annual meeting of the International Network of Engaged Buddhists at Phutthamonthon, not far from Bangkok. We had borrowed earphones for Thai participants to listen to translations of the discussions in English. The chap in charge of the earphones must have been bored because he put on the radio to listen to the news and music. He whispered to me during our meeting that there had just been a coup in Bangkok. I joked with the INEB participants that coups d'état in my country are nothing unusual—it is how we change governments. An unsuccessful coup is like a reelection, a successful one is like a general election.

Afterwards, I told some foreign journalists that most of the Thai public prefers coups d'état because the governments the politicians set up democratically are always full of corruption and infighting. The Thai public likes a new government for the first three months, but after six months they start criticizing it. I added, of course, that we must continue working toward democracy, however bad things may seem. Eventually, perhaps, we can develop a real democracy. Going back to a dictatorship is no good. What I said was true, and there was nothing original in it, but no Thai newspaper would ever publish such remarks.

The coup leaders, the National Peace Keeping Council (NPKC) were very strict to begin with. They imposed censorship, but after three days, in the usual Thai style, they relaxed. The people all loved General Suchinda Kraprayoon, one of their leaders. Suchinda selected Mr. Anand Panyarachun to become prime minister. Everybody was happy. He was a good technocrat, aristocrat, and had a good team devoted to the affairs of the state—all honest people. But I wasn't happy. Mr. Anand's merits were beside the point. He came to power illegitimately because a coup is illegitimate. Again, nobody published my remarks.

But about one month after the coup, on my way home from a visit to the U.N. University for Peace in Costa Rica, I was interviewed by *Siam Media* in Los Angeles. L.A. has the largest Thai community abroad and many Thai newspapers. I criticized the coup very strongly. I said Mr. Anand had no legitimacy, and that however well-intentioned he may be, this was not true democracy. The NPKC had taken hold of power above the law, which is not right. Around that time, Mr. Thanong Po-arn, a labor leader, disappeared. He had said that the coup destroyed the labor movement and that he would bring the case to the International Labor Organization. I remarked that his disappearance was very serious, a flagrant abuse of human rights. My remarks were published in America and some copies sent to Bangkok. Quite a number of people read them there. The NPKC was very upset.

Meanwhile, I had been writing regularly for the *Matichon* daily and for the weekly magazine. After the coup, the publisher, Khanchai Bunpan, wrote that the new government was a *dhammika* dictatorship—a righteous dictatorship. He urged people to give them a chance to develop the country, to avoid criticizing them. Of course, the NPKC had supreme power and could shut down his presses at any time. Thammasat University banned both the *Matichon* daily and weekly. Students put up posters saying they would not read propaganda sheets. I wrote a polite letter to the paper saying I would no longer write for them. I didn't want it shut down and the staff to become unemployed due to my criticisms. I said, "I don't regard the government as a righteous dictatorship. I think they are just rogues and opportunists." Khanchai's assistant warned me that I should keep my mouth shut. They said it was good that I had stopped writing for the paper, that they wouldn't have published my column anyhow.

General Suchinda was very upset. He had helped me seven years ago during my lèse-majesté charge and felt I was now attacking him personally. The NPKC's number two—Air Marshal Kaset Rojananin of the royal air force—had been friendly with me before this, but he now remarked that the press should remind intellectuals that they are not above the law. They can criticize within the limit of the law, but if they go beyond, they'll be arrested. Obviously, he meant me. This relationship also became strained.

My speech at Thammasat

I was invited to speak many times. No matter what the subject, I would attack the NPKC. I spoke in May at Thammasat University along with Mr. Puwadon Songprasert, General Secretary of the Social Science Association. He was very outspoken and attacked the NPKC much more strongly than I. I denounced the coup leaders in principle, but he knew all the background facts. *Matichon* reported it in one small column.

In August, big workshops and lectures were held at Thammasat University to remind people that the NPKC was no good for them. I was invited to speak by the National Student Federation of Thailand, the Thammasat University Club, and the Coordinating Group for Religion and Society. It was not a large crowd—just over two hundred people. In my lecture, I reviewed the reasons for all the coups, beginning with the first coup in 1947 all the way down to the recent 1991 coup. I said that every coup was bad—bad for the country, bad for the monarchy, and bad for the Buddhist religion. I said the law of lèse-majesté must be abolished because it traps the monarchy by making it inflexible and unable to accept criticism. If we want to protect the monarchy, everything should be discussed openly. Real loyalty demands honesty, open criticism, even dissent. We must protect against manipulation by politicians, businessmen, and multinational corporations. (See Appendix III.)

Mr. Sunnai Chulapongsathorn, one of my lawyers in the previous lèse-majesté case, happened to be at my lecture. In fact, it was in his car that I had been arrested seven years before. He drove me home. "This may be your second case, you know. But if they dare arrest you, it'll be a very tough fight." By the next morning, the NPKC was very angry. Before I went down to Pattani to deliver another lecture, a reporter from *Matichon* called me: Had I heard that Suchinda had sent his staff to the police station to file two cases against me, one for defaming the king and another for defaming Suchinda himself? I said I had not heard; it had not been in the news. The next day, *Matichon* reported it. Defaming the commander-in-chief of the army is a fairly moderate charge with a maximum punishment of only two years. But Suchinda twisted my talk to charge me with lèse-majesté, which is much more serious and carries a punishment of up to fifteen years in prison.

I thought I could fight this case and went on to Pattani. When I returned to Bangkok, my wife was waiting at the airport. She said, "You are not going to speak anymore." She sent me up to Chiang Mai to hide. She thought that if I kept quiet—no press reports—perhaps it would be possible to resolve the conflict. I went to Chiang Mai for one week, during which time a search warrant was brought to my house. My wife said I wasn't home.

The people who hid me in Chiang Mai considered matters to be quite serious. Once arrested, I would not be treated well. I would be taken to the headquarters of the Crime Suppression Unit, run by Boonchu Wangkanon, an army classmate of General Suchinda. He was known to be a dreadful man. In fact, it had been broadcast about me on the army radio: "The old intellectual doesn't realize he is not young anymore. He has a foul mouth. We must knock his teeth in. We must beat him and get blood out of him." This was all on the radio. It didn't please me. My friends said I should get out of the country before an arrest warrant was issued. But I figured that the search warrant meant there was probably already an arrest warrant out. They argued, "This is a weekend. The Thai are not that efficient." I reminded them that it had also been a weekend the last time they arrested me.

When rumor had it that they were about to arrest me, my friend Michael Baumann telephoned me from Germany. I asked him to contact my friend Reinhard Schlagintweit, now chief of the political affairs department of the foreign ministry in Germany. Schlagintweit telephoned the German ambassador and asked him to do everything he could to help me. I called the ambassador late at night to explain my predicament, and he said, "Please come to the embassy. I will help you." But how could I go? I was in Chiang Mai, six hundred kilometers away from Bangkok. He said, "All right, I will send my car flying the German flag. The car is bulletproof. No one will arrest you. You will have diplomatic immunity." His number two man flew up to Chiang Mai, and the car was sent separately. He joined me in the car, and we drove together to the embassy.

In hiding at the German Embassy

As I happened to be under contract to write an article for the U.N. University, I thought this connection could help me. I contacted the university rector's office, but my friend Soedjatmoko had died, and the new rector couldn't care less about me. I looked up the law and found that those who are employed by a foreign embassy are also exempt from being arrested. I asked my friend Schlagintweit to ask the German ambassador to employ me. Schlagintweit replied, "Sulak, if you were in Burma, I would tell the ambassador to do that. But Thailand is not that bad. They will not kill you." I said, "Mr. Thanong, the labor leader, disappeared and was certainly killed." "Well," he reasoned, "with your status, they wouldn't kill you." "Yes, but they broadcast that they would knock me around," I argued. "Sulak," he said, "we simply cannot employ you, but we will invite you to stay in the embassy as long as you wish."

Baumann, being very clever, asked *Der Spiegel* in Germany to talk to the German foreign ministry. They said, "Yes, we are happy Mr. Sulak has decided to come to the German Embassy, and he is our guest for as long as he wishes. It's an honor for us to protect an intellectual who fights for democracy. We believe the charge against him is trumped up." At first, the German ambassador was happy to help, but he eventually became unhappy. His wife was very nervous. He said, "If the Thai government throws me out, the German government will send me somewhere in Africa. I don't want to go to Africa. I want to stay here." He advised me to give myself up.

Before submitting myself, I called Schlagintweit again. He happened to be in New York, and it was two or three o'clock in the morning there when I called. I told him my options were to stay locked in the embassy and make the ambassador unhappy, or to give myself up and make my friends unhappy. He said, "It's up to you—it's your case. But why don't you escape?" I said, "How can I escape? They're listening to our telephone call right now. There are three police cars in front of the embassy. There are two in front of my house and one at my office. There's even a police car in Chiang Mai." He said, "Well,

Sulak, how can I advise you? I'm in New York. You do the best you can for your own reputation, for your own safety. Whatever you do, I'm with you." So I told the ambassador, "All right. I'll turn myself in." He made the telephone call to the chief of police. They asked the ambassador to take me to the local police station.

Meanwhile, three of my friends came and told me that I must not go. Dr. Prawase said that on no account must I submit myself. He had talked to various people and found out, in the Thai way, that they would be rough with me. Mr. Khanchai was very upset with me; General Suchinda was very upset with me—they were all very upset with me. They felt that they had to teach me a lesson. But I told my friends, "I gave my word to the ambassador. I must go now." I asked them to hold my passport and my Buddha image for me because by the next day I would be in jail.

The ambassador went to have a nap; he was relieved that I wouldn't be staying. I went for a walk in the beautiful embassy compound. There were geese and deer and peacocks. My people came back. They said, "By hook or by crook we're taking you out of here. If by luck we can get away, we will." In my weakness, I said, "Okay, I'll go." I went without anything. I left my diary in my room at the embassy. Luckily, since my wife had told my lawyer to meet me at the police station to bail me out and everything seemed confirmed to make my arrest, the police had removed the car from in front of the embassy.

Fleeing from Siam

We left the embassy on a Sunday, so there were no traffic jams. My friends drove me straight to Chaiyaphum in the northeast. They had planned everything. They had sandwiches and extra petrol. We arrived in Chaiyaphum at night, and one of our friends there took me in. He was wonderful. He had been a minister in the Prem Cabinet before and was a local MP. He said, "You can't stay in town. You are too well-known. I'll take you to my factory upcountry, but you can't stay there long. You must cross to Laos tomorrow." We got to the factory at midnight. Since the next day was Siamese All-Souls' Day, the border was closed. There was no way of crossing, and at night, they shoot. But the local headman went to talk to the village headman in nearby Udornthani. He said, "People sometimes cross to buy cheap cigarettes or cheap liquor to smuggle back in. Just dress like a fisherman. It will cost you one hundred baht to cross." We decided to try it.

We left for the border at four o'clock in the morning. We pretended the car was stalled and loitered by the roadside until the afternoon. Then, I crossed by boat to Laos by myself, with my passport, one bag of chocolates, and one bottle of water. By the time we had negotiated everything, they realized I was somebody important—not a fisherman—and charged two thousand baht. I had left the embassy at three o'clock in the afternoon on Sunday. Twenty-four hours later, I was in Laos.

Strangely enough, a Laotian chap spotted me because he had seen me on television. He saw my bag. It said "S. Sivaraksa" on it. He took me to a friend, a government minister in charge of the Institute of Social Science, a partner of our Santi Pracha Dhamma Institute in Bangkok. When my friend saw me, he said, "Ajahn Sulak, Laos is not safe for you because the Thai coup leaders and our prime minister Kraisorn Promviharn are friends. Laos has no rule of law. They can arrest you and send you back. We have to get you out of Laos as soon as we can." I had thought I was escaping to freedom!

Luckily, I had many friends. They loaned me money to escape to Sweden, since I didn't need a visa to go there. Only Aeroflot flies to Sweden without stopping in Bangkok, but the flight was completely booked. It was October, the opening of the new term, and a lot of Lao students were returning to Moscow. With the help of friends and a little bit of bribery, I managed to get a one-way ticket on Aeroflot. It was the most expensive first-class ticket, and I had to pay with American dollars at full price. We also had to bribe immigration in order to get me out. We even had to pay the Aeroflot captain not to list my name on the passenger list. It turned out our first stop would be Rangoon, and the Burmese insisted that every passenger must get off. Everyone deplaned except me, since I was listed as a crew member. I could have been detained because I had denounced the Thai junta for collaborating with the Burmese junta, SLORC. I was also helping the Burmese students on the border. Luckily, everything was quiet for the rest of the flight. We spent a few hours in Moscow, and then I flew to Stockholm. I was free at last.

In exile

My passport was to expire in February, but the Thai Embassy in Sweden would not renew it for me. I continued on to London. Amnesty International invited me to England to give lectures at the School of Oriental and African Studies, London, and at Cambridge and Hull Universities. As earlier, they considered me a prisoner of conscience. Fortunately, the embassy in London renewed my passport. I traveled to Germany, France, and Ireland. I even went to the Nobel Peace Prize ceremony for Aung San Suu Kyi in Norway. In my lecture at Thammasat in September, I had predicted she would receive the Nobel Prize. Her chances of winning had been considered quite remote, since the prize had recently gone to the Dalai Lama, another Asian Buddhist. When they announced she had won, a journalist from Berlin called me and asked, "How did you know, Mr. Sulak?" I joked with her that I wasn't a Buddhist for nothing. I had some foreknowledge. At the ceremony in Norway, the Burmese invited me to have my photograph taken with them. All the young ladies were in their national costume. They said, "You are one of us." I felt very good to be welcomed by the Burmese.

I was in Europe for two months while my American friends tried to help me. At this time, Parallax Press was completing my book *Seeds of Peace*. When I landed in San Francisco in February 1992, they presented me with the first copy. I gave a lecture in the Bay Area that was broadcast on radio and television and carried in various magazines. My wife joined me, first in Honolulu, then on to Seattle and Vancouver. Afterwards, I was a keynote speaker at the West Coast meeting of Amnesty International. Over five hundred people came. From there we went to Los Angeles to meet with the Thai community. I gave a lecture on the one-year anniversary of the coup d'état, and the Thai newspaper reported it. After Los Angeles, my wife returned home to look after the business and take care of our children. I stayed in North America for six months. I worked my way across the country, traveling to every U.S. university that offered Buddhist and Southeast Asian Studies. After visiting the new Thai Studies Department at Arizona State University, I went on to the University of Chicago, Northern Illinois University, University of

Iowa, University of Wisconsin, University of Michigan, and Windsor University in Canada.

I spoke with the Thai students at every university I visited. I realized that they knew very little about American society. They didn't know about the new movements—the aspirations of the Native Americans, African Americans, or the Greens. I told them they must be aware of what is happening in the U.S. They should not study only their academic disciplines and miss the opportunity to learn about the strengths and weaknesses of the U.S. They would risk going back home thinking they knew America. Of course, what they knew would be based only on the mass media and their own counterparts in the ivory tower—middle-class Americans. This knowledge is superficial and deceptive. If they remained unaware of the issues of social justice, democratic rights, and human rights, they would return home and end up serving the dictatorial regime. Their education would bring them only social mobility. As an old Chinese sage said, "The more one studies, the less one becomes useful to one's country and Mother Earth."

The Thai students also knew very little about what was happening in their own country. Some of them read a Thai newspaper, but some didn't even do that. I told them that our country was getting much worse off, that the environment was being destroyed in an alarming way. They must find a way to relate meaningfully to the issues in their own country.

The Sixtieth Anniversary of Thai Democracy

Everywhere I went to speak, many students resented what I said, but others asked what they could do. It was 1992, the sixtieth anniversary of democracy in Siam. One year earlier, I had begun a project in Siam called "The Sixtieth Anniversary of Thai Democracy" to alert people to the state of our democracy and to remind them that we still had to work for real democracy with the NPKC now in control. When I started the project, Pridi's widow, Lady Phoonsuk, was the honorary chair, and I was chair of the working committee. We planned to have seminars in colleges and universities throughout Siam with the collaboration of the Social Science Association. Many NGOs became involved in the anniversary.

I also saw a need to bring spiritual depth to Thai democracy. I felt that we must link it with Buddhism. One month before our democracy began, on the full moon in May 1932, Buddhadasa Bhikkhu had started the forest monastery Suan Mokkh, the "Garden of Liberation." His purpose was to revive Buddhism and return to the original teachings of the Buddha. He wanted to initiate a "Dhammic" socialism, not the socialism of the Soviet Union or China but a socialism of real democracy, fraternity, equality, and liberty, like the Sangha the Buddha had founded. Our democracy since 1932 has been in imitation of the West, and we never looked for answers in our own Buddhist culture, so I thought our sixtieth anniversary of democracy should be linked with the sixtieth anniversary of Suan Mokkh. Since I could not be home for the anniversary, I suggested to the students that we have a celebration in America. They agreed. It was set for the last week of May at Wat Buddhadhamma in Hinsdale, near Chicago.

Bloody May of 1992

During this month we had a dreadful crisis in Bangkok. General Suchinda had installed himself as prime minister, proving himself to be a dishonest, ambitious man. Ex-MP Mr. Chalad Worachat began a public fast to demand a democratically elected prime minister. I communicated with our people there to support and encourage him. It started peacefully. Then Mr. Chamlong Srimuang, former governor of Bangkok and a more well-known figure, became involved. A big demonstration was organized very peacefully by many of our people. But on May 17, the military brought in outside agitators to throw bricks and bottles, giving them an excuse to start killing peaceful demonstrators. The killing lasted for four days. Finally, the king intervened and the killing ceased, but hundreds of people had died or vanished, and many more were badly treated. It was just like the massacre of October 6, 1976.

I was in Canada. I arrived after Mr. Chalad had started fasting, and my Quaker friends there told the media that something bloody might take place in Siam. They asked if anyone wanted to interview me, a well-known man involved in this nonviolent struggle. Nobody was interested, but when the violent event took place, they all called. I was on television in Canada and on the radio in America. I was quoted in the Canadian newspapers, in *The New York Times*, the *Boston Globe*, and in the *Independent* in London.

As a result of this crisis in Siam, all the students I spoke to became interested in our meeting in Chicago. They came from Ann Arbor, Cambridge, Ithaca, and from as far away as Los Angeles, San Francisco, Seattle, and Washington, D.C. Over three hundred people came—not only Thais, but Americans and Canadians. Alan Senauke, director of the Buddhist Peace Fellowship, came from Berkeley, and our Quaker friends came from L.A. and New England. We came together to see what we could do. I wanted to link the Thais abroad with the Burmese, Tibetans, and others who had been oppressed by dictators and had to confront suffering. Although the Thai students were far away from home, they could also learn about the suffering of people here in America. I told the students to visit the slums to have a look and share with the people suffering there. Through dialogue with each other, we know we are all fellow sufferers in *samsara*. This is how we can overcome suffering.

Around this time, I met a man somewhere near Chicago who predicted my future back home. He was half white, half Native American. He brought his feathered hat and put it on me. He was quite serious. He smoked the ceremonial pipe with me and asked the Almighty to help. Then he said, "You won't go to prison. The smoke is telling me." It didn't matter whether or not I believed in the smoke. When you are depressed and see people showing that they care about you sincerely by including you in their ceremonies, it creates mutual trust and support.

After my stay in North America, I traveled between Germany, Japan, Italy, and France, giving lectures and attending conferences. In France I found out that a Canadian organization had decided to sponsor all the leading Nobel Peace Prize laureates to travel to Burma to support Aung San Suu Kyi. But they weren't allowed in by the Burmese, so it was changed to Siam. Unfortunately, the Thai government would not allow His Holiness the Dalai Lama to come. I had been fighting for His Holiness for so long. I told my host in Paris, who happened to be president of the France-Burma Association, "We supposedly have a democratic government. Why don't you try to get them to change their minds?" He said they had already talked to the prime minister. It was not possible. I said, "Don't give up. Write an open letter and send it to the *Bangkok Post*. Publish it openly to pressure the Thai government. Say that they very kindly invited the Nobel laureates to come to Siam because the Burmese did not want them. Why would they bar His Holiness from visiting a Buddhist country? Are they under the protectorate of the Chinese? Put it in a polite way." I had a copy of the letter sent to Mr. Dhamrong Padamapas, head of my production company and honorary secretary of the Thai-Tibetan Study Group. It was published in the *Bangkok Post*. I think the king must have read it. His Holiness was invited.

Returning home to trial

There was a rumor that I could now return home. Mr. Anand Panyarachun had resumed his second premiership after the resignation of Suchinda in May 1992. He said it would be better to have me criticize the Thai government inside the country than from abroad. It was a false alarm, though, since the public prosecutor would not follow his orders. The civil service listens only to the military, and, since Mr. Anand was running an interim government, the public prosecutor knew that within two months Anand would be gone, and the military would remain. Many people in the army didn't like me because I denounced them and criticized their corruption, and the public prosecutor didn't want to step on their toes.

Mr. Chuan Leekpai was the next prime minister. I had known him since he first became an MP in the 1960s. In fact, I had proposed to the Fredrich Naumann Stiftung, a German foundation, that he be invited for a study tour in England and Germany in 1971. Mr. Chuan said I could come home, that he would clear my passage from the airport, and that I could be prosecuted straightaway. I arrived back in Siam in December 1992, and they allowed me free on bail. I tried to argue with Mr. Chuan to withdraw my case as they had the last time, since it was not good for the government. But he was famous for assuring that things are done according to the procedures. Even though many people sent petitions to the king, Chuan, being a weak man, wouldn't do anything. My friends in the legal profession predicted that in a case of lèse-majesté, there was a ninety-nine-percent chance

I'd end up in jail, and that my imprisonment would last at least six years.

I came home for the trial, although I wasn't quite sure whether I'd stay home for good. Ryukoku University in Kyoto, through Mr. Yoshiyuki Tsurumi and Mr. Higashi Nakamura, invited me as a research scholar for six months, and I felt I had to honor their request. The court was very kind and allowed me to go. But they added, "You must come back to appear in court every month or two." It was very costly to keep flying back. Some of the Protestant churches in Germany raised money to help me pay my legal fees. Some of my Thai friends also helped me by raising money, so I had no financial difficulties.

My case was quite unusual. Many monks came to court, and it was full of yellow robes. This had never happened before, since monks are not supposed to concern themselves with political affairs. We had much international attention. This time the court was open, so the International Commission for Jurists sent their observer, and Amnesty International kept a close watch. Perhaps because the court wanted to show they had become more liberal and truly cared for justice, they allowed me to make a personal closing statement. Legally, I had always been entitled to one, but it had not been allowed for the last thirty years. I asked my lawyer to request it, and he said, "No, it's never been allowed." I replied, "Try anyway. They can only say no." So we did, and they allowed it. The president of the criminal court himself came to listen with care to my statement. In fact, the final judgment quoted many passages from my closing remarks. (See Appendix Four.)

Several witnesses had much influence on the court. One was my own witness, Dr. Pridi Kasemsap, former rector of Thammasat University, dean of the Faculty of Law, and a former judge. He agreed that I had tried to argue that in a civilized country people must have free speech. He also agreed with me that crawling is certainly a symbol of barbarism. This was in reference to one of the contending passages from my speech. I had quoted King Chulalongkorn's 1873 prohibition against crawling before the king, in which he said that crawling is a symbol of oppression and barbarism. I argued that crawling came back in 1957 with the dictator Sarit Thanarat. Dr. Pridi added that the judges should decide my case strictly by rule of law and not due to politics or outside pressure.

Two of the prosecutor's witnesses also helped my case. One was Mr. Sawet Thanapradit, a ninety-year-old man and an expert on the royal court. He said he was too old to go to court, so they examined him at his own home. He gave evidence in my favor, saying, "Mr. Sulak is a very well-known scholar. He has written many books, and I have read them with care. He knows all about court etiquette. He knows the royal language. I've known him for thirty years. Princess Jongjit, Prince Dhani—these leading members of royalty were very close to Mr. Sulak. He simply could not defame the king." A second, Mr. Dhongthong Chandrarangsu, although he was not even very friendly with me and felt that I used impolite language concerning royalty, testified that General Suchinda would do anything to beat his opponent. My lawyer tried to argue that General Suchinda might have altered the tapes of my lecture. He certainly hadn't listened to them even though he lied to the court that he had.

These two witnesses were very strong. A third witness, also for the prosecution, took three or four months to be tracked down by the police. He was a nobody. He claimed to have heard my lecture, but he couldn't even describe the place where I had given it. I recalled in my closing remarks the regicide case of 1946 when the judges relied

In front of the courthouse during the trial

Monks and laypeople offer their support

on false witnesses. That was fifty years ago, and the police had still not changed. Fortunately, the judges have changed, and when judgment of the court came, I was acquitted. Even more, I was praised for defending democracy, defending the monarchy, and alerting students to the dangers of consumerism. This was a first in Thai legal history. The judgment was quoted in the law report of Thammasat University. I hope my case has set a new trend.

To top it off, the new public prosecutor did not appeal. He had the right to appeal within one month, and he even extended the period of appeal for another month. But in the end, he was very brave and did not appeal. Normally, the case would have gone through two more courts. It could have lasted at least three more years. Of course, there had also been international pressure. The International Commission for Jurists wrote a nice letter to him asking him not to appeal and praising the judgment. Legally, my case ended on June 26, 1995.

On December 8, 1995, I received the Right Livelihood Award in the Swedish Parliament. The award committee cited the judgment from my recent acquittal in which the court stated, "He warned the students not to live a luxurious, consumer lifestyle, not to worship being rich, not to admire people in power, and to be concerned about justice and righteousness." The Right Livelihood Award is widely considered the alternative Nobel Prize (an award I'd been twice nominated for but didn't win). I felt very privileged to receive the Right Livelihood Award on the same day the Japanese Buddhists celebrate the Buddha's enlightenment. In fact, "right livelihood" is itself a Buddhist term meaning a livelihood that is nonexploitative to oneself or others. A group of four Buddhist monks chanted in Pali at the ceremony—probably the first time there was Buddhist chanting in any Western parliament.

Alternatives to Consumerism

This award reflects my recent concern for developing an alternative to consumerism—the new, demonic religion. It reduces life to only one purpose—to acquire money in order to consume, to put it very crudely. This new religion is very powerful. Even the churches and temples are building more and larger buildings, and the monks are leading a more luxurious lifestyle. The media teaches people to be aggressive, offering violence, crime, and sex. People learn to look down on their own family and cultural heritage. We are urged to consume more, and this leads to the destruction of the environment.

My main work has always involved alternative development because I believe the present model of development is wrong. The rich get richer, the poor get poorer, and the rich do not even become happier. I have come to see that alternative development will not work unless we tackle this core of consumerism. Of course, we cannot match their promoters with money or technology. But they don't have spiritual depth. That's why I created a project on Buddhist, Christian, and Muslim alternatives to consumerism. I feel that these three leading world religions should collaborate to wrestle with this issue.

I planned the Alternatives to Consumerism project ten years ago with Chandra Muzaffar, Uthai Dulyakasem Chaiwat Satha-anand, David Chappell, and George Willoughby. It was not funded back then, but just like anything I start, I kept pushing for it all these years. A small Swiss and French group called Foundation for the Progress of Humanity agreed to support us as part of their commitment to environmental balance and social justice. The Catholic Comité Contre la Famine et pour le Développement, also supports us, and we have the collaboration of quite a number of friends from the three religious traditions. The project tells the stories of simple, self-reliant, spiritual, and harmonious lifestyles that confront consumerism.

We bring people together in Asia, Europe, and America. It is a more or less practical forum to meet people. In 1997 we held a big "Alternatives to Consumerism" conference. We invited all kinds of people—Native, African, and European Americans; Europeans; Africans; and Asians. The whole gathering was about spiritual reflections. We need spiritual force for social justice and environmental balance. There are many people around the world seeking something beyond the usual development model or the usual intellectual approach. We are seeking something that reaches deep down into our common roots. We all need the earth, the water, the clouds, the sun. If our organizations can learn something spiritual, we will cultivate more love and less hatred. In fact, I think the world should concentrate on peace and the spiritual dimension of life throughout the next century. Although we have some differences, we can work with each other to do something for the benefit of all beings.

We have also been working on alternative media for the past few years, since the mainstream press and media promote violence, greed, and lust. Our friends Chee and Sok Nai from Malaysia are producing alternative images. The so-called primitive people in India; Christian communities such as L'Arche in France; and the Muslim Baan Krua in Bangkok and Luang Pho Nan in Northeast Siam are all struggling within their own religious traditions against consumerism, although they don't call it that. We hope to televise some of these struggles.

The Spirit in Education Movement (SEM)

At home in Siam I recently began the SEM. The idea for SEM arose out of the need to counter a mainstream education that promotes a compartmentalized, "head" learning. Education has become a means to a certificate or a job. It doesn't matter whether that job is a right livelihood or a wrong one. The only thing that matters is how much money you make. Education has lost its ethical dimension. SEM is based on Buddhist principles, encouraging teachers and students to learn from each other and the environment. We work to develop and strengthen meditation practices and artistic creativity. We must all find our inner strength and learn who we are in order to cultivate inner peace. Education, for us, is building friendships and having time for more than intellectual pursuits.

We try to integrate alternative politics and alternatives to consumerism into our courses. Our first course, Alternative Development from a Buddhist Perspective, ran for three weeks. It was open to everyone and was very successful. We had professors from Canada, Germany, and India, and *maechi* (nuns) and monks with almost no education. They all loved it. We do not limit ourselves to Thais and Buddhists. We have Quakers, Mennonites, and Maryknoll priests. We run courses for Cambodians, Sri Lankans, and Bangladeshis. We recently trained thirty Baptists from Burma. Most of our SEM courses are very small. They are intensive and allow deeper discussion. The subjects are all interrelated and non-compartmentalized. We do not address the usual issues taken up by academic institutions. Our courses always include meditation practice. We try to link the heart and the head.

We are developing dialogues with existing educational institutions and alternative thinkers and educators who believe in inner spirit and environmental balance. Some of these have included The Naropa Institute in America, Schumacher College in England, and the Institute of Total Revolution in India. I often teach at these places, and their teachers and students come to us. We hope to link with institutes in Japan and Taiwan. Mainstream educational institutions are also linking with us. They have asked us to teach courses for them. Some business groups have asked us to run courses on conflict resolution because they feel they lose too much time on infighting.

As part of our work, we have revived the *Pajarayasara* magazine started by Bibhob Dhongchai over twenty years ago. He started it to give voice to new ideas in education, but we focus now not only on alternative education but alternative economics, politics, and environmental issues. We have a related project focusing on alternative politics. The prevailing politics promotes hatred and violence. Most political regimes around the world, especially in Asia, are a heritage of the colonial past. I'm looking for alternatives. We Buddhists are working with like-minded people from different cultures and religions. Luckily, there are a lot of people thinking in these terms— Maurice Ash in England, Chandra Muzzafar in Malaysia, Helena Norberg-Hodge in Ladakh, Abdulrahman Wahid of Indonesia, Bishop Labayan and Walden Bello from the Philippines, and Satish Kumar of India, now living in England.

Lately we have been fighting the gas pipeline coming from Burma into my country. As the local people become aware, they want to fight for their own safety. Then, they want to fight to preserve the forest for their children and grandchildren. Finally, they realize that they are fighting not only for the local people in Kanchanaburi but for the entire country, the region, and even the world. They are concerned about the ethnic Burmese who have been deprived of basic human rights and forced to work without pay, for the villages that have been uprooted, and for child laborers. It's a fight for human dignity all over the world.

I only play a small part because ultimately people have to empower themselves. Perhaps I can help them by reminding them not to hate the oppressors. I speak with fellow Christians and Muslims, as well as Buddhists. I don't have the ability or network to destroy consumerism, globalization, the World Bank, the World Trade Organization, or the International Monetary Fund. But if these things don't change to serve the people, they will destroy themselves. They have no moral legitimacy but only greed to drive them, and this will be their downfall. Meanwhile, I hope that the small people, with alternatives, can survive.

CHAPTER **21** | *Reflections*

These memoirs are being published for my sixty-fifth birthday. Sixty-five is old by Asian standards, where you're an old man by the age of sixty. The average life expectancy in Siam is fifty-seven for men. I feel I have lived eight surplus years already.

When I reflect on my life and my achievements, I see that I have managed to make many good friends. The Buddha said, "Good friends are the whole of the holy life." Good friends become your other self. They help you, encourage you, and are critical of you. For me, encountering new people and strengthening old friendships has been a wonderful part of life. I have many good friends who, like me, are critical of the mainstream, especially friends in the West. More people misunderstand me in my own country because I am a challenge to them, but I am gaining more Thai friends among the younger people.

Some people might ask if I am not wasting my time attending so many meetings and talking with so many people. We waste a lot of fuel flying to and from conferences. We eat junk food. Sometimes we use too much paper, wasting the trees. But I want to expand my work to include more people who think alternatively. We must come together to speak out. The more you talk with people in power, the more chance that they will eventually listen. Eventually they will be fair. We can make good friends and listen to each other. When I go to talk with the Archbishop of Canterbury or the president of the World Bank, I don't think they can change things overnight. But it is always good to talk. It is a sign that they are ready to listen. That kind of exchange is essential. Sometimes you can change things for the better. That is why I develop and maintain my international connections.

One of my contributions to this process is that I can bring the best from the various traditions. I recognize that my people are not really just the Thais. My ancestors came from China. We are in debt to the Indians and to the Sri Lankans for our Buddhism. I try to look profoundly into my own cultures with all their positive and negative elements and to bring them into the modern world. My aspiration is to help my people discover their roots—our spiritual and cultural heritage. Our most fundamental starting place for this project is the breath. There is no denying that this is one thing we all share. If we can begin here, many beautiful things will grow. With breathing, I feel we can even overcome consumerism. "I breathe therefore I am" means that everyone is important, not only human beings but animals, trees, rivers, the land.

In the Buddhist tradition, development toward happiness is an important aspect. We develop towards bringing our body and mind into harmony with our heart, with our environment, with society. This is not development at the expense of the environment or of the poor. It means development in a useful fashion. This past July we had an economic crisis, and the value of our currency dropped drastically. Many people were unhappy. They didn't realize it is all an hallucination. Even the dollar might become scratch paper within a few decades. So why worry? Our ancestors existed on fish, rice, water, the fields, and the trees. These are our roots. We should look to the poor, to the people who are self-reliant. Why concentrate on money?

The West cut off its roots the year that Columbus claimed to have discovered America. Of course, people had already been there for hundreds of years, living with their own local wisdom. But when the West claimed superiority, they began to look forward without ever looking back. I am very critical of the mainstream Western approach—technology, capitalism, consumerism. Even so, I learned a great deal from my Western education. I am indebted to writers of Western literature for their social commitment and analysis of society. My tradition alone would have made me very conservative, even as an engaged Buddhist. English writers really helped me to become concerned about the poor. While our Buddhist roots are very important, these roots must spring into contemporary society. In much of our forest tradition in this country, there are wonderful monks. However, they have no idea about social justice. They don't know that the forests are being destroyed. I think the West has that awareness of social justice.

But ultimately, for me, Buddhism has always come first. We

Buddhists must not only become aware of unjust social structures. We must try to eliminate or overcome them with awareness and non-violence. We must be mindful. We must see suffering with understanding, and with that understanding, perhaps we can be skillful in doing something. Just this past New Year's Eve several of us were on our way to a party at my in-laws' house. On the way, the car spun out of control and went straight into a ditch. Fortunately, no one was hurt. As we were waiting for a truck to come haul our car out, a neighbor came out of her house and told us this is called "death corner." The tow truck driver was amazed that no one was hurt and wanted to know if I had a special amulet. I said, "Yes, I have the Buddha. The Buddha kept me alive. If you know the Buddha, you have mindfulness, you have peace." This is the message I am always sharing with others. I guess it's not time for me to stop yet.

Appendices

Siamese Calendar

The Siamese calendar was originally based on the lunar system, the New Year being the first waxing moon of the fifth month (around the end of March to early April). Later, Siam adopted the Indian sun-based system, which designated Songkran as the New Year festival—that is, April 13 was New Year's Eve, the sun rests for one day on April 14, and the New Year begins on April 15. This was called the Chula Saka Era, which is 1,181 years after the Buddhist Era (BE).

When we adopted the Western calendar around one hundred years ago, giving Siamese names to January, February, etc., King Chulaongkorn declared April 1 to be the New Year, with the Bangkok Era dating from 1782, the year the city was founded. His son, Rama VI, discontinued using the Bangkok Era.

In 1939, the government officially changed our New Year to begin on January 1. They claimed that we had used the first waxing moon of the first month to be our New Year before it was changed to the fifth month to coincide with the Songkran Festival. The beginning of the lunar first month approximates the first of January.

Normally, our Buddhist-Era calendar is reckoned to begin in 543 BC of the Christian era, although the Singhalese and Burmese regard it as 544. Western scholars differ greatly over this issue. I was born on March 27, 1933, or BE 2476. Officially, my birthday is in BE 2475 as it falls after April 1. However, since I was born on the second day of the waxing moon of the fifth month, I embrace the New Year by our lunar calendar, and the year 2476. Hence, I was born in the year of the rooster, not the year of the monkey.

‖ *Siamese Government*

After Ayuthaya ceased to be the capital of Siam, a new capital was established in Thonburi, across the river from Bangkok. The king of Thonburi reigned from 1767 to 1782, after which the capital was moved to Bangkok and the Chakri Dynasty was established. The nine reigns of the Chakri Dynasty are as follows:

1782 – 1809	Rama I (Phra Buddhayotfa)
1809 – 1824	Rama II (Phra Buddhaloetla)
1824 – 1851	Rama III (Phra Nangklao)
1851 – 1868	Rama IV (Mongkut)
1868 – 1910	Rama V (Chulalongkorn)
1910 – 1925	Rama VI (Vajiravudh)
1925 – 1935	Rama VII (Prajadhipok)
1935 – 1946	Rama VIII (Ananda Mahidol)
from 1946	Rama IX (Bhumiphol Adulyadej)

Up until 1932, Siam was ruled by an absolute monarchy. From June 24 of that year until the present, the government has been a constitutional monarchy. The prime ministers since 1932 are listed below. Most of these prime ministers have had several administrations, but these are not noted.

1932 – 1933	Phya Manopakonnitithada (Kon Hutasing)
1933 – 1938	Phya Phahonphonphayuhasena (Phot Phahonyothin)
1938 – 1944	Luang Pibunsongkram (Plaek Pibunsongkram)
1944 – 1945	Khuang Aphaiwong
1945	Thawi Bunyaket
1945 – 1946	Seni Pramoj

1946	Khuang Aphaiwong
1946	Pridi Banomyong
1946 – 1947	Luang Thamrongnawasawat (Thawan Thamrongnawasawat)
1947 – 1948	Khuang Aphaiwong
1948 – 1957	Plaek Pibunsongkram
1957	Phot Sarasin
1958	Thanom Kittikachorn
1959 – 1963	Sarit Thanarat
1963 – 1973	Thanom Kittikachorn
1973 – 1975	Sanya Dharmasakti
1975	Seni Pramoj
1975 – 1976	Kukrit Pramoj
1976	Seni Pramoj
1976 – 1977	Thanin Kraivichien
1977 – 1980	Kriengsak Chomanand
1980 – 1988	Prem Tinsulanonda
1988 – 1991	Chatichai Choonhavan
1991 – 1992	Anand Panyarachun
1992	Suchinda Kraprayoon
1992	Anand Panyarachun
1992 – 1995	Chuan Leekpai
1995 – 1996	Barnharn Silpa-archa
1996 – 1997	Chavilit Yongchaiyut
1997 –	Chuan Leekpai

The pioneer for democracy in Siam was Mr. Pridi Banomyong, but his reform movement to introduce social welfare services for all was considered too radical, and he was eventually forced into exile. Field Marshal Pibunsongkram, who was more dictatorial than democratic, took over power. It was under Pibun in 1939 that the name of our country was changed from Siam to Thailand, in imitation of Deutschland. Pibun admired Hitler, and he claimed that the Thai were a superior race. He demanded that other ethnic people in the kingdom must conform to the Thai language and culture. He prohibited the wearing of our national dress and the chewing of betel nut, and instead forced people to follow Western fashions. I have steadfastly refused to follow his decree both in using the official name of the country and in wearing Western dress while in Siam.

With Pridi Banomyong

||| *Regression of Democracy in Siam*

Speech delivered at Thammasat University, August 1991

Why did the 1991 coup in the Soviet Union fail in less than sixty hours while the February 1991 Thai coup shows no sign of ending? One important difference is that we Thais are not interested in democracy.

In 1973, hundreds of thousands of Thais overthrew the military regime. Like the Soviet people, they felt angry and frustrated with tyranny. This time, however, we did not take to the streets because, since 1973, the military has used every means possible to undermine the people's movement. They have used the schools, universities, and mass media. Those who have resisted—leaders of the farmers' movements and labor unions—have been arrested and even killed. The movement for democracy was destroyed with the bloody coup of October 1976, and the movement is still dormant today. If the student and people's movements are not revitalized, the current National Peace Keeping Council (NPKC) will remain in power for many years.

Since the first coup in 1947, the military in Siam has not had one new idea. Unfortunately, the civilians are not much better. Deep down they seem to admire those in power, kowtowing as servants to the military. I wish I could name even one person who is respectable and worthy of admiration, but I cannot.

In 1957, Field Marshal Sarit Thanarat, the worst tyrant we've ever had, abolished the constitution and dissolved the Parliament. He arrested and killed almost all the progressives, including intellectuals, journalists, and opposition politicians. Despite this, people still call him a great man. Why? Because we Thais have been completely brainwashed by our educational system to respect dictators and admire those in power, even if they are cruel and evil. As long as we retain this mentality, there is no hope for democracy in Siam.

The NPKC made five declarations regarding the need for their coup. First, they accused the former government of corruption. This is true. Several ministers are commonly known to have gained inordinate amounts of wealth. But is the NPKC free of guilt? They are certainly more clever, because they do not divulge much to the public. But how much profit did they make on arms deals with China and other countries? Just before the coup, its leaders went to Burma. Did they go there to learn how to carry out a coup? What did they receive there? The NPKC decide their own salaries. How much do they make a month? What are they doing to deserve it? These questions are never asked.

Second, the NPKC announced that the elected politicians abused their power over the civil servants. But the Secretary of the NPKC is also the Minister of the Interior. Although he launched a program to teach democracy to the people, he simultaneously abolished the system of local elections. Is this not a case of a politician abusing power over the civil servants? This kind of act destroys the very basis for democracy in our society.

Third, the NPKC accused the former government of being a parliamentary dictatorship. Is the NPKC *not* a dictatorship? The senators appointed by the NPKC are worse than dictators; they are serving the dictators. In the last administration, although many MPs were involved in vote-buying scandals, some did have dignity. This cannot be said of any present senators.

Fourth, the NPKC accused the former administration of failing to look into the plot against the queen. However, six months have already passed, and what has the NPKC done to solve this case?

Fifth, the NPKC declared that they needed to take one step backwards in order to go ten steps forward for democracy. I was willing to accept this reasoning and give the NPKC a chance, knowing that in the last Parliament there was very little chance for real democracy. The former Prime Minister himself admitted that his last election campaign had cost him the most ever, and that the next campaign would have cost him more. Clearly, only the richest politicians can win an election, but if the NPKC is serious about this point, they must have something to show us after six months of rule. They have done nothing because they are preparing to use one of their own people to be the next Prime Minister and to control a political party from behind the scenes. For six months, the NPKC has not tackled any issues of social justice, despite all the power they wield.

What should a good government do? We always mention three areas: nation, religion, and king. Before the 1957 coup, we also used to mention the constitution, but Field Marshal Sarit removed it when he destroyed the Parliament. So, as a symbolic action, when we appeal for democracy, we must call for all four. And the constitution must not be drafted by the sycophants of dictators, because it would serve only the dictators and the military.

The constitution is a supreme set of laws that will bring equality to the people. It must state clearly that any declarations by ruling coups are invalid and unenforceable as laws. It is unfortunate that the legal and judicial institutions in this country accept these declarations as law based on a German legal theory that whoever controls state power has authority to issue laws. The traditional Thai system of justice required all laws to be sanctioned by the king and administered and enforced by the government, but the declarations by this or any coup have never gone through this traditional process. Therefore, the leaders of every coup, and especially the last one, should be accused of lèse-majesté. But no one has arrested them.

In a new constitution, freedom, equality, and fraternity must be guaranteed. We always forget that our present laws are unjust because they benefit only the rich. The whole process of justice in our country is shaky; the police, the public prosecutors, and the judges are not upright and are easily influenced. These are the issues of equality and equity that urgently need to be addressed. It is not easy, but it can be done if the political will is there. Unfortunately, we have not had the will.

A constitution is the core of democracy and must be respected. To have a real constitution, the whole educational system must be democratic, which means the headmasters must be willing to listen to the teachers, and the teachers must be willing to listen to the students, and vice versa. We do not need to send soldiers to the villages to teach them democracy. The Thai people are already democratic, but they are taught to be afraid of the authorities, military dictators, and local mafia. We must overcome this fear so that people will say what they think.

We must also abolish this law of lèse-majesté. While the monarchies in most of Europe survived by adapting themselves to change and accepting criticism, the German and Russian monarchs were inflexible and unable to tolerate criticism, and they collapsed. We have to accept that the king, the prince, and the princesses are ordinary people. I believe that the king does not want false respect and that he is open to honest criticism. The monarchy is necessary as the center of unity in the country. Its status must remain above politics and economics. It must be above manipulation by politicians, businessmen, and multinational corporations. We must somehow help the monarchy to exist meaningfully in contemporary Thai society. If the NPKC and the government are truly loyal to the king, they should be helping to prepare for the succession of the current king in an orderly way.

Third, the institution of Buddhism has been weakened and corrupted in present-day society. This can be traced to the ecclesiastic law of 1963, issued by Field Marshal Sarit, who wanted to control the monks under his dictatorial system. Those monks who are in the Council of Elders (the governing body of the monkhood) are very old and without any political or social awareness.

Recently, the junta of Burma (SLORC), in cooperation with the Thai military, tried to bestow an award of the highest honor on the Supreme Patriarch of Siam and to give secondary honors to the rest of the Council of Elders. Originally, SLORC wanted to invite the monks to receive the awards in Rangoon, but some people protested their visit because it would legitimize SLORC's cruelty both to their monks and their own citizens. Burmese monks, people, and students are all disgusted with SLORC. The monks in Mandalay even refuse to accept alms from military families! But SLORC and the NPKC are working together in logging, fishing, and arms trading. When General Chavilit Yongchaiyut was Supreme Commander of the Army, he sent Burmese student refugees back into the hands of the Saw Maung government in exchange for logging concessions in Burma. And before the February coup, the leader of the NPKC shamelessly went to Burma to visit SLORC. Every country in the world, with the exceptions of China, Japan, Siam, and some other ASEAN countries, has condemned SLORC for killing its own people. But China, Japan, and Siam want to cooperate with SLORC for deals that will harm the environment. Cutting trees in Burma will inevitably adversely affect Siam. Clearly, the NPKC intervened to have the awards delivered to the monks in Siam instead of in Burma. Was this an act of loyalty to the religion or merely to advance their own interests?

Another example of the NPKC's lack of sincerity towards religion is their treatment of Phra Prachak. Phra Prachak is a conservationist monk who has tried to protect the forest in Buriram Province. But because the military works with local capitalists to log there, even to build golf courses, Phra Prachak was arrested. These military people say they believe in Buddhism, but they don't understand the Buddha's teachings, and they ignore authentic monks like Buddhadasa.

Fourth, the institution of the nation. The army is a state within the state. They are like termites destroying the house they inhabit. They only know how to carry out coups and kill unarmed people. I ask the good people in the military to see themselves as ordinary people who have to relate with other ordinary people. We need dignity and morals, but we have none. We allow the strong to exploit the weak. We allow parents to sell their own daughters. We allow the poor to sell their labor in Saudi Arabia, Singapore, and California. But our elites ignore these people and their struggle.

Because we lack dignity and morality and neglect our own cultural roots, our society is inundated with consumerism. We have fast foods, Western eating habits, Western dress, condominiums, and golf, all of which oppose our traditional values. We want to be industrialized and powerful, but at the expense of our suffering poor. If the government had morality and courage, all of these problems could be solved. The ministers must be ready to resign if the military opposes them and their policies.

These days Europe is moving in a new direction. Democracy is being taken seriously. The Soviet coup in August failed because it ran against this trend. In democracy, we must pay attention to ordinary people and to everyone's human rights. The Burmese students have taken refuge in Siam because they have been chased and killed in Burma. Aung San Suu Kyi has been under house arrest for two years, but Prime Minister Anand has never said anything on her behalf. I believe that if Prime Minister Anand had been detained for more

than two years, Aung San Suu Kyi would have stood up and demanded his release! We Thai people are just not interested in human rights.
I believe that by the end of this year, Aung San Suu Kyi will receive
the Nobel Peace Prize as she has already been awarded the Prize for
Human Rights by the European Parliament, while we remain a nation
of submissive people without moral courage. We are not in step with
the democratic trend of the Western world. We mold ourselves according to their economic and technological development, destroying our
environment and basic human rights, but we fail to join them in valu-
ing democracy, human rights, animal rights, and environmental rights,
all of which are embodied in the teachings of the Buddha. If we look
at the essence of Buddhism, we can apply it to democracy with self-
respect.

What I have said will be ignored by the NPKC. Though Mr. Anand
may understand, he cannot do much. So my hope is that the young
people and those who suffered on October 6, 1976, will not join the
NPKC or any other military party or even form a new political party
within this rotten system. Instead, we should cultivate political awareness and understanding based on our indigenous culture and fight
for social justice and ecological balance in a nonviolent way. Please
think about what I have said, even if you do not agree. If we consume
less, practice democracy in our lives, learn to respect the poor, uphold
human rights, support the Burmese students and others who are
oppressed, then we will have self-respect, and we can appeal for
democracy. If we do this, the NPKC will not last. But if we are submissive, they may be in power for many years. Long live democracy.

IV | *Closing Statement*
on the Second Case of Lèse-majesté

Criminal Court of Siam, April 3, 1995

Honorable Judges, I am Sulak Sivaraksa, the defendant of the black case number 1901 /2536. I was charged with lèse-majesté and defaming General Suchinda Kraprayoon on August 22, 1991. I would like to make the following statement:

1) The charge against me is political. Politicians have used this kind of political charge to get rid of people they consider opponents since 1947. In Siam, when the military stages a coup to get rid of elected governments, that coup is rebellious and severely destructive to the country, the religion, the monarchy, and the constitution. Suchinda and his colleagues in the NPKC (National Peace Keeping Council) must also be considered rebellious. I would like you to consider my case as part of the process to destroy innocent people who stand up against corruption of military dictators. These dictatorial governments always issue new laws to destroy their opposition whom they could not fight in a democratic way. Before 1947, Phya Mano closed the Parliament and deleted some articles of the constitution. A law was also issued against being a Communist. This law was used to force Mr. Pridi Banomyong, the father of Thai democracy, to leave the country even though he was not a Communist.

Field Marshal Pibunsongkram, the prime minister after the Second World War, used a charge of defaming the U.S. Ambassador and being rebellious against his opposition leader, M. R. Kukrit Pramoj. Field Marshal S. Thanarat, another Military Leader in power from 1957 to the early 1960s, arrested the Venerable Phra Vimaladhamma, the Abbot of Wat Mahadhatu, in 1962 on charges of being a Communist and destabilizing the country. He was put in prison without trial until 1966, after the Field Marshal died. He was released with a statement from the court saying that evidence showed he was completely innocent and unjustly charged. During all the military regimes many intellectuals, journalists, and social activists were put in prison, forced to leave the country, or assassinated. Mr. Krong Chandawong and Mr. Ruom Wongpan, both social activists, were charged with being Communists and sentenced to death. Mr. Kulab Saipradit, a journalist, was forced to leave the country and die in exile.

In the time of General Pao Sriyanon, four ex-ministers, Mr. Chamlong, Mr. Thawin, Mr. Tongin and Mr. Tongplaoy, who each contributed a great deal to society, were shot dead at Bangkhen. Another very important ex-minister and freedom fighter, Mr. Tieng Sirikhan, was also assassinated by government orders. No Thai government has shown any regret for any of these actions. Worse than that, monuments for these generals have been built without any pangs of conscience. In his testimony, Suchinda said that he respected cruel dictators like Field Marshal Sarit Thanarat.

When King Rama VIII was found dead in his royal bedchamber, the government created fake witnesses, and three innocent people were sentenced to death although the case was appealed to the highest Supreme Court. Later on, one of the main witnesses, Mr. Tee Srisuwan, became a monk and confessed that he gave a fake statement that condemned the three victims to death. Mr. Pridi, the main political opponent of the prime minister at the time, was accused of being an instigator of the regicide case and forced to leave the country.

In 1973, Field Marshal Thanom Kittikachorn pressed charges against eleven leaders of the People's Movement that was demanding democracy. The charge was for organizing political meetings of more than five people. Later on, they were charged with being rebels against the government. These charges were the cause of a mass uprising against the military regime which resulted in the exile of three top military leaders and the disbanding of that government.

After this, despite democratically elected governments, the army was still a dictatorial element in the state machinery. This element became more and more active and resulted in the Bloody Coup in 1976. The charge of lèse-majesté was used as a political tool to suppress both students and others involved in the democratic movement. Hundreds were killed and thousands put in jail. In response to this, many students left Bangkok and other big cities to join the Communist movement in the jungle. At the time, the maximum punishment for lèse-majesté was increased to fifteen-years' imprisonment, and many innocent people became victims of this law.

The latest case of lèse-majesté was against a French businessman named Lech Kissielewicz, who was arrested upon stepping off an airplane on December 17, 1994. He said something to defame the king when he was informed a princess was on the same plane. He was out on bail on January 4, 1995, with a 400,000 baht guarantee. Fortunately, on February 15, 1995, the court threw out the case, saying that he had no intention to defame the king. This case is a good sign for me, as I believe that the judges also understand that I had no intention whatsoever of defaming the king.

In my case, I was charged many days after my speech at Thammasat University by General Suchinda, who had tremendous power during that time. He also threatened my life, which is why I left the country in 1991 until the end of the military junta in 1992. Many other politicians and activists had to leave the country at this time. Worse was the disappearance of labor movement leader, Mr. Thanong Po-arn, after saying he would appeal to the International Labor Organization when the NPKC dissolved the Workers Union. His family believes he was assassinated under orders from the military junta.

I mention all these cases because I want to make it clear that my case was one in a chain of political maneuvers where the military junta has used the laws and courts to suppress its innocent political opponents. I did ask the public prosecutor to reinvestigate my case because the investigation by the police under the NPKC supervisor was not fair.

However, this request was not considered because the powerful supreme public prosecutor was appointed by the NPKC. I believe that otherwise it would not have been necessary for my case to burden the court for so long. However, I believe in the justice of the court and am looking to the compassion of the judges. It was clear that witnesses of the prosecution contradicted each other on many details. Both Mr. Sawet Thanapradit, a prosecution witness, and Mr. Sathirapong Wannapok, a defense witness, stated that I would not say anything to defame the king.

2) I want to make it clear that I am loyal to the King and the Royal Family as recognized by prosecution witnesses Mr. Sawet Thanapradit and Mr. Dhongthong Chandrarangsu. I want to add that if I had not coordinated the repair of the library which was the former home of King Rama I, the building would have disappeared. The initial money for repairing the library came from the present King, and it was finished in time to celebrate the bicentenary of Bangkok and the Chakri Dynasty. Moreover, the Crown Princess came to the celebration of the main hall of my local monastery, Wat Thongnopphakun, and I drank tea with her on this occasion.

I organized the funeral of Professor Fua Haripitak, the artist who supervised the conservation of the above-mentioned library, and the Crown Princess attended the funeral as guest of honor and talked to me personally. This was after the charge of lèse-majesté, which suggests she doesn't believe in the charge.

As one of my defense witnesses stated, the Princess Kalyanivadhana donated funds to build a library in Ladakh to commemorate the centenary of the King's father. This again was after the charge, and she was well aware that I had initiated the project. Her secretary sent me a letter on my 60th birthday sending blessings from Her Royal Highness.

Moreover, I was invited to give a public talk at the Government House on the occasion of Her Royal Highness' seventy-second birthday.

This briefly informs you of my consistent loyalty to the Royal Family. On the fiftieth anniversary of the King's reign in 1996, the Supreme Patriarch has accepted my invitation for him to cast 1,000 Buddha images to be installed in a Tibetan monastery in South India. With all this evidence, I hope that the court will recognize my loyalty to the monarchy.

3) I am regarded by the press as an author and thinker. Some call me a leading Siamese intellectual. I would like to let you know that an intellectual must play a prominent role in the field of culture, development, and democracy. An intellectual would not submit to a dictator nor respect a person like Field Marshal Sarit Thanarat or General

Suchinda, no matter how strong they are when in power. He or she must also have a deep empathy for the suffering of the small people. Because of this stand, I have been oppressed by dictators since before 1973 and since 1991. However, I am in a much better position than many other people in this country, especially those who have to sell their daughters as prostitutes, their children as slave laborers. On top of these social ills, the natural environment is deteriorating, the forests are being destroyed, pollution is increasing, and the gap between the rich and poor is widening.

Six decades ago, George Orwell, the famous British author, said that if the U.S.S.R. didn't turn to democracy, the whole empire would collapse because the ruling Communist elite had no legitimacy whatsoever to rule the country, and the small people would win at the end. No one believed him at the time, but now there is no more Soviet Empire.

I also believe that, ultimately, the commoners will win, and the dictators will be destroyed. Even those who claim to be democratic, if they govern without moral legitimacy, will also be finished. Of course, I know that to attack the dictator or the people in power is to bring harm to myself, but I regard it as my duty to encourage the people to see the value of the commoner. I feel that ordinary people should be aware of their own dignity, equality, and self-confidence—the basic elements of democracy. I have never submitted to any authority and have challenged corrupt authority all through my life. Society will fail if people submit to corrupt authority. This is especially true nowadays with multinational corporations intervening in state power and using the consumer culture to intoxicate people. This makes people feel they have no value unless they earn money and buy the unnecessary goods advertised in the media. Our youth is seduced by junk food and alcohol; whisky sales in Siam are the second highest in the world. Even worse is the large part of the national budget spent on armaments. The taxpayers' money should be used for basic health care and mass education.

As an intellectual, I have to criticize the wrong direction of development which worships greed, hatred, and delusion—the root causes of suffering. I have to make known to the people the value of *sila, samadhi,* and *pañña* so that they will fight nonviolently against unjust authority following the Eightfold Path of the Buddha.

Society can survive with dignity and real democracy only when people have the basic freedom to speak, write, and criticize. Since I was charged with lèse-majesté, the intellectual community has expressed concern about how legal procedures in Siam have been abused by corrupt politicians to get rid of anyone who stands in their way. My case and Phra Prachak's case were quoted as examples in a seminar on legal procedures and political maneuvers in July 1994 at the Faculty of Law of Thammasat University.

I have suffered a great deal during the legal proceedings surrounding my court cases. Friends and I have used a lot of energy, time, and money that could be spent on other things. I hope the court will give me justice.

Although the NPKC has been dismantled, there are still people who continue exercising its power to oppress people, using twisted legal procedures. Our neighbors are still exploited and oppressed, be they Burmese refugees or others. Meanwhile, Aung San Suu Kyi is still under house arrest, and SLORC is still recognized by the Thai government without shame or political legitimacy.

I also would like to tell you that the present army commander and General Anusorn Krisanaserani, who pressed charges against me, are still attacking me as if I were an enemy of the army. Actually, I only want to warn the army to be professional in its actions and not to interfere in state matters. Fortunately, these people have not nor could not take over the government. Otherwise, I would have been charged with lèse-majesté again or might have disappeared like the Labor leader.

Even if I am judged innocent, Thai society will not move forward to freedom, equality, and fraternity while the law is abused for the sake of political maneuvers in a context of structural violence. This opens opportunities for the rich and the powerful to oppress and exploit the poor and the powerless. However, if the court declares my freedom from the oppression of the NPKC, it will be one step forward to a legal victory for the ordinary people in this country.

4) In an academic paper by David Streckfuss, University of Wisconsin at Madison, in the U.S., entitled "Kings in the Age of Nations: The Paradox of Lèse-majesté as Political Crime in Thailand," he concluded that:

> "It appears that lèse-majesté will remain a potent political and cultural issue in Thailand for the foreseeable future. This may seem odd in light of the growing middle class, a growing awareness of the importance of the right of free speech, and the gradual spread of the idea of equality. It is ironic, then, to note that throughout the country's modern history, the punishment for lèse-majesté has edged ever upward.
>
> "As a part of a Print Act in the late 1890s, the sentence for the first Thai law of lèse-majesté was limited to not more than three years imprisonment. Although in 1908 it was increased to up to seven years imprisonment, after the 1932 revolution, lèse-majesté as a crime seemed to go into a decline. But with the revision of the criminal code in 1957, in which lèse-majesté became not merely a crime against the reputation of the royalty but a national security offense, and with the revitalization of the monarchy under Sarit Thanarat and successive militarily-dominated governments, the charge has resurfaced to become the epitome of political and cultural subversion. In 1976, the law was revised to make the punishment not less than three and not more than fifteen years. This means that the ever-heightening punishment for lèse-majesté has gone hand-in-hand with the military's ascendancy within Thai politics."

At the end he concluded that, "Although the present King seems to enjoy a great deal of popularity—the lèse-majesté law making this impossible to accurately assess—even ardent monarchists cannot but warily look toward the future and the question of succession."

At present in Siam, ordinary people do not dare criticize the Royal Family or associated offices such as the Bureau of Crown Property and the Bureau of HM Private Property, even though they treat people unjustly. Mr. Sahachai Supmitkrisna was unjustly treated by the two bureaus for more than two decades and has appealed to the King ten times. Every time the King has said he will grant justice. In his most recent appeal, the King's secretary wrote a letter saying that the King has asked the Bureau of Crown Property to give him justice. Up until now, no action has been taken. Hardly any media has reported news about this case. Was this because of fear of lèse-majesté charges?

Many people don't understand why I was charged with lèse-majesté or why I am always attacked by those in power. Recently, the public relations officer of the army has announced that, "Sulak has created uneasy feeling among the army, and this may lead to violent action." Others criticize me of always repeating myself. I would like to let you know that if there is more justice in society and small people are less oppressed, a person like me would not need to speak out. An example of injustice is the Muslim community of Bankrua, whose residents are going to be kicked out of their homes where they have lived as long as the Bangkok dynasty. Their homes are in the path of a new highway. Although the government promised the road would be redirected, it has reneged on this. Another example is the case of former Phra Prachak, who was arrested while still in robes, because he wanted to protect the forest. Those from the elite circle invaded the forest to make golf courses and resorts with seemingly little restriction from the laws. General Suchinda is an honorary chairman of one of these golf courses.

This is why I can't keep quiet. I hope you who have access to justice understand a person like me who only seeks righteousness in society. If you grant me freedom, you will support the movement for freedom and human rights in this country.

5) During the celebration of the second coronation of King Rama V in 1873, a new law against crawling on the floor was issued with the following statement:

> "In Siam there are many oppressive traditions that need to be changed…the tradition of crawling on the floor in front of royalty is very oppressive. The junior people who crawl on the floor have to suffer to give respect to their seniors. His Majesty sees that this tradition is useless to the country; it is the sym-

bol of the origin of all kinds of oppression. So this tradition needs to be stopped. His Majesty wants all his people to be happy and not to suffer by crawling on the floor anymore. So he orders to change from crawling to standing up and bowing as a way of paying respect. Those with status may question what is the good of changing from crawling to standing up and bowing. The reason is that His Majesty wants to make sure there is no unjust oppression in this country. Any country in which the powerful does not oppress the powerless is sure to be prosperous."

This law is an important document for the promotion of human dignity according to the view of King Rama V. Field Marshal Sarit Thanarat brought back the tradition of crawling on the floor against this law in the name of loyalty to the Royal Family. I will not mention here how fake his loyalty was in this and other actions. However, I would like to quote Professor Pridi Kasemsap, one of my witnesses, saying in the court that: "Kings Rama V and VI wanted all their people to have equal dignity and for Thailand to be equal to other civilized countries so they got rid of the tradition of crawling on the floor."

A further quote from Professor Pridi Kasemsap in an introduction to *Using Law for Political Purposes* states that:

"Ultimately, speaking about the issue of using law for political purposes, I would like to remind you that society can be stable only when the application of legal procedures is based on the Rule of Law. In other words, in order to use law for political purposes, you need to keep in mind the principles of justice. You should not use law to destroy those who disagree with you in the name of giving benefit to the majority."

In the *Far Eastern Economic Review* of March 2, 1995, Rodney Tasker quoted the Royal Secretary of the King as saying that using the charge of lèse-majesté will decrease progressively as Thailand develops. I hope this is the case, but not as Mr. Tasker predicts that this law is aimed at Thai people rather than foreigners. There should not be double standards in using a law—one for Thais and one for foreigners. We can see that foreigners do not crawl in front of the King, but why did General Suchinda crawl in front of the King when there was a crisis as in May 1992? A few days prior to that, he ordered the shooting of many people who only wanted him to resign as prime minister.

The essence of being a human is having the courage to confront truth without pretension. All that I have said is for you to consider to give me justice. I respect truth over power or status. I hope your judgment will be similar to the case of the Venerable Phra Vimala-dhamma in 1966, where the judgment proclaimed the innocence of the defendant.

6) In December 1994, I was invited to be a judge at the Permanent Peoples' Tribunal in England. The judgment was made at the British Parliament to punish the system of multinational corporations which aims to maximize profits without considering the welfare of the work-ers and natural environment. An example of this is Union Carbide Limited from the U.S., which was responsible for the explosion at Bhopal in India, causing many deaths and much sickness. After ten years, these people have not been rightly compensated. The Courts of India and the U.S. did not do anything, so the people have to rely on the Permanent Peoples' Tribunal. Although this tribunal has no legal power, it has moral and cultural influence. The Tribunal also condemned the modern medical system that only benefits the rich and abandons the poor. This medical system encourages fear of death and reliance on expensive medical treatments.

Strictly speaking, the World Court or the International Court of Justice at the Hague has no jurisdiction over any government either, as you may recall from the Khao Phra Vihara case in the early 1960s when we lost at the World Court, and Sarit Thanarat refused to hand Phra Vihara over to Cambodia. His Majesty the King had to per-suade him gently that he should obey the World Court, which gave our country much prestige then.

This Permanent Peoples' Tribunal was started in Sweden in the 1960s by Bertrand Russell, an important English philosopher, to con-demn the U.S. for invading Vietnam without any legitimacy. This war caused huge losses of life and resources for the Vietnamese, the Americans, and many other people in the name of American Imperialism. Though the judgment had no legal effects, it encouraged people all over the world to protest against the Vietnam War. This resulted in the big American Empire losing the Vietnam War.

In 1992, I was also a judge on the Permanent Peoples' Tribunal at the European Parliament in France, condemning the invasion of Tibet by China. This invasion totally destroyed the freedom, human rights, culture, and environment of Tibet.

Ironically, I am recognized in the international community to be an honorable judge, but in my own country I am being tried for a serious criminal offense because of the oppression of dictators. I hope that the criminal court of Siam will understand me and give me justice according to the rule of law.

I asked my lawyer to submit a written document to the court outlining the contradictory nature of the testimony of the prosecution witnesses and how those witnesses benefited my case.

Finally, I would like to thank the judges and public prosecutors who expressed loving kindness, patience, and gentleness all through this long court case. I would also like to thank the Thai and international media for accurate reporting of my case. Also, thanks to the many people, including monks and foreigners, who came to listen to the trial on so many occasions. This has been an important support for me, especially the representatives from international organizations like the International Commission for Jurists (ICJ). However, I believe in your consideration to make a judgment in my case with justice and compassion.

Yours respectfully,
Sulak Sivaraksa

V *Acceptance Speech*
for the Right Livelihood Award

December 8, 1995

I feel very privileged to be here at the Swedish Parliament to receive the Right Livelihood Award—especially today. Everyone knows that the awards are widely considered the Alternative Nobel Prizes. What everyone may not know is that December 8, according to some traditions, is Buddha's enlightenment day—the day an ordinary human being awoke from attachment to greed, hatred, and delusion to become fully enlightened and compassionate. Selfishness was transformed into selflessness and intellectual arrogance into a real understanding of the self and the world—the kind of real understanding necessarily accompanied by loving kindness toward all sentient beings.

Right Livelihood itself is a Buddhist term, a key element in the Noble Eightfold Path, or Middle Way, the Buddha taught as a way for all of us to transcend greed, hatred, and delusion—or at least to lessen them. The stages on the Path are Right View, Right Intention, Right Speech, Right Action, Right Livelihood, Right Effort, Right Mindfulness, and Right Concentration. Right Livelihood means a livelihood which is nonexploitative to the self or others, and, as a Buddhist, I am happy to be recognized as one who tries to lead this kind of life. In my own country I am usually known as a trouble-maker or rabble-rouser, one who challenges the economic and tech-nological "development" destined to make Siam the fifth "Tiger" among the newly industrialized countries modeled after Japan. This "Gang of Four" already includes Taiwan, South Korea, Hong Kong, and Singapore.

This model of development has no ethical or spiritual dimension, and its technological advances involve massive ecological devastation while its economic progress widens the abyss between rich and poor, even while subjecting whole populations to the voraciousness of the barely masked greed called consumerism. There are no human rights within it, especially economic, social, and development human rights, even as it sometimes pays lip service to civil and political freedoms. This model of development is called "progress," which comes from the Latin root meaning madness. Since I want to be sane and to live in a saner world, I have spent my life attempting to offer alternatives, not only in my country but throughout Asia and beyond. To paraphrase Shumacher, my efforts are "small" but attempt to be "beautiful."

The Thai authorities do not always find my criticism of the status quo beautiful, however, especially when we have military coups, which we do quite often in my country. The powers that be become very angry with me; sometimes they burn my books, and sometimes I am forced into exile lest they put me in jail. I have been persona non grata with the Thai authorities since 1967, and in 1976 the Thai military junta wanted to arrest or perhaps kill me. Fortunately, I was in England at the time, so they only drove my business into bankruptcy. Many of my contemporaries and students were murdered, maimed, or imprisoned. The lucky ones managed to flee abroad. I remained abroad for two years. I wish to thank the Swedish government and people who were most generous to Thai refugees. The Swedish Ambassador in Bangkok took personal risks to help Thai intellectuals reach Sweden, and then-Prime Minister Olaf Palme was friendly and helpful to many of us.

In 1991 my open criticism of the military junta again drove me into exile. Unofficially the junta tried to kill me; officially they charged me with lèse-majesté, an extremely serious crime in Siam with a maximum penalty of 15 years. I was fortunate in that the German Ambassador in Bangkok helped protect me. When I was able to escape abroad, my first destination was, of course, Sweden. My Swedish friends did not disappoint me. We have now formed a Thai Studies Association among my Thai friends in Sweden and elsewhere in order to help people within Siam work for social justice and social welfare. Friends provided me with hospitality and arranged teaching work in Europe, North America, and Japan. Among other positions, I was a Distinguished Visiting Professor at the University of Hawaii and received the Naropa Institute Founder's Award, as well as giving courses there. My alma mater, the University of Wales, Lampeter, also provided me with an honorary fellowship. Both International PEN Centres in London and Toronto elected me their honorary member. Not only did the Thai PEN Centre ignore me, ten years ago its former president was the instigator to bring the case of lèse-majesté against me.

I remained in exile for fourteen months this time before being able to return to face court hearings on the charges of lèse-majesté. Compared with my friends from Indonesia, Burma, Tibet, Sri Lanka, Cambodia, and elsewhere, this is very light. Yet exile can be miserable; only friendship, hope, forgiveness, and the practice of mindful deep breathing helped me to keep my head above water. I must admit that when I see senseless killing and human rights abuse, I sometimes become angry. But Thich Nhat Hanh, my Vietnamese Buddhist teacher, taught me to become aware of anger in order to surround it with mindfulness. He says that anger is like a closed flower which will bloom when the sunlight penetrates it deeply. If you keep breathing mindfully, shining compassion and understanding upon it, your practice will penetrate the anger, and you will look into its depths and see its root. When this happens, the anger cannot resist. The flower will bloom and show its heart to the sun. The same is true of greed, lust, and delusion.

With this mindful practice of breathing, I learned not to hate the military junta, nor the corrupt politicians, nor even the executives in the multinational corporations. I became more aware of the unjust social, political, and economic structures as the source of injustice and violence. The rich and powerful benefit economically and legally from the system, but they are also trapped by it, and neither they nor their families are made happy.

My court case on the lèse-majesté charges lasted almost four years, during which time many friends and organizations assisted. They included Amnesty International (London); the International Commission of Jurists (Geneva) and the Human Rights Desk of Bread for the World (Stuttgart), among many others. My attorneys were wonderful, fighting the case patiently, courteously, and courageously; and my colleagues gave me much encouragement. My wife has always been and continues to remain a tremendous support to me.

I was acquitted on the charges of lèse-majesté, which is very unusual. My acquittal made me proud of our judiciary system, making me believe that our progressive judges no longer blindly follow oppressive laws, many of them decrees of the military junta, but now care more for justice and mercy. The judges went so far as to praise me in court stating, which is unprecedented within living memory, that, "It is clear that the defendant aimed at teaching the students to be conscious of the essence of democracy. He warned the students not to live a luxurious, consumer lifestyle, not to worship being rich, not to admire people in power, and to be concerned about justice and righteousness." I was pleased when the Right Livelihood Award Committee cited this part of the judgment and encouraged me to go forward with new projects.

My latest projects concern interfaith Alternatives to Consumerism and the Spirit in Education Movement (SEM). The Foundation for the Progress of Humanity (France, Switzerland) has helped initiate the first project which calls for Buddhists, Christians, and Muslims to work together in developing awareness of the problems of consumerism and demonstrating viable alternative ways of living. The second project, SEM, has already begun with assistance from the Sharpham Trust (England) and the Heinrich Böll Foundation (Germany). We have already given courses and will initiate SEM formally with a public event on December 12, with the Head of Shumacher College (England) as keynote speaker. I hope SEM will provide an alternative to prevailing educational trends which concentrate on the head rather than the heart and reward cleverness without regard to ethics. The Naropa Institute (Boulder, Colorado) already attempts to introduce engaged Buddhism as part of its curriculum, that is, to teach its students how to confront suffering and be mindful of ways of overcoming it nonviolently both at the personal and the social, economic, and other structural levels. The Institute of Total Revolution (Vecchi, Gujarat, India) also trains in a Gandhian method of education.

At SEM we try to develop friendship in the Buddhist sense of kalayanamitra, among students and teachers—to learn from each other and from the environment; to develop meditation practice and artistic creativity; to understand and respect indigenous cultures; to plant seeds of peace within ourselves and our world; to develop beauty, goodness, and critical self-awareness in order to become transformed personally. This, in turn, will lead us to care less for ourselves and more for others; to combine understanding and compassion; to work for social justice and ecological balance; and to develop Right Livelihood as part of our Buddhist practice.

SEM participants will not avoid contact with suffering or become separate from our awareness of suffering in the world but will find ways to alleviate suffering wherever it is found. Above all, they will try to understand the ways in which prevailing economic, social, and political systems contribute to suffering, to violence, and to the culture of violence that surrounds us, in order to provide a countervailing force of nonviolence, compassion, and understanding.

At the deepest level, the causes of suffering are always greed, hatred, and delusion. At the more immediate level, these causes have become embodied in consumerism, militarism, compartmentalization of thought and practice (e.g., the use of such strategies as "social engineering"), and the separation of efforts to resolve social problems from the process of personal transformation.

In SEM we hope to understand that the knowledge we presently possess is not changeless so that we can learn and practice nonattachment to views, to become open to receive the truth that resides in life and not simply in conceptual knowledge. I hope SEM participants will be able to learn throughout their entire lives and to observe the reality of the world and within ourselves at all times.

In order to do this, and not to lose ourselves in dispersion in our surroundings, we need to practice mindfulness, especially the breathing which brings us back to what is happening in the present moment—with what is wondrous, refreshing, and healing both within and around us. We hope to continually plant seeds of joy, peace, and understanding in ourselves in order to facilitate the ongoing work of transformation in the depths of our consciousness.

I am very grateful to be in this wonderful company, to be accepting this Right Livelihood Award, and to be able to share with you some of my work, my hopes, and my dreams. I welcome all participation in our projects, especially in the new work on Alternatives to Consumerism and in the Spirit in Education Movement. It would be wonderful to welcome any of you as teachers and/or students in our SEM courses.

Before I thank you all, both for this wonderful award and for your interest in our work and projects, may I ask the four Buddhist monks—constituting the Sangha—from Burma, Siam, England, and Germany, to chant words of the Buddha for peace and happiness of all sentient beings.

Sulak Sivaraksa
Stockholm, Sweden
December 8, 1995

Acronyms

ACFOD: Asian Cultural Forum on Development

AFSC: American Friends Service Committee

ASEAN: Association of Southeast Asian Nations

BBC: British Broadcasting Corporation

BPF: Buddhist Peace Fellowship

BIS: British Information Service

CCFD: Catholic Comité Contre la Famine et pour le Développement

CGRS: Coordinating Group for Religion and Society

ICJ: International Commission for Jurists

INEB: International Network of Engaged Buddhists

IPI: International Press Institute

NGO: nongovernmental organization

NPKC: National Peace Keeping Council

PEN: Poets, Playwrights, Essayists, Editors, and Novelists

SCONTE: Society for the Conservation of National Treasures and the Environment

SEATO: Southeast Asian Treaty Organization

SEM: Spirit in Education Movement

SLORC: State Law and Order Restoration Council

TICD: Thai Interreligious Commission for Development

VSO: Voluntary Service Overseas

WCC: World Council of Churches

WCRP: World Conference on Religion and Peace

WFB: World Fellowship of Buddhists

Glossary

Ajahn—title meaning teacher

bhikkhu—a fully ordained Buddhist monk

Buddhadhamma—the teachings of the Buddha

Dhamma—truths referred to by the teachings of a Buddha; application of these teachings

Eightfold Path—the practices leading to the cessation of suffering as taught by the Buddha, including Right View, Right Thinking, Right Speech, Right Action, Right Livelihood, Right Effort, Right Mindfulness, and Right Concentration

lèse-majesté—the crime of defaming or criticizing royalty

Mahayana—generally referring to the Northern tradition of Buddhism

Pali Canon—one of the earliest recorded written collections of the Buddha's discourses

pañña—wisdom or insight

Phra—title meaning venerable

samadhi—meditative concentration

samsara—frustrating, repetitive cycle of birth and death

Sangha—community of people committed to the practice of the Dhamma; sometimes referring exclusively to ordained monks or nuns

sila—morality or ethical teachings; precepts

sutta—a discourse attributed to the Buddha

Theravada—the tradition of Buddhism prevalent in Southeast Asia

Vajrayana—the tradition of Buddhism prevalent in Tibet

vihara—a Buddhist monastery

vinaya—the rule followed by Buddhist monks and nuns

wat—a Buddhist monastery

Index

Note: Thai names are entered in Thai name order, personal name before family name.

Parallax Press publishes books and tapes on mindful awareness and social responsibility, "making peace right in the moment we are alive." For a copy of our free catalog, please write to:

Parallax Press
P.O. Box 7355
Berkeley, California 94707

E-mail: parapress @ aol.com
www.parallax.org

Other recent Parallax Press titles:

Dharma Gaia edited by Allan Hunt Badiner

Engaged Buddhist Reader edited by Arnold Kotler

In the Footsteps of Gandhi edited by Catherine Ingram

Learning True Love by Sister Chân Không

Love in Action by Thich Nhat Hanh

The Path of Compassion edited by Fred Eppsteiner

Seeds of Peace by Sulak Sivaraksa

Step by Step by Maha Ghosananda

Thinking Green! by Petra K. Kelly

Worlds in Harmony by His Holiness the Dalai Lama